# With the
# *Kama Sutra*
## Under My Arm

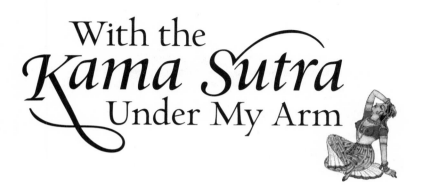

# With the Kama Sutra Under My Arm

My Madcap Misadventures Across India

Trisha Bernard

STERLING

New York / London
www.sterlingpublishing.com

STERLING and the distinctive Sterling logo are registered
trademarks of Sterling Publishing Co., Inc.

**Library of Congress Cataloging-in-Publication Data**

Bernard, Patricia.
[With the Kamasutra under my arm]
With the Kama sutra under my arm : my madcap misadventures across India / Trisha
Bernard.
p. cm.
Originally published: With the Kamasutra under my arm : an Indian journey. New Delhi :
Bluejay Books, 2005.
ISBN 978-1-4027-5712-9
1. India--Description and travel. 2. Bernard, Patricia--Travel--India. I. Title.
DS414.2.B4 2008
954--dc22
2008018356


2   4   6   8   10   9   7   5   3   1


American version published in the United States by Sterling Publishing Co., Inc.
387 Park Avenue South, New York, NY 10016
© 2008 by Patricia Bernard
This edition of *With the* Kama Sutra
*Under My Arm: An Indian Journey* is published by arrangement with
East Street Publications, Australia.

Previously published as *With the Kama Sutra under my arm: An Indian journey*
© 2006 Patricia Bernard

Distributed in Canada by Sterling Publishing
*c/o* Canadian Manda Group, 165 Dufferin Street
Toronto, Ontario, Canada M6K 3H6
Distributed in the United Kingdom by GMC Distribution Services
Castle Place, 166 High Street, Lewes, East Sussex, England BN7 1XU

Sterling ISBN 978-1-4027-5712-9

For information about custom editions, special sales, premium and
corporate purchases, please contact Sterling Special Sales
Department at 800-805-5489 or specialsales@sterlingpublishing.com.

Thanks to one of my dearest and oldest friends, Jeannie,
for making me laugh.

# Contents

To quote the elderly gentleman I'd met in the Taj Mahal:

*"A warlord class exists as long as it goes to war."*

Mogul emperors existed as long as they returned to their cold and windy homelands for a dose of annual hardship, doing a bit of conquering on the way.

Once they settled on the Ganges plain, the insidious heat got to them, and eagles turned to chickens. In other words, the descendants of the sword-wielding Babur turned into indolent and vacuous wearers of voluminous muslin skirts who dallied away their lives and fortunes with wine, women, and song.

We should be so lucky.

Islamabad ⊛      Leh ●
                 JAMMU &
                 KASHMIR

**PAKISTAN**      Shimla ●        C H I N A

                              Rishikesh
                              Haridwar        *TIBET*

*Corbett Tiger Reserve* &
*Sonanadi Wildlife Sanctuary*            H I M A L A Y A S    Mount Everest ▲
*Fatehpur Sikri Palace* ★ **New Delhi**  N E P A L                    Thimphu
Bikaner ●  ★    ⊛                                              ⊛ **BHUTAN**
        ★ *Deshnok-Rat*          Kathmandu ⊛
*Sam Sand Dunes*    *Temple*         Agra      Darjeeling ●
*National Park* ★
        ★                   ★ *Taj Mahal*
Jaisalmer ●  *Thar*  ● Jodhpur  Jaipur ●  ★                  **BANGLADESH**
*Desert*                         *Keoladeo Park*
**RAJASTHAN**                    *Bharatpur Bird*  *Ganges R.*
*Mount Abu* ▲ ● Udaipur          *Sanctuary*
                                         Varanasi ●          Dhaka ⊛
Gandhinagar ●                                      Kolkata
                      Bhopal ●                     (Calcutta)

            **I N D I A**              ● Bhubaneswar

Mumbai ●
(Bombay)
                  Hyderabad ●           *Bay of Bengal*

Panaji ●                    ● Vijayawada
Goa ●
            *Arabian*
            *Sea*
                  Bangalore ●    ● Chennai
                                   (Madras)
            Mysore ●
                                                    N
                                          W ✦ E
            Kochi ●                                 S
            (Cochin)
                                          0    250    500 km
      Kanyakumari ●                            Scale

                  **SRI LANKA**

                  Colombo ⊛            ⊛ Capital City
                                       ● Other City

            *INDIAN OCEAN*

# *Chapter 1*

## Thar Desert

Our windowless, wooden-seated bus rattled past kilometers of red hills, which eventually became green wheat fields, squares of dry, cracked dirt, and finally, piles of plastic that smothered the earth so that nothing grew and might never grow there again.

We saw a one-legged scarecrow in a *dhoti* lording it over a bare field, not winning the battle against a flock of determined crows; a woman in an orange sari washing a baby in a purple plastic dish on top of a manure pile; two men, their day's work done, gossiping, with their wooden plows over their shoulders; and a woman in a sapphire-blue skirt and rose-pink scarf balancing two brass bowls on her head. As she walked, the sun's rays hit the bowls, turning them into flames, making it seem as if she carried the internal fire of life upon her oiled black hair. Finally, the bus stopped at a large roadside chai shop.

The chai shop, stuck out in the middle of nowhere, had three ovens, many rickety chairs with legs wired together, a dozen tables, and a scattering of male clientele who seemed to have walked there. There were no toilets.

Everyone left the bus to pee. Sally and I were about to walk down the road when the man in front of us kicked a ragbag of bones. The unfortunate dog yelped in pain and Sally exploded. Marching up to the man, she kicked him in the shins and shouted, "How do you like it?"

The man gaped at her. His friends gaped at her. All the passengers and men in the chai shop gaped at her. And I gaped at her. I couldn't believe she'd done it. Hadn't I just told her about the missionary and his two sons who had been burned alive by rioting Indians?

The dog kicker tried to explain that he had kicked the dog to get it out of our way, but Sally wouldn't listen. She was bent on lecturing him on cruelty to animals. I tried to interrupt, to get her away from the crowd of mismatched jacket-and-trousered men who were gathering around us, four circles deep. In the end, I yanked her away and dragged her towards the shed.

"Are you out of your mind? We are in the middle of nowhere and you kick an Indian in his own country." Not that kicking anyone anywhere is acceptable, but we were the tourists.

"Don't you care about the dog?" she retorted.

"Of course I care. I have two dogs! But kicking someone is not going to change a lifetime habit. Dogs are not important to Indians. They are not holy cows, milk-giving goats or rubbish-eating pigs. As far as they're concerned, dogs are vermin."

"Then why don't they put them to sleep?"

She knew the answer already. Orthodox Hindus, Jains and Buddhists cannot kill a living thing, and a Muslim's interest in a non-profit-making animal is minimal. So the dogs live and die in abject misery. But then so do a lot of Indians.

Sally stormed off behind the shed. I stood guard.

Suddenly, some intuition made me turn, and I saw the dog kicker's friends removing our bags from the bus. With visions of being left in the middle of a desert with only the chai shop for shelter, I took off like Superwoman, arriving as my bag was tossed onto the road. I snatched it up and clutched it to my bosom, covering the broken zipper with my arms.

On top of my clothes lay a very explicit copy of the *Kama Sutra*. One look at the semi-naked entwined bodies on its cover and these austere men with their down-turned moustaches and parakeet-colored turbans would freak. It would be no good insisting that we were not modern-day Jezebels (which I am sure are in the Koran as they are in the Old Testament). No good explaining that the *Kama Sutra* was much loved by their Muslim Moguls of old. No good telling them I was a writer and the book was for research. Its brilliantly colored pages would be shredded and thrown to the desert winds, and we would be left behind. And that was the good scenario.

"*Sidi, Sidi,*" I cried, while bowing with my hands held in prayer position in front of my bag. "I am very, very sorry for what happened. My friend ..." I gestured towards the shed with my head, "... is not well." I then did the international sign of twisting my right forefinger to show she was loco, nuts, insane, brain scrambled, etc. Bowing again and with many more *Sidis* (where had that come from? Was it from my grandfather who'd brought back many words from Egypt after World War II?), they let me put my bag back on the bus.

Just then Sally rushed up. Completely ignoring the men, she berated me with, "You left me there unguarded. Anyone could have come along. I always watch for you." Then, noticing the multitude of men blocking her entry to the bus, she demanded with a glare, "What's going on?"

"Smile please, Sally. They are about to leave us here."

More glares. "They wouldn't dare!"

"They would. Your bags are over there." I pointed to her bags lying in the dust.

Then while bowing, smiling and *Sidi*-ing, I grabbed her and her bags, all four of them, and hauled her through the men and onto the bus.

"Sit there and don't move until I get back," I ordered.

"Where are you going?"

"Behind the shed! I still have to pee."

# *Chapter 2*

## MONSTER CASE

**B**ack on the bus, I relaxed into a reverie that went something like this: What the hell was I doing in the middle of Rajasthan with an Indian-kicking, dog-loving maniac? Because this was not the first time we'd had trouble with dogs. Why wasn't I traveling on my own as I normally did? What had possessed me to come to India after having flown over it so many times without the slightest urge to do so? Not that I don't like Indians. I do. And they like me, normally. To quote my Indian female friends, I am an Indian's Delight.

I had first discovered this when in Sri Lanka; a handsome young jeweler gave me a silver ring as a memento of our meeting while professing his undying love (I imagine there are many of those silver rings floating around the world). In London, if there was a Kashmir gentleman at the same pub, then he was at my elbow within minutes of my arrival. In a disco with two hundred stunningly beautiful, mini-skirted British girls gyrating, it is me who the Delhi fellow asks to dance. Should I be on the French Metro and there are thirty empty seats, the handsome Sikh sits beside me. In Hong Kong, a girlfriend and I were chased around the Chinese Emporium by four turbaned Romeos, and in Fiji, while queuing in the bank, I was proposed to by a charming Indian who informed me he was a millionaire and well worth considering. Believe me, I considered.

My Indian female friends say that this attraction is due to my resemblance to Lord Vishnu's consort—the short, plump, bosomy Lady Lakshmi, goddess of fortune and opportunity, and mother of the world. They also said that I would have a great time in India. Especially as I was suffering from a broken heart, and India is a great place to get over yesterday's romance.

So off I went to buy a guidebook and a copy of the *Kama Sutra.* Because if I was going to India, I was going to learn all about why my boyfriend had left me for another, how to seduce a new lover, how to train a hawk (supposedly to carry love letters), how to furnish a house seductively, and how to seduce other women's husbands. All in the name of a writer's research.

I also bought a small red zip-up bag. Red (ninety-nine per cent of luggage on any airport conveyor belt is black) and small in case I need to run and carry it at the same time. This being a leftover habit from my youth, when Sally, my backpacking companion and I shot through from a place. Not because we hadn't paid the hostel bill but because we'd been out with princes the night before and did not want to be lumbered with frogs in broad daylight.

Into my bag went silk trousers and top and a pair of high-heeled sandals in case an Indian maharajah wined and dined me, two pairs of well-worn cotton trousers and two T-shirts for looking too poor to be begged from or robbed, some flat sandals, a swimsuit, a cheap camera so that if it is stolen I wouldn't be bankrupted, and a diary. Packing light is essential if one doesn't know what to tip porters, or if, as in India, a stray male grabs your bag and insists on carrying it for you in the opposite direction to the one you are going in.

I then rang the cheapest airline. My friends, who travel business class on respectable planes, predict that one day, I will book a seat on a plane that either drops out of the sky or is hijacked and forced to land by the Caspian Sea. Not so. The planes I catch are not worth hijacking, and landing by the Caspian Sea would be awesome.

I had my injections and booked a short Rajasthani camel tour. Short because I do not find camels romantic, and tour because all my "have been to India" friends agreed that traipsing alone over a Rajasthani desert with a turbaned and moustached camel driver would be unwise.

In retrospect, one should never listen to one's friends. My camel driver turned out to be a virile twenty-five-year-old Omar Sharif look-alike.

Back to my travel plans. Where to go after Delhi?

Stretching 3214 kilometers from north to south, India resembles a blunt stalactite. First are the mystical Himalayas forming a dragon-tooth wall between it and China. Next are the intriguing principalities of Nepal, Bhutan, the tea regions of Darjiling (formerly Darjeeling) and Sikkim, followed by the Ganges Plain, which contains Agra and Delhi, the Deccan Plateau famous for its Hindu and Muslim kingdoms, and the infamous crumbling metropolis of Mumbai, the once mighty bay-side city of Bombay. It was a hard choice.

Then there was the jungle-covered south with its monkey temples and Hindu fishing villages, so different from the wind-swept Rajasthan forts and the gold-tipped Buddhist temples. Not to mention Goa with its tasty Portuguese cuisine and hordes of English tourists searching for the perfect beach. How could I see it all? I couldn't. Not in one go anyway.

So, because there is nothing so romantic as men in buttercup-yellow turbans and peach-pink sunsets over golden deserts, I decided on Rajasthan, with side trips up north to the birth of the Ganges and south to the holy city of Varanasi. If I fell in love with India, as my friends promised I would, I would return to visit the rest.

All was arranged. I had even been to see the famous film *Bandit Queen*, a rape-and-bash shocker about the cruelty meted out to low-caste Indian women when, out of the blue, I received a phone call from Edinburgh. It was my long-lost backpacking friend, Sally. Long lost because she never answers letters, emails or phone messages. Sally was coming for a visit. I told her I was off to India.

"India!" she screamed. "I'd love to go to India."

How quickly the charm of koalas and kangaroos faded beside the lure of the Taj Mahal as Sally rabbited on about gold-trimmed saris, nose jewelry and cheap leather sandals, all of which should have warned me that she had become a shopping freak.

Let me explain about Sally. In our twenties, Sally and I hitchhiked through Europe, Northern Africa, Asia Minor, England and Ireland. Then, after losing our virginity in the same week, I sailed for New York to become a writer and she flew to Jerusalem to plant trees. Since then we have married, given birth and divorced. I live in Sydney and write books; she lives in Scotland and protects plants. I have been inviting her to visit me for years. But traveling to India with her was another thing. Since our traveling together, I had discovered the joys of traveling alone.

How else could I have spent four days in Jerusalem sitting on a wall reading James Michener's *The Source*, while behind me Orthodox Jews and born-again Christians prayed shoulder to shoulder, standing above two layers of earth that hid toppled Roman columns and what's left of King Solomon's palace?

How else could I have walked around a volcano gazing at the blank-eyed, red-stone, hatted statues, while conversing with a handsome Easter Islander who suggested we strip off and swim in a volcanic pool that resembled the lair of the Creature of the Black Lagoon? I declined. He went ahead. They're beautifully made, those Easter Islanders.

Finally, how else could I have spent a day speaking excruciatingly bad French and drinking yak tea, the most unpleasant brew ever invented, with charming Jean Claude and a group of Tibetan road workers while gawking at the Potala palace in Lhasa?

I like traveling alone.

Sally would not be put off. Three weeks later, she arrived with a pile of luggage that she quadrupled during her three-week stay with me in Sydney. Hence our mad rush to find a suitcase large enough to put everything in for our flight to India. Sally intended leaving this "one size fits all my life" suitcase in Delhi Airport's baggage storage department. It seemed a good idea at the time.

All her unwanted clothes, her brown paper bags containing tourist pamphlets, maps, newspaper articles, magazines, postcards and secret Sally stuff, her carved African chess set (bought in Sydney. Why?) and a cloth drawstring bag full of knotted plastic bags (that resembled gigantic blowflies, don't ask) were jammed into this monster case.

Her extra jumper, scarf, woolen hat, bottled water, Kleenex, plastic bags in case of air sickness, instant camera, toilet rolls and bag of oranges were distributed between a large backpack, a small backpack, a Bali-print bag and a tapestry bag from Peru.

Getting the monster case into the trunk of the taxi was accomplished with the help of two weight-lifting male neighbors and a reluctant Lebanese taxidriver with a bad back. And let me tell you, if he didn't have one to start with, he had one when we finished. At the departure lounge, the case was too big for the airport trolleys, so we dragged it to the booking desk. Here we were informed that it was thirty-three kilos overweight and that a union law prohibited the handling of such gigantic luggage.

Having just hauled the case half a block this made sense to me, but not to Sally. So with a mere fifteen minutes before take-off (we'd arrived late—enough said), with a long queue behind us, and a booking clerk whose attitude said she knew we had a chopped-up body in the case and we were not going to get it past her, Sally began arguing her rights as a global traveler.

It got her nowhere. Especially after she used the dreaded words "In Britain, they would ... blah, blah, blah."

"Is that so?" said the airline clerk, her eyes as flinty as the Simpson Desert during the winter solstice.

So I handed over my precious zip-and-expand bag. The one that folds up to nothing and unzips to the size of a suitcase. The one that was as scarce as hen's teeth. The one ... forget it! It didn't survive the flight. It arrived in Delhi with a split in its bottom and thirty-three kilos of Sally's travel pamphlets, news-paper articles and plastic blowflies most likely scattered over the Indian Ocean by a frustrated thief.

With minutes to go, her case and my zip-and-expand bag were accepted and we raced through customs.

"I'll buy gin. You buy rum," I shouted, as we galloped towards the duty-free shop. "It'll help kill malaria bugs."

"I don't drink rum or gin," she shouted back.

Wouldn't you know it?

The flight was great, except for the constant flicking of a sari scarf in our faces whenever we asked the flight attendant for assistance. Continual films of the sugary romantic kind left me plenty of time to read my guidebook and discover how to say *Namaste* while holding my hands together in prayer position, and how nose-pins and bindis, those red dots made with vermilion powder worn between the eyebrows, were once worn by married women as symbols of purity, but now ... I almost heard a sharp sniff of disdainful disgust coming from the guidebook's pages ... adorn many an unmarried nose and eyebrows.

"Being human a woman has desires," I read aloud. "Consequently, if a woman is unmarried, she must be impure and unchaste; otherwise what does she do about her desires?"

"Impure and unchaste things," giggled Sally from beneath her red woolly hat, her way of combating the fierce air conditioning.

"So where does that leave divorced us?"

"Impure and unchaste! And would we have it any other way?"

"No!" we chorused.

We arrived at 10 p.m. and Delhi's international airport's cleanliness and efficiency surprised me.

My apprehension was due to having traveled via Air India once before and having to stop over at Delhi's domestic airport. This airport smelled so strongly of urine that I breathed through my mouth for the next three hours, completely reassured that the overload of ammonia would kill any germs I inhaled. There was nowhere to sit but on a litter and piss-covered floor, nowhere to buy a coffee, and the toilets were such that the entire passenger body decided to wait until they reboarded the plane.

Indira Gandhi airport is a large modern airport with five customs and immigration queues all moving quickly. Not the one I was in, nor the one I moved to. But when I joined the "Indians Only Queue" I was through in a jiffy. "In a jiffy" being the official's words when I asked how long it would take to get to Delhi.

Next came the collecting of luggage. There was my red bag and disembowelled zip-and-expand bag sitting in the middle of the airport floor. The monster suitcase was nowhere in sight. I was not surprised. It had probably fallen off the trolley and crushed some unsuspecting baggage-wallah or ten unsuspecting baggage-wallahs. Or, as it had no doubt weighed down the tail end of the plane, it had been jettisoned over New Guinea.

There's an interesting thought. Out of the sky hurtles an enormous case, which bursts open at the feet of one hundred astounded New Guinean natives. Out spills a remarkable array of unknown objects, especially the African chess set and the knotted blowflies. Bingo! The suitcase cult is born with the original hundred devotees swelling to thousands, each holding a copy of the monster suitcase woven in palm fronds, each wearing a plastic bag blowfly in their hair, and all staring skywards for the next arrival of manna from heaven.

At last we found Sally's case. Mainly because we realized that we were wrongly standing at the Nepal Airline's luggage outlet. So what were my bags doing there? Lugging the monster case into the exit hall, we were assailed by an amazing din as a gallimaufry of screaming males, turbaned and not, surged forward, holding up placards printed with the names of lost passengers. We staggered on, heaving the case into a second hall full of tourist touts. Pre-warned not to negotiate for a taxi outside the airport, I asked four young men, standing behind four different counters, how much a taxi to Delhi would cost. I then chose the one who quoted half what the others quoted. Did they think I was deaf or daft? I was neither. What I was, was utterly stunned at how handsome they all were.

We paid our money to our chosen slicked-back-haired lad who handed us over to an ancient, toothless grandfather wearing a large, loose diaper. Grandpa handed us over to a taxi driver, who beckoned for Sally to follow him. She did so, dragging her case over a crossing, up a gutter, over a second crossing, into a dark car parking lot, and past dozens of battered and bruised cars to a leaning tin shed shrouded in the lime-green mists of polluted time. I followed, carrying my red bag, her two backpacks, her two cloth bags, and a plastic bag of information she'd collected from the plane.

The baggage storage depot's interior, lit by one lone swinging hurricane lamp, was even less inviting than its collapsing exterior. Everything was covered in dust, including the ghostly attendant. I suggested taking the case with us. But Sally was adamant. Tomorrow it would go home via Lufthansa. So the case was abandoned. I'm sure I heard it whimpering as we left.

The taxi driver led us to his dented grey Morris Oxford, or Ambassador as they are called in India. Forty minutes later, we were at the Arnpit Hotel. But not before we'd been off-loaded at three other hotels, and not before our driver did a lot of "question asking" of passing rickshaw men.

The Arnpit Hotel is not in the center of Delhi. Nor is it in the famous backpacker Paharganj market area near the railway station. It is in the north of the city close to the Karol Bagh Markets. *Bagh* means gardens. There are no gardens. But there is a long greasy road where Delhians go to buy motorbike, refrigerator, car or sewing machine parts. The Arnpit Hotel looked as if it was either under construction, under renovation, or falling down. Once inside we were told, repeatedly and proudly, that it was being renewed at the cost of $90,000.

Our fourth-floor room was reached by the two of us squashing into a tiny elevator with a polite and silent operator, who, when the three of our knees and hips touched, pretended they didn't.

Our room had two single beds jammed together, which we parted immediately, two armchairs, a coffee table, a bay window overlooking downtown Delhi, and no toilet paper. Did we care? We did not. Sally was carrying six rolls in her Peruvian tapestry bag.

# Chapter 3

## First Day in Delhi

Next morning, over tea and toast brought to the room by a handsome waiter who Sally fell instantly in love with, we discovered why there was such a plethora of young men cluttering up the hotels of India. They are not paid. They are given a place to sleep and wash and the chance to earn tips while gratefully working an eighteen-hour day for nothing.

"They should thank their lucky stars," added the hotel owner, a plump, rosebud-lipped Brahman in white muslin who spent his day lounging on a sofa in his hotel foyer watching his builders work.

Their graceful slow-motion movements as they chipped away with hammers and chisels; their gentle pushing of brooms while they removed dust from one area so it could settle on another; and their willingness to stop and stare at anyone entering or leaving the foyer did not instill enormous confidence in a swiftly renovated hotel. Nevertheless, the owner seemed happy. Perhaps all he was paying them was a bed on the roof and a bowl of rice.

After having been carried over the newly cemented front steps by two workmen (every day should start so regally), we discovered that the hotel was built on a five-road traffic intersection. In the middle, stood a bare hill lorded over by two billy goats gruff chewing plastic bags. Around them, swirled a gritty cloud of exhaust smoke out of which spun over-packed buses (going to work on one of those must give the word *intimate* a new meaning); battalions of rattle-trap trucks loaded so high that the men on top appeared ready to tumble off at the next swerve; dozens of rickshaws with tatty stroller hoods and riders in minimum clothing chewing betel nut which they spat like globs of fresh blood, onto the road; auto-rickshaws with carpeted seats and turbaned drivers, their heads turned to talk to the five or six schoolgirls crushed into the "backside" seat; and motorbikes with sidecars full of sari-clad, bejeweled wives and spotlessly clean school children.

Amongst this hooting, tooting, not always driving in the same direction mob, strolled a haughty grey Brahman bull followed by his harem of four unconcerned cows, and I mean "unconcerned." You'd have thought they were on the set of *The Sound of Music* strolling up a Swiss hillside eating daisies, they were so unconcerned.

The reason for the lack of alarm shown by these large beasts, with their cast-iron stomachs and come-to-bed eyes, was explained to us by a nearby taxi driver. "Until recently, anyone who killed a cow was executed. Now, they are only given lengthy prison sentences."

No wonder these daintily stepping bovines with the fluttering eyelashes were so nonchalant. Or could it be that they were so high on exhaust fumes that they really thought they were on a Swiss hillside eating daisies?

As crossing the road looked precarious, we hurried around the corner to Ajmal Khan Road and discovered a shopping street crowded with stalls selling saris and *salwar kameezes*, and a hole-in-the-wall yogurt shop called Punjabi Sweets where we decided to have a second breakfast. Here we ate yogurt called curd with small balls of dough dripping with honey called *gulab jamun* (*gulab* meaning rose, because the honey is made from bees that only visit rose bushes); *ras malai*, a cheese, milk and nut pudding; and *samosa* pastries filled with vegetables plus enough chili to burn the skin off the back of a rhinoceros. It was the last samosa Sally ate.

All was washed down with a glass of chai which had been stewing over a flame for an hour, and for which we have the British to thank as they were the first to put milk into their tea to stop the boiling water cracking their imported China tea cups. Sweet milky chai takes a lot of getting used to if one doesn't take sugar or milk in one's beverage. But boiled to buggery tea is better than bottled water when one isn't sure the water doesn't come from the local well.

On leaving Punjabi Sweets, we discovered a beautician's shop with prices that could not be refused, so we made appointments for the next day, then we hailed an auto-rickshaw to take us to the government tourist bureau.

So began Indian lesson number one. Which is, where you say you want to go and where your driver takes you does not have to be the same place. In fact, the chances of it being so are nil. Our driver, who spoke no English, took us to Connaught Place because that is where all non-Indians go.

Connaught Place consists of three concentric circles. The outer circle is Connaught Circus, now renamed Indira Chowk after India's Madam Prime Minister, and the inner circle, formerly Connaught Place, is Rajiv Chowk, named after the Madam Prime Minister's favorite son.

Rajik Chowk with its classical Doric-columned walkway and two-storied buildings is Delhi's Fifth Avenue. It even overlooks a Central Park. This park appears to have no entrances, but there must be a way in because as we cycled around it three times in an attempt to get off without being run down by trucks, numerous cows gazed down at us, giving us a condescending "I'm the King of the Castle" stare. How had they gotten there? Did they do a midnight trek across an empty road? Was the six-lane Rajiv Chowk ever empty? Or did they stroll through the wheel-to-wheel, bumper-to-bumper hooting traffic, knowing that the threat of a prison sentence was enough to save them from being bowled over and sold to a non-Hindu butcher?

Our pedaller turned down a back lane packed with rickshaws and sleeping or dead people and stopped outside the travel office of his second cousin on his first wife's brother-in-law's side. Here a slim patent-leather-haired man, with teeth Colgate would pay a fortune to advertise, insisted on sending out for chai while he assured us that he would only charge $56 each to take us to Rishikesh (the Ganges River town made famous by John Lennon) and Haridwar, a holy town favored with a footprint of the god Vishnu.

"Why so cheap?" we asked.

"Because you are special. You both look like my aunts."

Big mistake, buddy! No one wants to look like anyone's aunt. Try Julia Roberts, Elle Macpherson, Meg Ryan. We drank his chai and left. We'll be back, we promised. We lied.

Had we but known it, his was a very good deal, but being annoyed at not being taken to where we'd asked to go plus the aunt compliment, we headed for the government tourist bureau, where we were greeted by a woman who swore all other tourist operators were crooks and that she was the only official agent.

We discovered later that she was related to the boss of the government tourist bureau and that he'd allowed her to set up business at the front door while the real government workers sat behind her, not daring to speak up for fear of being fired.

Now came Indian lesson number two. Where business is concerned, no Indian ever says no. Even if the task is impossible. This is where we came undone. We asked for an English-speaking guide. "Certainly, Madams." We asked to go to the two holy cities in the foothills of the Himalayas. "Certainly, Madams." Sally, who'd read Jim Corbett's book, *Man-eaters of Kumaon* asked if we could include the Corbett Tiger Reserve. "Why not, Madams?"

Why not, indeed! The fact that the tiger park was hundreds of kilometers of spine-shattering roads in the opposite direction to Rishikesh and Haridwar and that this sales woman was saying that everything could be done in four days, which was impossible without a helicopter, didn't matter to her. What did matter was that we must pay her immediately.

Off we went to change our dollars. On the way, we were accosted by a third tourist operator, who quoted a cheaper price for the same trip, and a fourth who was cheaper still. There is always someone who will do it cheaper in Delhi.

Having unnecessarily circled Rajiv Chowk while dodging shoe cleaners, fruit sellers who peel the fruit for you with their vermilion fingernails whether you want it or not, persistent beaded-bag sellers, and crippled beggars who scoot, crab-like, along on their amputated or twisted limbs, always attended by someone ready to grab any money thrown at them, we fell into the entrance of the Imperial Hotel. One foot on its white-pebbled driveway and all patting of arms and purring of "Madam, Madam," stopped.

The Imperial Hotel is a lovely colonial-style hotel where Imperialists hide away from the hoi polloi, where one can have a guilt-free gin and tonic sitting on a green-columned, marble-floored verandah under green awnings while outside the hubbub goes on unabated. We hurried up a driveway flanked with palms and flowerbeds of lilies and geraniums to a columned portico guarded by two grey-bearded Sikhs wearing glittering cockatoo-crested turbans, gold-buttoned uniforms, and matching cummerbunds holding in their regal tummies. They were extraordinarily grand and we gazed in admiration at them as one pointed out the entrance to the bank.

My dollars were changed quickly. I always carry cash hidden in a belt resembling a leather belt. It can hold $5000, and was once stared at in amazement by four Russian customs officials when I was ordered to open it at Moscow's airport.

"That is the most money I have ever seen," whispered one.

"It's the most money I've ever seen," I informed her.

It was also the belt holding $3000 that I'd left under a pillow in a dodgy hotel in Nairobi, and only discovered my loss when on the plane to Zimbabwe. I got the money back, but needless to say this is one very traveled money belt.

Sally's credit card was harder to access. So while she argued with the teller, I went to explore. One step into the hotel's impressive foyer and I was in love with its pink marble floor and Brunswick green walls decorated with etchings of Delhi's British Colonial days. My favorite was an etching showing the British governor-general galloping between two rows of richly decorated elephants, all kneeling with their trunks raised and their turbaned *mahouts* holding aloft fringed red-and-gold umbrellas. Now that's the kind of power I want.

I sauntered past a marble table holding a vase of purple orchids, trying to look as if I was staying there even though I was wearing my "don't beg from me" clothes, and headed for the ladies' rest room. A common old loo it was not! It was a plush, lush ladies salon de toilette with hot and cold running water and a hot and cold running attendant who wiped the seat before I entered and after I left, and who handed me an embroidered hand-towel with her left hand while holding out her right hand for ten rupees. Obviously, my poverty-stricken clothes did not work in the Imperial Hotel.

Still no sign of Sally, so I strolled down a broad corridor, past a bubbling fountain, through French doors, and out into the garden where I discovered an Olympic-sized swimming pool with six Olympic-sized young men standing behind a tower of fresh towels, each panting with anticipation for someone to wait on. But the pool was swimmer-free. It would take a brave woman to peel off to her swimsuit with those six pairs of glittering prune-colored eyes watching her.

Sally caught up with me at the outdoor restaurant and we decided that, after our sweaty, noisy morning of negotiations, we deserved the buffet lunch set out on the manicured lawn. So there we sat, in our dusty T-shirts and trousers, sipping iced water, already unknowingly infected with the British disease of "Imperialitis," or to use the more commonly known term, "The Raj."

First we had a gin and tonic while watching the falcons swoop over the adjoining rose garden (so that's where the honey for the *gulab* comes from). Then we had another while trying to guess where the other patrons came from. There was a girlish middle-aged woman in floral dress, white socks and sandals that had to be a resident of the Isle of Man caught in a time warp; three Germans in heavy winter suits speaking heavily accented English with two charming, whippet-thin Indian men who looked as if they were capable of outwitting the Germans in the blink of a languid eyelid; and a very beautiful European woman wearing a turban and long tunic and trousers made of white shantung silk, with four waiters fawning over her. We could almost hear her jewel-laden, golden-painted fingernails clashing like sabres as she flicked away their murmured suggestions. Was she the Swedish wife of a rich Indian? Was she a wealthy American on her first visit to India? Did she own the hotel? Whichever. She was a joy to behold.

Sally went to photograph the falcons while three young waiters, whom I decided to adopt on the spot, escorted me to the hibiscus-decorated tables set out under twelve green-and-white striped umbrellas. They did this, they said, so they could explain the food to me. The food was marvelous and there was enough of it to feed an Imperial army.

What a lovely way to live. It wasn't hard to see why eighteenth-century Englishmen settled in to this glorious lifestyle so readily. The heady power of wall-to-wall servants, the unending platters of food, the intoxicating possibility of acres of near-naked dancing girls, would have turned the head of any East India Company official. Who, it is said, poor things, were forced to employ between fifty and seventy attendants, simply to get through the day. Mind you, if they worked at the pace of the Arnpit Hotel's renovators, fifty to seventy servants was understandable.

But what of our lady in the government tourist bureau? We decided, influenced by the gin no doubt, if she wasn't there when we got back, we would see her tomorrow.

She was there, and our driver and car were organized for three days hence. She took our money and was gone before we'd picked up our backpacks, or in Sally's case, a backpack, two drawstring bags and a plastic bag of information that she had collected from the hotel.

Then the dreaded specter of the monster case reared its head and we went in search of Lufthansa Airlines.

"I am sorry, Madam, but we do not send luggage off in all directions," said a tight-lipped receptionist with a penciled-in moustache.

"Just one direction," corrected Sally. "Edinburgh."

"No, thank you. We do not send suitcases to Edinburgh. Edinburgh is frightened of terrorist's bombs."

"There is no terrorist's bomb in my case!" snapped Sally.

I wondered how she could be sure. Her case was so large it could have been a breeding ground for all sorts of things. Who was to say it hadn't picked up the seed of a bomb while flying over Indonesia where revolutionary uprisings were going on all the time? Who was to say that a baby bomb wasn't growing away inside her case just waiting to explode? Fed by all the "stuff" she had jammed in on top of it.

"We don't know that," said penciled-in moustache.

How perceptive of him.

"In Britain they would ... blah, blah, blah."

The Indian representative of Lufthansa didn't give a guru's begging bowl about what they did in Britain, unless we wanted to discuss cricket, and anyone who could afford such a large suitcase could afford to look after it. What he did say was that the airport baggage storage department was not a safe place to leave anything.

It was dark when we arrived at the mist-covered tin shed. Pitch black by the time we trundled the monster case across the car park to the taxi rank and lights were flickering on all over Delhi by the time we reached the Arnpit Hotel. The staff was most helpful. They didn't mind fighting to fit the monster case into the tiny elevator. They didn't mind racing up five flights to be there when the groaning elevator eventually arrived. They didn't even mind heaving the case up the last flight of stairs to the roof where they put it in their cramped bedroom/kitchen which doubled as the hotel's baggage storage room. Here, like some malignant growth, it took up residence, where it was probably used as a mini-billiard table or a bed for a very short waiter.

That night, we decided to drink gin and practiced our first Kama Sutra position. We were doing this, we told each other, as a form of exercise and for education as Sally also had lover problems.

"Kama is the god of love," I read aloud, while clutching my pillow which was to be my surrogate lover. Sally did the same. Beggars can't be choosers, and she hadn't managed to lasso the handsome waiter yet, although it looked promising. "Unlike the Western Eros or Cupid, who is portrayed as a cute little baby, Kama is a beautiful youth married to Rati, the goddess of sensual desire."

"A married god of love!" exclaimed Sally. "That's new. Go on."

"The *Kama Sutra*, dedicated to the god Kama, was written by Vatsyayana in the fourth century a.d. To quote from the flyleaf, it is a description of exotic practices written without guilt, shame or sense of sin."

Sally raised her eyebrows and sipped her gin.

"In 1883 it was translated into English by Sir Richard Burton, the famous British explorer. Which makes one wonder what he was exploring."

"Don't run British explorers down," snarled Sally. "Without them, there wouldn't be half the Anglo-Indians there are today."

Sometimes her logic escapes me but I am sure there are many Anglo-Indians who would agree with her.

I read on. "Coming from a sexually repressed Victorian England where wives were advised to lay back and do their duty, Burton was astounded at the liberal sex education afforded to both sexes in India. During his eight years working for the East India Company, he took three mistresses (one, an expensive prima donna dancer, was speedily fetched back by her dancing teacher). On his return to London, he formed a gentlemen's club to study the *Kama Sutra* with its philosophy of sensuality, fun and frolic. Not that his gentlemen friends ever showed the book to their wives, nor that their wives were ever expected to perform the Kama Sutra positions. Heaven forbid!"

"And heaven forbid that their wives ever mentioned how they'd probably seen the book already. Especially those who'd been in India," added Sally. "So tell me a position before I lose interest in this pillow."

I flicked through the *Kama Sutra*, searching for a picture of the right position to copy and knew it immediately. It was a beautiful illustration of a bearded man, naked but for his silk turban and jewels, sitting on a swing with an exquisitely shaped female wearing only a scarf and as much gold jewelry around her ankles, wrists, neck and through her ears and nose as she could wear and still remain upright under its weight. Sitting astride the man's lap, this doe-eyed damsel gazed fiercely into his dark eyes while holding aloft a white flower, symbolizing pure love. He gazed back at her, holding aloft a hookah water pipe, symbolizing that there were pleasures in this world other than her. Together, they rocked the swing. They did not look in the least bit romantic.

We stared passionately at our pillows while holding our gins aloft, and I laughed so much that I fell off my bed.

"I need a red velvet swing like they have," I complained.

Sally stared up at our ceiling with its wobbling rotating fan. "You'd need a stronger rafter."

"I wonder if they ever swing too hard and fall off."

"Never," announced Sally, confidently waving her third gin about. "There would be slaves to do the pushing."

"Which would give community participation a new slant," said I.

Sally didn't answer. She'd fallen asleep. I don't think she is used to gin.

Next morning, we negotiated a price for a rickshaw for the day. But as the idea of being pedaled around by a fellow human caused us twinges of guilt, we searched for a strong-looking pedaller. We found one but he didn't speak English, so pointing to the Delhi map, we showed him where we wanted to go.

He nodded vigorously and we were soon scooting along through the bell-jiggling, hooting traffic, dodging placid cows chewing unrecognizable things that will not pass through their first stomach let alone end up in their second, and barely missing a family of pigs rooting through rotting fruit, and a crippled dog dragging its backside behind it.

"Calcutta used to be the capital," I read loudly, hoping that animal liberationist Sally hadn't seen the dog. "Delhi became the capital in 1911 when visited by King George V and Queen Mary, the then reigning Empress of India. She wore a crown allegedly sporting six thousand diamonds, twenty-two emeralds, four rubies and four sapphires."

But my description of the sumptuous crown could not block out Sally's screams of, "Oh God! Look at that dog!" as she almost upset the rickshaw while twisting around to commiserate with the lame animal.

"Want to know how the Muslims came to Delhi?" I shouted in her ear. "From the tenth century, India was attacked by small, highly disciplined Muslim forces which demolished the larger, undisciplined, caste-riddled Hindu armies, and ..."

"Oh God! Look at that poor cow," she shrieked as we swerved around a cow with a torn udder and under the scaffolding of a five-story tall statue of Hanuman the monkey god.

The builders' scaffolding was made of bamboo poles tied with palm fronds. It looked incredibly flimsy and I instantly imagined a plasterer plunging through it and landing on us. Sally didn't notice and our pedaller probably ran the gauntlet of falling plasterers on a daily basis.

Then a hooting limousine purposely bumped our rickshaw wheel. Where driving is concerned, Indian men have no conscience. I yelled "back off" and gave the driver "the finger." After this universal insult, he fell in behind. Sally was still bemoaning the plight of the cow.

Most of the accidents we saw, as we tore around Connaught Place with a multitude of thousands like bath water down a plug-hole, were between cycle-rickshaws and auto-rickshaws. Where the tossed-out passengers ended up was a puzzle as there were no mangled legs sticking out from beneath the rickshaws. Only harassed drivers struggling against the tide of traffic trying to right their vehicles. Did rickshaws only tip over when empty? This was a comforting thought.

What became infinitely transparent as we hurtled down Kasturba Road, as if participating in the Melbourne Cup or the English Derby, was that larger vehicles had right of way over smaller vehicles, a road sweeper's donkey cart had right of way over our cycle-rickshaw, and pedestrians had no rights, thus becoming expert leapers and dodgers. So why aren't Indians winning

Olympic gold medals for high jump and long jump?

After tearing along a dozen one-way streets, we eventually arrived at a mighty stone arch called the India Gate on which is carved the names of 85,000 Indian soldiers who died fighting for Britain in World War I, and those who died in the 1919 Afghan uprising.

We sped around this gate at top speed. Obviously having made the bargain to take us to A, B and C, our driver intended on doing so as fast as he could.

"Can we stop and see the gate?" shouted Sally, hanging onto the side of the rocking rickshaw with knuckles whiter than snow.

Our driver took one hand off his shaking handlebars and pointed to it, indicating that she must be blind if she couldn't see the enormous thing. There it was, engulfed in traffic fumes. What more could she ask for? In other words, if you can't eat it, wear it or sleep under it, and no one can sleep under it because there are guards to stop one doing so, what bloody use was it?

Before Sally could insist, we were rocketing along Dr. Zakir Hussain Road towards Emperor Humayun's Tomb, while I wondered why there were no Indian bicycle riders competing in the Olympic Games.

"Emperor Humayun's Tomb," I read aloud, to keep Sally's mind off having missed visiting the India Gate, "was built in 1650 a.d., eight years after Humayun's untimely demise, by his devoted senior wife, the beautiful red-headed Empress Haji Begum. He fell down his library stairs."

"Drunk?" queried Sally.

"Opium," I said.

I'd read that, with the exception of Aurangzeb, all the great Moguls were addicted to the poppy.

"Humayun ruled for ten years, most of which were spent in exile. During his time in Delhi, he cruised up and down the Yamuna River on a floating palace known as one of the wonders of the world. The palace's halls, gardens and bazaar rested on connecting platforms which were kept afloat by constantly moving barges, thus making an attack difficult."

"Obviously a popular ruler," grunted Sally.

On arriving at Humayun's Tomb, we left our pedaller in the rickshaw parking area, and entered the tomb's gardens through a huge sandstone archway. Once inside, the silence, interrupted only by the faint buzz of insects, swallowed us up, and the symmetry of the tomb's forty-four arches, green dome and double-storied petal-shaped windows and doorways instantly transported us into the tales of the Arabian Nights.

"Aladdin and the magic carpet," whispered Sally.

"Ali Baba and open sesame," I whispered back.

So eerie was the feeling of hurtling back in time that I expected any second to see the pale face of the Empress Haji Begum peering down from one of the delicate cupolas that topped the tomb's four towers. Or, as we entered through an archway, that we would stumble upon a ghostly cluster of royal wives, sisters and aunts, their heads bent over a plan of the tomb while they sat cross-legged on a silk woven carpet beneath a purple-shadowed ceiling. It was easy to imagine the instant halting of their murmured gossip. Their gasps and the quick covering of their startled faces, leaving only their kohl-rimmed eyes staring at us, as they faded into the mote-filled sunbeams.

Under the dome, we found a room containing two black-and-rose marble tombs. "These are not the real tombs," I read. "Humayun's and Haji Begum's tombs are in the vaults below surrounded by one hundred and seventy Islamic believers. Although entombed with her Muslim husband, it is possible that Haji Begum was not of the Islamic faith. Coming from Persia, she might have been a follower of Zoroaster."

"Who's Zoroaster?" Sally asked.

I read on. "Indian Zoroastrians have been in India since the tenth century when their homeland was annexed by Muslims. They are called Parsees and it is against their religion to be buried in a tomb. When a Parsee dies, his body is taken to a Tower of Silence. The tower is made up of three circles, one for men and one each for women and children. The bodies are left on top of the tower to be picked clean by the vultures, then the bones are swept into the tower's well. These funeral rites are similar to those of the Tibetan Buddhists, only in Tibet after the bones are picked clean, the eldest child has to smash them to dust with a hammer."

I heard Sally's sharp intake of breath, and I agreed; it seemed a gruesome task for a son or daughter to have to do to a parent, and I doubted if my first-born would be up to it.

"One thing is certain," I closed the guidebook. "Her red hair could mean she had Macedonian blood. Alexander the Great's armies marched through Persia to India and it's recorded that they left a lot of red-haired babies behind."

"Do you think I am a descendent of Alexander the Great's armies?" asked Sally, pushing her own red hair behind her ears.

"No. You look more Irish. Alexander didn't make it to Ireland."

On our walk back to the main gate, I remarked that had the fountains been playing and the reflection pool full as Empress Haji Begum had intended, her husband's tomb would have been perfect. But Delhi is short of water and so were we, so we bought some (which we later found out was bottled from the local tap), and a Coca-Cola for our driver.

Like the Basque people with their goatskin wine bottles, Indians hold their drinking vessels above their mouths, tip back their heads and aim so that only liquid touches their lips. Our pedaler didn't waste a drop. Being bad at aiming, I would have worn the Coca-Cola.

After drinking our water with mouths pressed firmly to the rims of our bottles, we began chatting with an Indian couple, who had come to see Humayun's Tomb. Because here, in the year 1857, the last Mogul emperor, Bahadur

Shah II, surrendered his empire to the British by handing over Humayun's ancient sword to a Major Hodson.

"How sad," I said, thinking that anyone called Hodson didn't sound half regal enough to receive an emperor's sword.

The husband agreed.

"But without the British we would never have had our extensive train system," his polite wife added for our benefit.

"And without the booty taken from India, London would never have afforded the building of its own underground railway," added her husband, determined to make his point.

"Seems like a good swap," said Sally. She's very touchy where colonial Britain is concerned.

We waved good-bye and climbed into our rickshaw. Five minutes later, we were circling the India Gate for the second time and again Sally shouted that she'd like to get out and have a look.

Our pedaller ignored her. One could almost hear his conversation with his wife that evening. "This red-haired woman wanted to get out. Now I ask you? Is this the request of a sane person? She doesn't know any of the names on the gate. It doesn't open to anywhere! And where would I park?"

"Can we stop at the gate?" she hollered.

He pedalled faster, turning a corner so abruptly that the rickshaw ricked, rocked and ricked again while we clung on like limpets. Then off we raced, along with thousands of others all determined to get to Parliament House before us.

Rajpath Road is very long and the uncut lawns on each side are home to herds of cattle and hundreds of squatters camped under tattered tents, their washing draped over bushes. After the noise of the old city, this unexpected space was exhilarating and I longed to run barefooted through the grass. If only I had the courage to fling myself out of our speeding rickshaw. And as long as I didn't mind looking utterly ridiculous in front of a multitude of hungry Indians who didn't have the energy to run anywhere.

It is along this road every 26th of January since 1950 that thousands come in from their villages on their garlanded ox and donkey carts, and even more thousands of city dwellers gather to watch India's Republic Day Parade with its wonderful pageantry of marching Gurkhas, bearded Sikhs, the camel corps, painted and flower-decked war-elephants, and modern day military might rolling along in jungle-green tanks. The 26th of January is also Australia's national day. Only there aren't any war-elephants.

Ahead of us rose Raisina Hill on which sits the copper-domed palace of Rashtrapati Bhavan. Built in 1929, it was once the residence of the British Viceroy. It is now the residence of the President of India. Our rickshaw pedaller stopped in front of its huge wrought-iron gates and we peered over the guard's shoulder at the last Indian palace built in the modern world.

It is enormous. It has a 180-foot-high dome, eight rooftop fountains, kilometers of porphyry slab floors, twelve enclosed courtyards covering four acres, and gardens which once challenged those of the Palace of Versailles.

"It is said, dear lady persons," said a taxi driver, bent on taking us away from our panting pedaller, "it cost the British Government one million pounds to build. During Lord Mountbatten's viceroyship, it took a thousand servants to clean its 340 rooms, and 368 gardeners and 50 bird chasers to keep the gardens tidy."

"Is that so," said Sally, who then told him what she thought of people who chased birds and how she expected better of a British lord. This completely confused the taxi driver.

We left our rickshaw and went to look at the twin Secretariat buildings built by the British to celebrate their own sense of power. These pompous red stone buildings facing each other have matching staircases. One flight of stairs was crowded with people. The others were crowded with hundreds of monkeys gorging on marigolds stolen from the Secretariat gardens.

There were green-haired monkeys with cunning faces

resembling tax collectors; big, old monkeys with rude bottoms and bleary eyes looking like Saturday night racecourse punters; soft-faced females with dewy-eyed babies clinging to their bellies; and infants with half-starved faces, venturing out into the world, but quickly running screaming back to mom should anyone come too close.

Off rushed Sally to photograph them while our pedaller chafed at the bit. She was hurrying through an archway when a nasty looking thug-monkey unwound himself from his sleeping spot and lowered himself down a column to stare at her.

"Isn't he cute!" she called back to me.

"Cute" was not the word that sprung to mind. "Bully," "mugger," "Mafia godfather" was more like it. I decided to photograph "The Don" from a distance. Sally decided to feed him a stale sandwich that she'd been carrying around to give to a deserving dog or holy cow.

She stuck her hand out and thug-monkey almost ripped it off at her wrist. Devouring the sandwich in one gulp, he hung there, examining her Bali-print bag, from where the sandwich had magically appeared, with red-rimmed, bleary eyes. Sally took his photo accompanied by cooing noises which thug-monkey was supposed to interpret as "Hello, brother. We are all one under the skin and within the universe. I love you."

Unfortunately, thug-monkey's mind was not on universal love so as she turned to photograph a smaller, cuter monkey, one that was attacking her leg, thug-monkey leaped. Landing on her shoulders, he wrenched at the strap of the Bali-print bag. Sally shrieked. This caused the smaller monkey, who was definitely into universal love of some sort, to scramble up and under her full Indian-print skirt while thug-monkey leaped onto her head, shrieking in chorus with her.

With thug-monkey's tail hanging over her eyes and his protruding red bottom dangling over her nose, Sally went berserk. Screaming like a banshee, she spun round and round in whirling dervish mode while slapping at her thighs and waving her arms like a windmill. This caused thug-monkey to nestle deeper into her long red hair; and lover-monkey, clearly a famous high-wire artist in a past life, to slide down her thigh and, clinging to the hem of her whirling skirt, swing its body and legs out in a wide arc, while screaming to the onlooking monkeys, "Look Mom, no feet."

While slapping at thug-monkey with her Bali-print bag, Sally dropped her camera. Thinking it to be a piece of square yellow fruit, lover-monkey abandoned her skirt and leaped for it. I leaped too. We arrived together and lover-monkey got a sharp slap around the ears to make him let it go. He did so, backing off, baring his tiny, razor-sharp teeth. I bared mine back. "Don't mess with me," I yelled. "I am a mother."

Meanwhile thug-monkey was fighting Sally for her Bali-print bag, much to the delight of a crowd of Indians while our pedaller, ashamed of the frisson we were causing, was edging away.

At last someone came to Sally's rescue. An Indian tourist, a well-known cricketer no doubt, waved a mandarin orange under thug-monkey's nose then bowled it over the lawn. The mandarin became a perfect spin ball. Thug-monkey became the perfect outfielder chasing after it. Sally, with her hair resembling a bird's nest and her face scratched and scarlet with embarrassment, raced for our exiting rickshaw, yelling, "Oh God! They have fleas! They have fleas!"

I did not doubt she was right and for a second, I contemplated taking a second rickshaw. But a true friend wouldn't do that, so together we leaped into our three-wheeled escape vehicle and after a quick wave of thanks to our rescuer, we made a quick getaway downhill towards the India Gate.

As we pedalled around it for the third time, I couldn't help myself. "Look, Sal. The India Gate! Want to get off?"

It was a wonder, after the momentous push she gave me, that the rickshaw stayed on its two wheels. Our driver glanced over his shoulder with a look that said, "Just my luck to pick up two nutters," and almost ran head-on into a donkey wagon.

The wagon driver and our pedaller were still shouting at each other when we were swallowed up by tens of thousands of scooters driven by men with sari-clad women balancing precariously in side-saddle mode on pillion seats. How the women stay on is a miracle, as they do not touch the men. Instead they clutch the side of the seat with their left hand while holding their saris over their heads with their right. All the time looking like beautiful, tropical flowers. Sally says it's genetic. That hundreds of years balancing on an elephant make balancing on a scooter child's play.

Two hours later, showered and shampooed, and with Sally's body decontaminated with the many strange concoctions that she keeps in her secret Sally stuff bag, and fortified by a pot of tea, we decided to go and see some Indian dancing.

Showing the pamphlet that advertised an evening of exquisite Indian dance to our hotel reception clerk, his offsider, and his offsider's offsider, we asked them to organize a taxi. There was an instant conference over whose cousin they would ring. How much to charge? And what percentage would they get from the deal?

The driver turned out to be new in Delhi. Four times we circled the ancient Ajimeri Gate which is too narrow for the traffic to go through so it swirls around it, horns blaring in complaint. Three times we saw the black muddy driveway and broken fence of the Russian Gulag-style tourist camp where braver than us tourists put up tents for five rupees. Four times we passed the horse and wagon parking station where horses are harnessed to their wagons at the beginning of their lives and unharnessed when they drop dead. Then we gave up.

"Take us back to the hotel," we yelled.

Indian lesson number three. It takes twice as long to get where you are going while you are paying than coming back after you refuse to pay.

Once in our room, I was too exhausted to read the *Kama*

*Sutra* and I thought Sally was too, so I was astounded to hear her ask for the monster case to be brought down.

Fifteen minutes later, there was a tap on the door and the case bounded into our room, dragging the handsome waiter behind it. I swear if that case could have wagged its handle, it would have.

I don't know what Sally was looking for? But after a half hour of the Japanese plastic bag game, which all backpackers recognize as the undoing of plastic bags, the doing up of plastic bags, the screwing up of plastic bags, and the stirring of plastic bags round and round, while repeating something that sounds like "Double, double toil and trouble, Fire burn and cauldron bubble," Sally hadn't found it. So I turned off my bedside lamp, leaving only the glow from hers for her to stir to. With an irritated click of her tongue, she headed for the main light switch.

"Not if you want to live," I growled.

The case lid was slammed shut and I believe I heard it gasp in pain. But it was not dragged to the door nor was the waiter summoned. The case settled in for the night.

# Chapter 4

## NAKED MONKS

We were descending the stairs to the underground beauty salon when a common Delhi occurrence took place. Delhi's electricity went off and the Dante-like cellar of scissor-waving beauticians was plunged into darkness.

Candle flames appeared within seconds, multiplied into infinity in the salon's mirrors. It was both pretty and creepy. But the hairdressers, all male, and the clientele, all female, didn't notice. No one but us thought it odd that such beautifully thick hair, that we would die for, was being cut and styled by candlelight.

We paid 400 rupees for a massage and 90 rupees for a pedicure and were led away. It was while being pummelled by a very small woman with fists of high-grade steel that I learned how "shampoo" and "bungalow" originated in India, and how all the money I'd paid at the reception desk went to the shop owner. Everyone else lived on their tips. Hint. Hint. I was remarking how unfair this was when my breasts were firmly grabbed and rotated vigorously in opposite directions. This energetic kneading was over before I had time to do more than gasp with surprise. So, I decided, Indian massages were different. That's all.

But it reminded me of a massage I'd had in South Vietnam when three of us booked into our hotel's beauty salon for an advertised relaxing sauna and massage. On our arrival, we were greeted by identical granite-faced triplets with ink-black hair and ink-black lacy underwear. We were led to three cubicles where we were ordered to undress and where, to my amazement, my marble-eyed masseuse stripped and entered the hot shower with me. Put off by her breathing on my neck, I explained that I preferred to sit in the steam alone. This caused her to flounce out, slamming the shower door. I'd been warned.

The massage that followed turned out to be excruciatingly embarrassing. I lay on the massage table as stiff as a new corpse, not a cell of my body relaxing as promised, while my mind searched for a way of escaping before the near-naked masseuse, crouching over my trembling thighs, pounced upon me.

In the next cubicle, Armard's triplet from hell suggested that he ditch his wife and come back for the real thing. His wife, Lizzy, in the third cubicle, remained rigidly speechless for the rest of the day. We never found out what happened to her.

With my Indian massage over, I was led towards my male pedicurist, a sweet young lad who sang to me while slicing off half my foot in an attempt to rid it of layers of dry skin lovingly built up on Bondi beach.

"A lady must have nice feet for husband," he said, with a smile that would have melted the Antarctic.

"I haven't got a husband," I said sadly. "Or a boyfriend anymore."

The look of pity he gave me was heart-wrenching, so I asked him if he had a wife.

"Oh no, Madam. I am saving up for a rickshaw for my father."

I nodded as if this made perfect sense. Then, as I gazed into his translucent black eyes while he kneeled beside the basin my feet were floating in, I wondered if he were a Dalit (the new word for Untouchables). Because if Hindus are not allowed to sit with their feet towards anyone, or prod anyone with their toe because it is insulting, then fiddling with women's feet would be considered such a lowly profession that finding a wife might be a problem.

After the hard-skin-slicing came the erotic-zone foot massage. From my toes to the back of my knees he scrubbed, pressed, pummelled, stretched, prodded, twisted, massaged and creamed. I had no idea there were that many erotic zones between one's knees and toes. By the time he'd finished, I felt I could have climbed Mount Everest barefooted. A pedicure and toenail painting followed. Every second was worth the tip I gave him, along with a promise to return.

Outside the shop, Sally turned on me with eyes the size of emu eggs. "Did she massage your breasts?"

"She did."

"Well? Don't you think that's suspect?"

"It was over too fast to be suspect."

"Don't you think it was sexual?"

"Not for me. I've breast fed."

Then I told her about my Vietnamese massage. That shut her up. With our tingling bodies and matching pink toenails, we decided to blitz Delhi's famous Red Fort. This time we took an auto-rickshaw driven by a handsome fellow with hennaed beard and moustache dyed in honor of the red-haired prophet Mohammed.

On the way, he informed us his name was Singh. Singh is the most popular name in India for all Sikhs and a few million Rajputs because it means "lion." We also learned that no matter how much we stressed that we did not want to go shopping, all auto-rickshaw drivers feel obliged to detour past their cousin's or uncle's souvenir shop, which is where we detoured to. Mr. Singh, who called me sister and who promised faithfully to look after me forever because we had met in another life, begged us to go inside. "Five minutes, dear ladies, then I will receive free petrol." As this is the same deal in Bangkok with the tuk-tuk drivers, we agreed to go inside but not to buy anything. Mr. Singh looked crestfallen as he would have received a commission on our purchases, then he nodded his opium poppy-colored turban at us. "Free petrol will do, dear ladies, and Allah willing, my next passengers will be Americans."

He need not have worried. Sally weakened within seconds of stepping into the cluttered-with-treasure-that-you-do-not-need-but-cannot-live-without shop. Ten minutes later, she exited with three miniature silk paintings, two rings, a pair of earrings and a Persian-style wall hanging. As we left the shop, she gazed longingly at a beautifully carved bookcase.

"Where will you put it all?" I demanded.

"In my case."

"You mean the case that is already bulging at the sides and needs six weight-lifting waiters and a mini-crane to move?"

Delhi's Red Fort is at the end of Chandni Chowk (Silver Street). *Chowk* means bazaar, and Chandni Chowk is one long bazaar as well as an extraordinarily busy thoroughfare smelling of sandalwood, rose and musk incense, and fried sweets, and full of shops, temples, yelling salesmen, hustling porters, hawkers, shoppers and cows feeding on cardboard boxes or plastic bags full of straw dust put down by worshipping vegetarian Hindus. First the cows eat the straw dust, then they eat the bags, boxes and plastic containers, followed by such luxuries as banana skins and vegetable peelings. In other words, they are living garbage disposal units which become manure manufacturers. The manure is collected and turned into fuel and so the recycling goes on.

My Sikh brother (in another life) dropped us off outside the Digambara Jain temple and bird hospital, which we would have adored to visit had we known what it was. But as the monks of the Digambara sect wear no clothes as part of their religious devotions, as covering one's body is considered unnatural, it's probably just as well we didn't pop in. My being an Indian's Delight combined with naked, freely swinging monks frolicking about feeding birds, plus our one night's knowledge of the Kama Sutra, could easily have been the undoing of all of us.

New Delhi, so I'd read, descended from eight different cities. The first, Lal Kot, was built about 1060 a.d. by the Rajputs. The second, Siri, was built in the eleventh century by a Muslim sultan. The third, Tughlaqabad, a massive walled ruin sprawling across a rocky escarpment about half-an-hour's drive from the center of New Delhi, was erected (built doesn't do it justice) in the 1320s by Ghiyas-ud-din Tughlaq, founder of a dynasty that ruled northern India for a hundred years. The fourth, Jahanpanah was built by Ghiyas-ud-din Tughlaq's son. Of the fifth, Ferozabad, built in 1354 by Feroz Shah, there is little to see except a 2300-year-old Ashoka pillar which was dragged there from its original spot by 8400 men. It is near Ferozabad that Mahatma Gandhi was cremated on the steps of the Raj Ghat. The sixth city was built by Muslim Humayun on the banks of the Yamuna, the same Humayun whose tomb we had visited yesterday. The seventh city, Shahjahanabad, was built by Mogul Shah Jahan. The eighth city was New Delhi, built by the British where the monkeys attacked Sally. It contained the National Museum and Connaught Place.

The Red Fort, where we stood now, was in Shahjahanabad. The Red Fort's Lahore Gate, so named because it faces Lahore in

Pakistan, is on the other side of a large square which was once a water-filled moat fed by the Yamuna River, the same river Emperor Humayun's floating palace sailed up and down on. Over time, the river moved a kilometer away, which puts man's attempt to leave his imprint on the earth into perspective, *n'est-ce pas?*

The square has always been a rallying place. It was here in the 1940s that Jawaharlal Nehru, India's first prime minister, and later, Indira Gandhi, India's first female prime minister, gave their "British go home" speeches. So with the imagined sound of an imaginary crowd cheering in our ears, we walked through Lahore Gate and into Chatta Chowk, a vaulted-ceiling, covered-in bazaar. During the seventeenth century, Chatta Chowk bazaar was full of gold merchants' shops that sold only to the royal family, or on a once a week male-free day, the female merchants of the Meena Bazaar took over the Chatta Chowk and sold solely to the high-class *begum* ladies of Shah Jahan's court. Now the bazaar shops sell silk prayer mats woven by children chained to their looms, and gorgeous beaded headdresses reminiscent of those worn by the femme fatale film stars of the thirties. Not only to overseas tourists either. Most of India's tourists are Indian.

Out came my guidebook. "In 1638, Shah Jahan moved his court from Agra to Delhi to an area named after himself, Shahjahanabad. He could do this because his armies controlled an area from Hindu Kush in the north to the Golconda diamond mines in the south, which is one large slice of India."

Sally wasn't listening. She was photographing three pink-and-red striped turnip-shaped domes, resembling three rose-tipped breasts, that belonged to the royal *hammams* or palace baths.

"Unfortunately, before the move from Agra to Delhi could be completed, Emperor Shah Jahan was knocked off his royal elephant, figuratively speaking, and imprisoned in Agra Fort Palace by his ambitious son, Prince Aurangzeb, who, after killing his four brothers and imprisoning his father, usurped the throne. Shah Jahan and Aurangzeb were the only two Mogul emperors to live in the Red Fort. In his later years, Aurangzeb slept in a tent for fear of being assassinated by his sons."

Suddenly I realized that my voice was the only sound I could hear. That my ears were no longer being assaulted by demanding taxi horns and conversations yelled from one silversmith to another. Noise is so prevalent in Delhi that one gets used to shouting over it or listening through it. When it is absent, one's ears tingle with the silence.

Ahead of us stood the Naubat Khana, an impressive three-floored, double-arched Drum House. The Drum House is the first building in any Mogul palace. Here on spring evenings, filled with the pungent perfume of jasmine and the twittering of caged birds kept awake especially for their song, Shah Jahan and his beloved empress listened with tearful nostalgia to the soft drum beats and flirtatious finger cymbals of their northern Mogul homeland.

Behind the Drum House is one of the fort's many gardens. These consist of low box hedges planted in geometrical shapes, spear-thin cypress trees, horizontal and diagonal pathways, and marble fountains. At its peak, this Mogul style of landscaping reached as far as Madrid, Morocco, and Windsor Castle.

How easy it was to imagine the ornate fountain overflowing with perfumed rose water filling the shallow canals, which ran through the garden and then into each of the marbled-pillared halls. The mournful wail of a lone flute. The sobbing into their silk cushions of the lovelorn and forgotten women of the *zenana*. Or, on a brighter note, the excited chatter of the begums, hidden behind their carved screens, discussing what they'd bought on their one-day-a week shopping spree.

On the other side of the garden stands the Palace of Colour. This was once the residence of the beautiful Empress Mumtaz Mahal for whom the Emperor Shah Jahan built the Taj Mahal. Here on a marble platform, beneath waving peacock-feathered fans, leaning on bejeweled cushions, used once then thrown away, the handsome Shah Jahan nibbled away at his Turkish Delight, sipped his fruit liqueurs, and gazed languidly at his beautiful wife, who, equally languidly, or was it seductively, paddled her feet in a large pool sprayed with cool water from a giant lotus flower fountain.

Leaving the emperor's favorite eating place, we visited the famous white marbled-walled Diwan-i-Khas, or Private Audience Hall. Here inscribed on the wall is the Persian quotation: "If there be a paradise on earth, it is here, oh! It is here." It is also in this hall 300 years ago, beneath a silver ceiling, and seated on the beautiful peacock throne, that Shah Jahan received his ministers, reviewed his ceremonial elephants, and discussed matters of great importance with his allies.

"A French traveler," I read from my guidebook, "called Jean-Baptiste Tavernier wrote that Shah Jahan had seven thrones, one covered in diamonds, the others in rubies, but that his peacock throne, with its six solid-gold feet inlaid with emeralds and diamonds and its gold-fringed canopy supported by twelve golden pearl-encrusted pillars, was his favorite. On the canopy's dome stood a peacock with an elevated tail made of blue sapphires, while on the throne's back were two more peacocks encrusted with sapphires, emeralds, pearls and 108 cabochon rubies (apparently Jean-Baptiste Tavernier had counted them all). Between the peacocks flew a parrot carved from a single emerald.

"When Shah Jahan was dying, his son Aurangzeb sent a messenger demanding the release of certain jewels as he intended altering the peacock throne. Shah Jahan sent a return message saying that if he was plagued once more, hammers would be provided to beat the jewels into powder."

Sally and I stared at the empty space where the throne should have been. "So who has the throne now?" asked Sally.

"In the year 1739, the Persian invader, General Nadir Shah, sacked and conquered Delhi and stole the peacock throne, taking it back to Tehran to have it melted down and the jewels broken up."

In solemn silence at such unbelievable destruction, we moved on.

I was watching a group of gossiping white-bearded, brightly turbaned men balancing on a garden wall like a row of rosellas (parrots), and Sally was photographing a small girl carrying a smaller boy, when an Indian tourist sidled up to me and whispered that the guards would take half of anything given to the children.

I gave the girl a packet of cookies which she opened and stuffed into her and her brother's mouths. Sally gave her money which she swallowed as easily as the cookies. So much for the guards' cut. But we hadn't given enough because with brother on hip and with huge eyes begging, she followed us past the monstrously ugly barracks built by the British after they had shot the sons and grandsons of Bahadur Shah, thus finishing off the once-proud Mogul line once and for all, and through three Mogul gardens to the Lahore Gate where we decided to visit our first Indian public toilet.

The toilets had just been showered with buckets of water carried from a hand pump by a man wearing a wet dhoti and an antique British pith helmet. Intent on doing his job well, he insisted I use the freshly splashed men's toilet. His insisting annoyed Sally so she sneaked into the women's toilet when he wasn't looking. Imagine her surprise when he returned with a bucket of water, pushed open the ladies' toilet door (there being no lock) and sloshed the water all over her exposed knees, trousers and feet. She exploded through the door dripping wet, furiously complaining that all he wanted was money. So? Everyone in India wanted money and the piffling sum he got for keeping the toilets clean wasn't likely to make him a millionaire.

Out in a humming, fume-choked Chandni Chowk, we hailed a rickshaw and were almost run down by a scooter carrying a driver, a pillion passenger, and, jammed between them, a large white goat. All three were helmeted. The goat-carrier had gorgeous eyes. So did the goat. Sally became upset about its well-being.

"It's wearing a helmet," I pointed out unnecessarily.

"The fumes can't be good for it."

"Can't be good for us either but we're still breathing."

Our rickshaw stopped at a set of traffic lights where we were set upon by a noseless, handless leper waving his scabby stump in our faces; two small dirt-encrusted girls; and a boy with eyes the color of mint leaves, who pushed the other three out of the way and stuck his hand in my face. Although he was dusty, he had obviously been sent out clean that morning, probably to go to school. Filth won and we gave the girls our small change. The leper wailed with desperate jealousy but the boy shrugged. He was probably their brother and they were working the spot from the clean and dirty angles.

The lights changed and our rickshaw took off. Looking back, I saw a row of swastikas painted across a wall and even though I know the swastika is an ancient symbol associated with the god Vishnu and his elephant-headed son Ganesh, and that Hitler borrowed it along with the word "Aryan," which means light-skinned race from Iran, the swastikas still gave me a shock.

Minutes later, we were at Jama Masjid mosque.

"I will wait for you, Madams?" announced our driver, sounding as if he had been rehearsing these words since he'd picked us up.

"No, thank you. We're going to walk back," I told him.

"But Madams, it is not safe to walk."

"Of course it is. Indians are lovely people."

That stumped him. He was unable to bring himself to say they weren't lovely people even though he wanted to earn more money. It was then I noticed how most of the auto-rickshaw drivers were well-fed, well-dressed Sikhs, whereas the cycle-rickshaw men were bare-footed, bare-chested, darker-skinned, thin Hindus. This one was so skinny I could count his ribs, so I told him to wait.

While taking off our sandals outside the mosque's northern gate, we met up with two Australian backpackers. Liesha and Tanya were the same age as Sally and I when we'd first gone to Morocco and we gazed at them with envy. How marvelous to be starting off for the first time! What amazing adventures they would have! They told us that the Nirula restaurant had the best ice cream in town and we told them that the Imperial Hotel was cheaper than Nirula's and too gorgeous to describe. Then we waved good-bye, promising to see them in Rajasthan which was where the four of us were heading.

Handing our sandals to the shoe-minder, we were given two modesty capes to cover our sinful bare arms before being allowed into the mosque that had been commissioned by Shah Jahan a mere six years after his workmen started the Red Fort.

Mosques are different the world over. Jama Masjid mosque looks nothing like the Blue Mosque of Istanbul or the ancient Mosque of Cordoba. To begin with, it is much, much bigger with a pink-and-rose-red walled courtyard so large that it holds 25,000 worshippers and takes ten minutes to walk across. Outside the courtyard's southern wall is a city of white tents accommodating twice that many pilgrims, and which, a guard told us, is never empty. He boasted that India has over 10 million Muslims, and should they all decide to pray at the mosque on the same day, the crowd would reach to the other side of Delhi. Now that would be a sight to see.

The eastern side of the courtyard, which faces the holy city of Mecca, is the most religious side. Here the main mosque is hidden away behind an elaborately carved red-and-white façade flanked by two pink-and-white striped barber-pole minarets. The turnip-shaped domes of this inner sanctum are not crowned with the symbol of Islam, but with the Hindu symbol of three diminishing water-pots balanced one on top of the other.

This is because Shah Jahan's builders were Hindus, who, high up there close to heaven and their own watching gods, had left their mark, which roughly translated says, "It is the same God towards whom all are directing their steps. Long live God."

Some mosques let all foreigners in. Some let foreign males in. Some only let Muslims in. I have had no problems entering mosques in Turkey or Egypt but was not allowed into a mosque in Morocco, so I was not surprised when we were not allowed inside Jama Masjid. Nor was I surprised when the guard refused to tell us where the women kneeled or where the keepers of the mosque kept the acres of red carpet that they roll out for the 25,000 worshippers to kneel upon. What he did say was that if we could find a man to accompany us, we could climb the southern minaret for a view of old and new Delhi. As it was too hot to accost a passing male and ask him, with suggestively raised eyebrow and a flick of the right shoulder, to "Come up the minaret, honey" we did not get to see the view. Although I did note that *Come Up the Minaret, Honey* was a great title for a book.

Instead, we decided to take a rickshaw to the famous Nizam-ud-din Shrine and watch the sun "die" over the city. On the way, for an extra forty rupees, our pedaller detoured through a posh suburb, and we glimpsed expensive cars parked in bougainvillea-decked car ports; bare-chested gardeners raking lawns with bamboo rakes that resembled the rakers' protruding rib cages; beds of yellow canna lilies tended by arched-over women sweeping up leaves with those ridiculous short-handled, back-breaking brooms, that if I had to use I'd burn first. Here, in middle-class suburbia, there wasn't a beggar in sight.

The Nizam-ud-din Shrine is not the burial place of the thirteenth-century Muslim Sufi saint, Nizam-ud-din. It is the burial place of Princess Jahanara, the faithful and loving daughter of Shah Jahan, who remained with her father for the eight years he was imprisoned in Agra by his wicked son, Aurangzeb.

One wonders how her brother treated her after their father died. After all, he'd done away with their four brothers, so of what value was a mere loyal sister?

The sunset over the city was beautiful. All hazy and smudged by a godly thumb in orange and grey pastel. From the Great Mosque came the high, ululating call of a *muezzin* floating towards us with its chorus of Delhi traffic. It left us feeling infinitely sad. As if, in this land of so many religions, we were missing out.

A woman placing flowers on the tomb said that if we returned on Thursday, the shrine would be aglow with candles and we could hear the Sufi devotional singers. We explained that we would not be in Delhi on Thursday, but that we were enjoying the quiet of the shrine as it allowed us to catch our breath after a very busy day. She nodded and agreed that life was busy, and Sally and I felt that we'd partaken in a deep and meaningful conversation.

As we were leaving this pretty shrine with its black-and-white striped domes and the black-and-white checked courtyard, the sun disappeared and night fell so instantly that, waxing lyrical, I described it as feeling as if I'd just had a kidnapper's black blanket thrown over my head.

"How would you know?" demanded Sally.

Sometimes waxing lyrical is an outright waste of time.

Back at the Arnpit Hotel, showered and with tea and coffee, and Sally's case open on the floor, I suggested that as we were in the land of 900 feature films a year, we should go to the cinema.

Sally didn't answer so I plowed on, "Once in Fiji, my nine-year-old daughter and I were the only non-Indians at an Indian cinema. The film had no subtitles so we spent the entire two-and-a-half hours trying to work out the plot. We never did, but we loved the costumes and the way the heroine wobbled her head, swiveled her eyes and twisted her wrists, and we fell in love with the dashing, singing hero. The next day, while walking along Nandi's main street, we were greeted by every Indian male we passed. One couple insisted we come home for a lunch of goat curry to show their appreciation at our going to their cinema."

"I don't eat goat, and I don't like Indian films," said Sally, wrist deep in her case. "Their love scenes are unrealistic and I hate high-pitched singing."

She was right. There is no kissing in Indian films, and all the heroines have the same high-pitched voices because these are dubbed by Lata Mangeshkar or by her sister, two of the most popular Indian film singers ever.

OK. No film. So how about we go out to eat. But Sally said her boobs hurt from her massage. At this unbelievable excuse, I poured a glass of gin and looked in the *Kama Sutra* for something to do with boobs. I found it.

"Refined in the fourth century A.D., the *Kama Sutra* is a summary of a gentleman's courtly life and a courtesan's daily life. It incorporates the knowledge of sensual pleasure while delighting in the mind, body and soul."

Sally stopped stirring.

"The *Kama Sutra* espouses that men and women should experiment to see what gives them the ultimate pleasure; that technique is no substitute for passion; and that passion and pleasure should be snatched whenever possible. Sally, perhaps you were being passionately snatched by your masseuse?"

"Will you shut up about it!"

So I read to myself how there were eight different types of kissing, and eight special G spot places to kiss. And how after marriage, a couple should sleep apart and only on the tenth night, when the woman has confidence that she has married the right one, should her husband expect all this G spot kissing and finally, marital congress.

Sally couldn't stand my silence. "What are you reading now?"

"A man who knows all the Kama Sutra positions is much loved by his wife, the wives of others, and by the courtesans. With such knowledge he will become a leader in society. But if he doesn't know the positions, even if he can speak on all other subjects, he will lose everyone's respect."

"Three guesses which modern-day politician fits into that category," said Sally.

# Chapter 5

## I Sikh Him Here, I Sikh Him There

New Delhi train station is Victorian in style, as are all the city stations of the largest rail system in the world. How odd to see such a London-looking building plonked down in the middle of swarming India. Obviously the English thought so too because they built an iron fence around it to separate it from the teeming millions. It didn't work.

Inside the fence awaits a battalion of rickshaw drivers, an army of dhoti-wearing porters, and a multitude of stray men primed to snatch bags and carry them off to whichever platform is needed in exchange for a coin. But as we had no baggage, they good-naturedly pointed to the stairs leading to the country ticket office and the station's resting rooms. Resting rooms are hotel rooms attached to railway stations. This is a custom left over from when there were few hotels to accommodate the British who were in constant need of refreshment and rest. I know exactly how they felt. One hour away from our hotel and I was already craving my next shower.

The ticket office was divided into Indians and "others." We filled out a form saying when and where we wanted to go and in which class, first, second, third, and another form saying when we wanted to come back and in which class. Then we joined the "others," along with four Japanese girls, in socks so white that their wearers must have arrived in India five minutes ago, two argumentative Dutchmen, and three solemn-faced, melancholy Finns.

Finally, it was our turn to sit in front of the chubby, turbaned booking clerk with the name of Mr. Singh displayed on his desk. Mr. Singh took our papers. "So you want two one-way tickets to Agra, correct?"

"Yes, please."

"But Madams! How will you return to Delhi?"

"We're going on to Rajasthan."

"But Madams! How?"

"We haven't decided yet."

"But Madams! What if you lose yourselves?"

"We have a map," said Sally.

"A bagful," I added. "My friend collects them."

He shook his head, "No. No. No, Madams. Maps are of no use. They are not correct. You will lose yourselves."

"Then we will have to find ourselves again," said Sally, in her most prim of schoolteacher's voices.

Amazingly, this logic quelled Mr. Singh's worries.

"You also want two sleeping berths from Delhi to Varanasi on the fifth and two sleeping berths from Varanasi returning to Delhi on the ninth, correct?"

We nodded.

"But Madams, it's a very long distance for such a short visit to such an interesting city."

"It is our last week in India," I explained. "But if we wanted to stay longer, could we change the date of our return ticket?"

He smiled sweetly at me, obviously thinking me some sort of brain-dead imbecile. "You could, Madam. If I were in Varanasi. But I am here." He raised his shoulders and opened his hands in a helpless, palms-up gesture. "Would you like upper, lower or middle bunks?"

Pre-warned that there were no ladders to the very high upper bunks and that they were so close to the ceiling fans that one risked decapitation; and that the lower bunks were too crowded and getting all the other passengers off them when you wanted to sleep was nigh impossible, we chose the middle. We then told Mr. Singh that he had been so helpful that he should come with us.

"Oh, Madams," he giggled. "There is nothing I would like better than to visit Varanasi. It is every Hindu's dream. But my wife is a very jealous woman."

I thought of enticing him with the fact that we carried our own *Kama Sutra*, but in the end, I told him that it was the same the world over, the best men were always taken.

On the way out of the station, we decided that someone should be told about how pleasant Mr. Singh was, so I stuck my head through the doorway of the manager's office and informed a Western-dressed woman that her Mr. Singh was a gem. She jumped up and invited us in, saying that so few people gave her feedback other than to complain, she was overjoyed to hear something nice for a change. Once we were seated, she gave us a short history of the railways, which turned out to be a compulsory examinable subject for all the railway's employees.

"Before 1850," she explained, "the poor people traveled by donkey, horse, camel or ox-drawn carts. The rich traveled by palanquins (litters) carried by bearers, accompanied by hordes of servants, tents and baggage, while the panjandrums (VIPs) of the British public service went in horse-drawn carriages."

Her voice rose dramatically. "All battled incredible distances with the ever-present danger of bandit attacks. Fifty years later, thanks to the British, more than 23,000 miles of track had been laid. These tracks carried over 11,000 trains a day which transported over 10 million passengers a day, thus Indian life has been greatly improved. Is it not amazing?"

Her grey-blue eyes, so at odds with her olive skin and pepper-grey hair, shone with pride, so we quickly agreed that it was indeed amazing. Then she continued with an intriguing snippet of gossip. "When my great-grandfather, a high-up British official, went abroad to oversee various British government projects, he took twelve armed guards, his carriage and his coffin. You see, although he had a British wife, he also had an Indian wife whom he hated to be parted from, but with whom he was unable to travel openly, due to protocol, you understand."

We nodded.

"The coffin, with air holes drilled into it, was placed in my grandfather's room each night while by day my great-grandmother lay inside it being jogged along on a wagon behind his official carriage. Can you imagine the shock bandits would have received if they had attacked his party and opened the coffin?"

She dissolved into laughter behind her cafe au lait hand. Then shrugging her shoulders, as if to say that was enough frivolity for one day, she handed Sally a pile of maps and wished us a happy journey.

"What about her great-grandmother having to lie in a coffin all day?" demanded Sally, as we descended to the street.

"They were in love," I said, feeling a pang of guilt because there was no way I would ever love anyone enough to lie in a coffin all day.

Across the very busy road was the Paharganj market. Once over, and still in one piece, we went in search of a cobbler. We found one. He'd set up business on the dusty pavement across the street from a tiny, two-table chai shop. The poor man didn't know what to do with us when we sat on the gutter beside him to discuss the cost of mending my sandal and Sally's backpack strap. The worker was indisputably an Untouchable. Who else in India would work on the lowliest part of the body, my feet, plus mend Sally's backpack which was made from the skin of a dead holy cow? Which also meant that by rights he should have been sitting lower than us for fear of his shadow polluting our bodies. Well, we sure messed up that bit of caste law.

"No wonder so many of them are becoming Christian," said Sally, as we sipped chai in the chai shop.

I agreed with her. Christ was an equalist. Well, almost an equalist. After all, it was Mary Magdalene who dried his feet with her hair, not Peter, Paul, Andrew or Judas. We drank more chai while watching the cobbler expertly use his big toe to hold my sandal while mending it. When he was finished, he gave us a look. That was all. Nothing as forward as a wave or beckoning gesture. Simply a brief, under the eyebrows glance. We finished our tea and crossed the street to pay him what seemed a reasonable amount to us but was probably a small fortune for him. Then off we went to Chandni Chowk again.

On arriving at Gurdwara Temple, we entered a reception room where we were given yellow scarves to cover our heads while we listened to a lecture about the Sikh religion. This comparatively modern religion was founded in 1469 by Guru Nanak, a gentleman who, not satisfied with the religions of his time, invented his own.

"Sikhs make up 1.8 percent of the Indian population," explained the young guide, who was wearing crispy clean Western clothes and a sparkling white turban. "In 1604 the Holy Scripture was compiled by the fifth guru. This guru also built the famous Gurdwara Darbar Shib or Golden Temple, at Amritsar. Amritsar is our holy city."

I'd read about Amritsar's Golden Temple. In 1984 after anti-government Sikh rebels had taken refuge in it, Prime Minister

Indira Gandhi had sent in Sikh troops to fetch them out. This hasty action ultimately ended her life as she was later assassinated by two of her Sikh guards. The moral being "do not send a Sikh to seek out another Sikh."

"Sikhs believe in one supreme God," continued our pristine guide. "In brotherly love and the salvation of honest work. But … when all else fails, they believe in the righteousness of the unsheathed sword."

As was discovered by Prime Minister Indira Gandhi.

"In 1780 due to the disintegration of the Mogul Empire and the invasion of the Afghan armies, the Sikhs established their own kingdom. This lasted sixty-nine years, until in 1849 they were annexed by the British."

"So there," mouthed Sally.

"I didn't know Afghanistan invaded India," I mouthed back.

"In Sikhism there is no caste system, no idols, no dowries, no divorce, no use of alcohol or tobacco, and no purdah. The birth of a daughter is celebrated and widows have never thrown themselves onto their husbands' funeral pyres. When Sikhs die, they are cremated and their ashes thrown into a body of water. Widows and widowers can remarry but a Sikh can only marry one woman at a time. Adultery is a sin and females wearing suggestive clothing are dishonorable. A Sikh husband must support his family and a Sikh wife must guide the family's spiritual life and pray daily for her husband's welfare."

I nudged Sally to stop her asking the obvious feminist question, i.e. what about the wife's welfare?

Our guide continued, "A Sikh is recognizable by five symbols. The *kesha* which means long hair. The *kangha* or comb worn beneath the turban. The *kara* which is a steel bracelet. The *kirpan*," he pulled a short sword from his trouser belt, "and the *kaccha*," he held up a pair of unbleached cotton underpants. "All five must be with him at all times."

"Do the women wear the same five items?" I asked.

"Not the turban, Madam, but the long hair, comb, bracelet and knife."

"And the baggy underpants?" asked Sally.

His dark eyes glittered cheekily at her. "Ah Madam, it is a wise man who knows what a lady wears under her sari. Now follow me, please."

We entered the Gurdwara Temple straight off the dusty pavement of Chandni Chowk by first washing our feet in a shallow trough of running water. The main hall was packed with men, women and children, all seated facing a golden canopy. Under the canopy sat a black-turbaned, black-bearded man reading at full volume from a holy script. Behind him sat three turbaned musicians playing mewling hand-pumped harmoniums. Surrounding them, visiting Sikhs talked and took photographs. The noise was deafening.

Our guide yelled over it, explaining that there was no Sikh priesthood and that any male or female could conduct the prayer. Then he led us into a kitchen where he explained that each day food was prepared for devotees, pilgrims and visitors.

"Here the high and low, rich and poor, learned and ignorant, share the same food," he explained. "But not enough to make refusing work a comfortable alternative. Just enough to keep a man alive while he searches for work. Widows and orphaned children are provided for indefinitely." Which decided me that if I were reborn an Indian woman, I would be a Sikh.

The kitchen was a large airy room with a spotless stone floor and three ovens in front of which sat a dozen well-dressed, bejeweled women with an equal number of small boys with long hair tied up in white scarves. All were busy rolling balls of flour and water. They smiled at us as if a string of curious foreigners threading their way through their kitchen was commonplace. Further along sat a white-turbaned man with a long grey beard tucked into his mandarin-orange cummerbund. He was in charge of a copper pan full of *chapattis*. Around the corner, more people stirred huge pots of dhal and a man in a pink floral turban turned roti on a hotplate. Everyone looked happy and everything was well organized and spotlessly clean.

Our guide took us out onto the temple roof where under the yellow flags that flutter over every Gurdwara temple, old men sat cross-legged praying or sleeping on their mats. One old man wearing a jacaranda-purple turban, baggy trousers and coat tied with an orange sash frowned furiously at us as he rearranged his bed over and over. Behind him rose the golden domes of a small mosque. Behind them towered the golden spires of a Hindu temple. Religion is shoulder-to-shoulder in Delhi.

That evening we ate on the roof of our hotel along with three French tourists who'd spent the day shopping in some very expensive shops. One of the women had bought a beautiful grey and lemon colored silk salwar kameez. With the lemon scarf wrapped around her neck, and her lemon leather sandals, she looked perfect.

Next morning, we decided to complete our religious tour of Delhi by visiting the Lakshmi Narayan temple. The one beside the scaffold-covered statue of Hanuman, the monkey god.

This modern-style temple was built in 1938. A successful Hindu industrialist who wished to find favor with the god Krishna financed it. By paying for such a large holy building he was investing in reincarnation insurance in a big way, and his prayer, that of being reborn to as comfortable a lifestyle as he already had, if not better, would surely be answered, or so said the man who took our shoes at the front door. The temple was fantastically ornate and crowded hip-to-hip with colorfully dressed devotees all willing to tell us about Hinduism and its five important beliefs.

First let me point out that as eighty percent of Indians are Hindu; this is no small religion. It started this way:

When the nomadic Aryan invaders overthrew the ancient civilizations of the fertile Indus Valley, they brought with them their chief god, Indra. Indra, god of storms, or to use his other title, Purandara, fort-destroyer, threw thunderbolts, much like

Thor of the Scandinavians and Zeus of the Greeks. In other words, he was a war god.

After the Aryans conquered the great agricultural cities of Harappa and Mohenjo-Daro, an area larger than Egypt or Sumer, they swallowed up the Indus valley's two chief cults of phallic lingam worship and sacrifice to the mother goddess (the ancestress of Kali). Over time, the Aryan god Indra became inferior to the triad of Brahma the Creator, Vishnu the Preserver and Shiva the Destroyer, all initially conceived as personifications of Brahman the immanent absolute, and Hinduism began, but still the most sacred image of a Hindu temple remains the *lingam* (the phallic symbol) within the *garbhagrha* (womb house) which is a small chamber in the center of the temple.

The five important beliefs of Hinduism barely touch on the enormous and complicated mythology that support this religion, but here goes.

One: that there are over a million Hindu gods and goddesses but Brahman is the Eternal One; that the Brahman wheel of birth, death and reincarnation encompasses the individual, the species, the social structure, the planet, the gods and the universe.

Two: that if you have an unrelenting, poverty-stricken life in the slums of Calcutta, Birmingham or New York, it is because you were a nasty person in a previous life and you are being punished, so don't expect any pity. Be humble, accept your lot, don't be ambitious, don't argue with your betters, bow low, and you might, just might, be reborn in a higher caste next time. But not if you are a woman.

Three: that cows, because they represent fertility, and bulls, because Shiva the Destroyer rides one, have been worshipped since ancient times. This is why Hindus do not eat beef, and why, in 1887, Hindus in the British Army mutinied when it was rumored that they were to clean their rifles with beef fat.

Four: that the Vedas scriptures, a collection of hymns written in 1000 b.c. by a Brahman, successfully divided the conquering upper-class Aryans from the conquered lower-class Indians by creating the four main castes. Which are the Brahmans, meaning the head of God or born out of the mouth of God, who were once priests but are now the wealthy upper class. The Kshatriyas, meaning the body of God, who were once exulted warriors, and are today's soldiers. The Vaisyas, the arms of God, who were once the traders and merchants and still are. The Sudras, the legs of God, who have always been and will always be the farmers. And the Dalits, who have had no caste for over 2000 years and are called Untouchables. Far below them, somewhere beyond even mentioning, are the Outcasts. One wonders what dreadful things they did in a past life to deserve such unending, unforgiving, unchanging misery? The four castes have sub-castes such as boat rowers, clay workers, cotton pickers, pedicurists and cobblers, and everyone is expected to marry within their sub-caste and do the same work as their father, grandfather, great-grandfather.

Five: that in all castes, including Brahman, women are less important than men. That to be born a woman is a punishment for a bad past life. Probably for being born a woman in the first place. This chauvinistic belief came about around the year of Christ's birth when a Brahman called Manu produced the first compilation of Hindu law which assigned women the status of chattel. Manu the Misogynist's exact words were, "Women are as foul as a falsehood." He continued with, "When the Lord of Creatures created women, he allotted them a love of their beds (sloth), of their chairs (laziness), of their ornaments (vanity), along with impure thoughts, wrath, dishonesty, malice and bad conduct."

Suddenly India's caste system made sense to me. If you were an Iranian general coming to conquer India one thousand years before Christ, what better way to do it than to convince the indigenous people that they weren't as high up God's social ladder as you were? Conquerors and colonists have been doing this for centuries. Then, if you wanted to keep men in their place you need only threaten them with being reborn a woman, who were all of a lower caste than men. It works every time.

As we left flower-decked Lakshmi Narayan temple, I was reminded of an old, red brick Hindu temple that I'd visited in Vietnam. At first sight, Cham Temple appeared derelict but as I climbed the path, I saw that the garden had been freshly watered and the blue-and-white tiled floors washed. Inside was a modest altar containing a gilded statue of Vishnu, two vases of lilies and some fruit. It was a peaceful, unadorned place. While I sat on some steps reading about the French colonization of Vietnam which made the English colonization of India look like a teddy bears' picnic, along came a group of Vietnamese worshippers dressed in long gowns of brown, maroon, deep pink and red, and all wearing large black necklaces resembling oversized rosary beads. I asked them if anyone spoke English. A schoolteacher did. He explained that centuries ago, Hinduism had been very strong in Vietnam and that there were still pockets of believers scattered throughout the hills. Cham Temple was their most holy place which was why he had rented a mini-bus and brought his villagers to see it. I took his address and promised to post him the photographs I had taken of them. Which I did.

Back at the Arnpit Hotel, we packed for our Himalayan trip, putting everything else in the monster case which went back to the top floor, whimpering all the way. I wouldn't have been at all surprised if that waiter didn't have arms stretching to his knees by the time we left.

# Chapter 6

## Rİshİkesh and Harİdwar

Our driver drove a cream 1950 Ambassador. His name was Umesh. He looked about twelve but was about eighteen and he spoke very little English and couldn't read Hindi, but he swore that he had driven to Corbett Tiger Reserve many times in the last six years. I calculated that this would have made him about twelve years old when he started. As Umesh couldn't read any of Sally's five maps and Sally couldn't find where we were, and her five opened maps were threatening to block the windshield, I became navigator. Why me? Because I can find north even if it is pitch black or raining. It's one of the survival techniques taught to me by my mother who believes that when the next world war comes we will need such skills.

Umesh did not eat during the day because he could not be sure the food was prepared in the right manner. We had to demand, quite forcefully, for him to stop so that we could buy water or fruit. Nor did he go to the toilet which was interesting because for the first three hours of our trip, it appeared that every other male in India was squatting along each side of the highway opening his bowels onto the brick dust, the bricks having been laid in rows of six on either side to widen the road. Or perhaps they'd been put there so that the entire male population of India could defecate in unison.

There are rules about performing one's toilet in India. One must be a bow's shot from anyone's home, a sacred banyan tree, temple, river, pond, well, field or footpath. Along a very busy highway is all that's left. There are also rules about how to do it. He (don't know what females do, as we didn't see any), must squat for everything. No standing up aiming at a haystack like a Frenchman, or spraying a wall and his shoes like an Aussie. While performing, an Indian must not look at the moon, sun, stars, fire or a passing Brahman and if he is an Untouchable then his crouching polluting shadow must not fall on any other caste. On completion a male must cleanse himself by using dirt or brick dust scooped up by his left hand. The use of toilet paper is considered filthy. Which is a good thing. Imagine a country ankle-deep in used toilet paper. Mind you, I still wouldn't be keen on using a handful of much used brick dust. Others must have come to the same conclusion as many of the males were washing themselves from plastic bowls. One wondered how clean they would end up, with the clouds of exhaust fumes belching from every passing vehicle and a plethora of plastic bags and bottles falling from the sky every time a vehicle drove past.

Suddenly we hit a traffic jam. Up ahead a truck had "eaten" a farmer's tractor. The mangled tractor was jammed beneath the truck's front wheels and although there were vehicles banked up on either side, there were no police, truck or tractor drivers. It was probably smart of the truck driver to disappear, considering how often lynch mobs assemble when there are accidents, such as in Rishikesh, where we were going, when a bus ran down two schoolgirls and the villagers killed twenty-five of the passengers in retaliation.

Following the car in front, Umesh nosedived down a dirt track into a creek bed, revved through knee-deep sand, then plowed towards a row of empty-fronted shops packed with curious-eyed men sitting in a row watching the mounting congestion. Outside the shops were two *charpoys* which are string cots set up for men to rest on after a cup of tea and a hard day's work. On them lay two men, wearing *lungis* (tubes of material pleated in the front at the waist), sleeping blissfully, unaware of the chaos around them.

In front of the sleepers, who were getting coated with dust, converged two opposing lanes of traffic. Buses full of calm-faced people squeezed past each other while carefully negotiating the narrow space between the shops and a row of eucalyptus trees. Bicycles dodged, ox carts trundled, cars hooted and threw up dust to hide that they were sneaking into the already jammed queue, and people stood about gaping. I got out for a walk. With one of his passengers disappearing into the traffic, it was amazing how quickly Umesh caught up with me. Still no police! It made me wonder how long the crippled truck and mangled tractor had been there. Six months? A year? Everyone seemed very used to the creek-bed detour.

Two hundred-and-ninety kilometers later, we arrived at Ramnagar, the gateway to the Corbett Tiger Reserve, where we were charged a toll to drive up the main street. This is the locals' way of making money. Another is to force the tourists' chauffeur to take an eye test, for which the tourist must pay, before the car is allowed to proceed along a road that without an eye test could be dangerous. They probably have man-made avalanches waiting for those who refuse.

While the toll collector thrust his greasy ticket book in our faces, we argued with Umesh that the government tourist bureau woman had sworn that all tolls and entry fees were included in the deal. He agreed that she might have said this but that she lied. Can't beat that logic. We paid the toll. Then we drove to the Ramnagar booking office to book two nights' accommodation in a tourist village in the center of the reserve. Here we came up against the town's second money-making scheme.

"Dhikala village is full, Madams. You had better stay in Ramnagar and drive into Bijrani tomorrow," explained the official, who was sharing his very small ticket office with five chai-drinking comrades.

"No accommodation. No entry," explained two Dutch backpackers, who were hanging around waiting for a lift.

Bijrani was not far enough into the reserve for Sally's liking, so we continued to push for Dhikala. Fifteen minutes later, we gave up. "OK, you win. We won't go to the tiger park. Can you please tell our driver in Hindi the fastest route to Rishikesh?"

This caused a mini-riot with the six men talking in Hindi all at once. Then the astounded official asked in English, "You do not go to the tiger park?"

"Not if there is no accommodation. We'll complain when we get back to Delhi and demand our money back."

That did it. Shouts at Umesh, who shook his head when we asked him what was wrong. But a guessed translation went like this: "A complaint to Delhi! My goodness me! Don't these silly foreigners know how to play the accommodation game?"

Of course we did because miraculously there was accommodation in Dhikala. "But it is very expensive," the official explained. "Which is why I did not mention it before. But you will see tigers I guarantee it."

So we paid for two nights and set off for Dhangarhi Gate,

which was twenty kilometers farther north, without the Dutch backpackers who refused to give Umesh a tiny tip if he took them, so he didn't. Naturally we missed Dhangarhi Gate. It did not look like a gate and its sign-post was in Hindi, a language none of us read. So how did Umesh get a car license if he can't read Hindi? And if he'd been here six times before, why didn't he know where the gate was? Don't ask.

The road to Dhikala village was a dirt track that twisted around and over many tree-covered hills before diving into countless steep-sided valleys and crossing what felt like hundreds of dry riverbeds full of round white stones the size of goose-feathered pillows. Although only fifty kilometers, it took us two hours with Umesh grumbling all the way about what his car owner would say to all the bumping, jarring and scraping of his exhaust pipe. We were unsympathetic. It wasn't our problem. Sally and I were learning the Indian trick of detachment. Whatever the problem, it's someone else's. Which could account for a lot in India.

It was during this tedious trip with nothing to see except what showed up in the beams of our bouncing headlights that Sally told me about Jim Corbett, the hunter turned tiger lover.

"Jim Corbett was idolized by the villagers because he killed the tigers that attacked them in their fields. Then one day he realized that if he, the maharajahs, the British royalty and the British upper-class, especially Lord Curzon who was famous for shooting anything that moved, continued shooting tigers and using them as library rugs, eventually there would be none left. So enlightened Jim threw away his guns, retired his trusty gun-carrier and took up wildlife photography. The result was India's first national park established in 1936. Which was no small feat in a country of starving millions, and considering the world was about to be plunged into the Second World War."

Sally continued, this time reading from a pamphlet she'd picked up in Ramnagar. "Corbett Tiger Reserve is situated beside the Ramganga River, home of the long-snouted, fish-eating

Asian crocodile and the much venerated by Hindus, Indian mugger crocodile that eats anything that moves. There are wild elephants, rhesus macaque monkeys, black-faced langur monkeys, tree-nesting peacocks, samba deer, monitor lizards, wild boars, jackals, Bagheera panthers and tigers."

I was impressed. This was some park.

On our arrival at Dhikala village, the keeper of the accommodation handed us a key and pointed into the darkness. "Third pink house. Film show in fifteen minutes. Everybody come."

"Unless they are eaten by a tiger as they search for their pink house," muttered Sally, who had to carry her own four bags as Umesh had disappeared into the drivers' quarters.

Our pink house had two apartments. One up, one down. As we climbed the stairs, we heard the woman below complaining to her porter in German-accented English that she did not want a ground floor apartment because a tiger might come through the window.

Her porter did the I'm-not-involved shrug but she kept on at him. In the end, he told her, "Madam, tigers are very rare and should one deem to visit you, you should consider yourself most honored. I have worked here all my life and never seen one yet. It is the water buffalo you have to be careful of. They will charge you."

So much for our guaranteed tiger sighting!

Dumping our bags on our beds, we headed into the water buffalo-filled darkness in search of a film screen. We found it inside an open-sided shed with seating ranging from ancient stuffed armchairs of a questionable health risk (they appeared to have been eaten in for centuries. I'm sure they had nests of mice, rats, spiders and other creepy crawlies inside them), rows of hard-backed chairs guaranteed to paralyze the bum and a row of straw mats for the children. We opted for the straw mats and the children, who promptly all called us "Aunty."

The film was old. Its music crackled and spat. Animals disappeared as the projector hit a piece of damaged celluloid then reappeared while a plummy British voice described, in spurts and starts, how the endangered bear, wolf, snow leopard and one-horned rhino were seldom seen nowadays. We were not surprised as he then continued with the description of how one maharajah had shot 207 rhinoceroses and 311 leopards in one day.

"But," he finished, happily, "there are spotted deer, hog deer, barking deer and wild asses, joyfully cavorting here in Corbett's Himalayan foothill reserve."

It might have been his accent or it might have been the "joyfully cavorting," but I got an instant mental picture of all the different animals dancing the congo through the jungle led by a fierce tiger and being hurried along by a snobby elephant with a swagger stick à la Disney.

"Will you stop sniggering," hissed Sally.

"I'm tired," I whispered back. "Although a bit of *Kama Sutra* might get me back on track. There have to be some wildlife positions in that book."

"They're all wildlife if you ask me. Anyway, I'm sick of the *Kama Sutra*."

This confirmed my suspicion that Sally was becoming dissatisfied with her pillow as a Kama Sutra partner and that she was missing her boyfriend.

Back in our pink house, I searched through the *Kama Sutra* and discovered the perfect wildlife picture. It was of the blue-skinned god Krishna, the cupid of Indian mythology, frolicking in a garden with a most willing damsel. Naked except for a sparkling crown topped with jeweled peacock feathers and many pearl necklaces, Krishna rested back on a pink satin pillow while the nubile sweetie, wearing only a gold-fringed red headscarf and her "making loving" jewelry, lay on top of him. But Krishna, looking quite bored and most disinterested with her pink plump buttocks and well-rounded thighs, gazed elsewhere. So she was playfully tugging at his long black tresses. Or considering how disinterested he was, perhaps the tugging was not so playful. Maybe she was trying to scalp him. The sweetie's heels were chained together with golden chains. Which meant she was unable to storm off if the hair-pulling ploy didn't work. Beside them were two green birds symbolizing freedom. Well, maybe not. Maybe I made that bit up because I don't like the idea of women's ankles being chained.

None of this was what I wanted to show Sally. It was who was in the garden with the amorous couple that interested me. Up in a tree sat a guard with a bow and arrow, below sat another with a monkey on his knee, the monkey was being lovingly familiar with the guard. Beside them lounged a third guard with a second monkey hugging and kissing him.

I held the book up so Sally could see. "Look Sally, that monkey who chased you in Delhi was definitely in love with you."

"Get over it!" she snapped.

I think it was her case she was missing, not her boyfriend. When she can't play the Japanese plastic bag game, she becomes very bad tempered.

Next morning we were woken by the complaining bellow of a bull elephant. It was 5 a.m. and we were booked on a jungle ride in search of tigers. We bounded out of bed, threw on our clothes, and raced outside.

The elephants were lined up at the elephant station. This is a platform from which one launches one's self onto the cloth-padded wooden saddle of whichever is your rocking mono-lith. Our rocking monolith's name was Rupkali. She had a black painted forehead with a white stripe across her eyebrows which continued behind her ears resembling a pair of John Lennon spectacles. The look in her large eyes reminded me of the painful eyes of women who are wearing shoes a size too small. It can't be much fun getting up at five every morning to traipse through a jungle that no longer holds any surprises. Especially if one's feet are hurting.

Rupkali carried six tourists. Sally and I sat at the back, facing backwards, because we wanted to pretend we were riding her alone. True, our view was of where Rupkali had been, and she and her brother and sister elephants "went" a lot, but I figured that if I were a tiger, and I heard an elephant tiptoeing towards me, the safest place would be to be behind it. Elephants make very little sound when they move, unless they're eating, then they sound like a crane knocking down a skyscraper. Do they care? No, they don't. Indian elephants have perfected the "It's not my problem" shrug long ago.

Rupkali left Dhikala village at a reluctant dawdle. Entering a forest full of peach-pink mist and tinkling bird calls, her mood bucked up immediately; up went her big grey head as she sashayed through chest-height pink-and-yellow lantana, making a noise like soft rain on a plastic raincoat. Every now and then she'd stop to rip up a rohni plant and eat its wide green leaves, or to pee, which, coming from immediately below us, sounded like the blast from a fireman's hose that left large soapy-water puddles on the path. Ahead of us yesterday's great globs of poo showed it to be a known route. What chance of spying a tiger? Practically none.

But nothing could spoil this enchanted morning. The rays of the sun slanting like hundreds of Mogul spears, the trees disappearing into the mist above our heads, my foot on my elephant's back feeling her rolling motion through my sandal, and the jolt of her hip as she took a short threatening run at three wild boars drinking at her personal waterhole. The boars bounded away, displaying no fear as their plump rumps bobbed up and down showing Rupkali exactly what they thought of her.

Rupkali's skinny tail had a few large black hairs growing out of an end that resembled a much-used toilet brush. It reminded me of the elephant-hair bracelets popular in my mother's day. She'd had one with a heavy silver clasp and thought it very exotic. I bet she didn't know it came from the elephant's tail.

Rupkali had a large sore on her left ankle from being chained up at night. I'd read that elephant trainers have to be cruel to break an elephant's will, and I immediately wished that I was hidden in a *machaan* observation tower watching this matriarch of her herd, unfettered and unsaddled, wandering along her own chosen path, not here with five others on her back participating in this act of passive cruelty.

Then as quickly as we'd dived into the damp jungle, we were out of it and swaying across a yellow elephant-grass plain towards a hillock crowned with five burned trees splayed like skinny fingers. Beside it stood an elephant.

"Wild," announced our elephant-wallah, a white-bearded man of about eighty. Would such a venerable old man lie? Sally and I thought so. The scene was too picturesque, too staged. If the elephant was wild, why didn't it move away as we approached? Instead, it stood there posing for our tourist cameras while six falcons swooped away on cue to fly over the purple water-mint of the Ramganga Reservoir.

"Tethered," I said.

"Cut-out cardboard," said Sally.

Either way we didn't get close enough to find out.

After a "never to be forgotten" two-hour ride, we returned to the elephant station where the elephants posed for photographs while we stroked their leathery trunks. Then while Sally asked Rupkali's mahout about a small green fruit called *amle* which she'd read was used to blacken elephants' toenails but which Indians also used in their pickles and jams, I went to look at the river. Not yet filled by monsoonal rain and reflecting a peerless blue sky, its string of water-lily filled pools looked like a necklet of sequins. I was admiring it when I discovered a very funny warning notice: "Ramganga River is inhabited by crocodiles. Swimming is prohibited. Survivors will be prosecuted." I should imagine they'd be pleased to be, if they survived.

Walking around outside the village is forbidden, so the rest of our stay was spent searching the river for snouts of crocodiles, bird-watching, talking to the rich Indian children who were there on holiday, and visiting the library which had the most amazing collection of old books and maps. Here I discovered that Corbett Tiger Reserve and the much larger Sonanadi Wildlife Sanctuary were joined together and that we would have to drive around them both to reach the holy town of Rishikesh, a fact our Delhi tourist agent lady had forgotten to mention.

Two days later, we left peaceful Dhikala without having seen a tiger but very happy to have been there. Back along the winding road we bumped. Over the riverbeds of stone with more complaints from Umesh, who, Sally pointed out, was a very unattractive man. Through Ramnagar, once again being caught by the toll collector, and out onto the main road, where having just passed a row of small cemented houses with bicycle parts holding down their plastic-covered roofs and a field full of women collecting cow pats, there came a loud bang from under the back seat.

"We are fractured," cried Umesh, pulling over.

It was clear by the way he waved his hands about that Umesh didn't change tires. He was a driver. Another caste, lower than his, dealt with tires.

"Have you got a jack?" I asked.

"Yes, Madam."

"Have you got a spare tire?"

"Yes, Madam."

"Where are they?"

"In Delhi, Madam!"

"That should be a great help."

We stood for half an hour, watching the lumber trucks roar past, then Umesh began walking back to town while we, much to his disgust, went to a street stall to buy something to eat. The stall sold curry balls served on a plate made from leaves sewn together. There were no knives, forks or spoons. Indians can't understand how we can put these utensils back into our mouths after they have touched our saliva. (I wonder how they feel about kissing). We ate with our fingers then threw the leaves away. All this cleanliness would have been admirable if after eating I hadn't seen the filthy, scum-covered drain that ran behind the food stall.

An hour later, two mechanics arrived. One carrying an antiquated jack, the other rolling a tire. Within minutes, the tire was changed and we were off. We never found out who paid for the tire, but it wasn't us.

We arrived at Rishikesh at dusk to find that all the hotels and ashrams of this famous town, where the Beatles discovered their orange-robed Maharishi Mahesh, were full. Even the Hotel Ganga, recommended for its yoga classes, could only offer a tent-with-a-view.

We ended up at the GMVN Tourist Bungalows, an antiquated set-up surrounded by a lovely garden. That evening we walked down a steeply cobbled alley, christened Urine Alley, to the Lakshman Jhula bridge. This picturesque bridge is a walking, scooter-riding, bike-riding, cow-strolling, single-span affair with two cables stretching from one side to the other. Beneath these cables hangs a plank walkway with wire safety-fences each side to stop devotees from throwing themselves into the water. Hindus believe the river Ganges flows from god Vishnu's feet.

To the north of the bridge was a semi-circle of purple hills blinking with low watt electric lights, paraffin lamps and candles. To the south squatted Swarg Ashram, the main temple district, where bell-tinkling ashrams lean tiredly against multi-colored temples, each with its own steps or landing facing the river or ghat, and each wearing a garish electric light necklace that is reflected like an upside down fun park in the river.

We crossed the bridge and were walking towards the temples when we saw a matted-haired, scraggly-bearded *sadhu* standing bemused in the middle of the street. Beside him stood an earnest young woman speaking German. This was surprising because the sadhu didn't look as if he was anchored to the planet let alone able to understand that distant language.

Catching hold of his filthy hand, she gazed into his vacant kohl-rimmed eyes and invited him to come with her. The sadhu remained motionless. I doubt if he knew she was there.

Farther up the hill, three Indian women who'd been watching the sadhu and the girl raised their eyebrows at us in a skeptical manner as we passed. We raised ours back. Enough said.

The restaurant catered to foreigners and Indians. The back-packers were clustered together eating bowls of porridge, honey and banana. The Indians were clustered around the television watching a popular soap based on the great Hindu epic, *The Ramayana*, which goes something like this:

When King Rama's Queen Sita was kidnapped by the evil demon King Ravana of Sri Lanka, handsome King Rama with his equally handsome brother Lakshmana and Hanuman the monkey god rushed to her rescue. During the war that followed, Lakshmana was wounded and Hanuman the monkey god flew to the Ganges on his flying cloud in search of lifesaving herbs. Unable to choose which would save the king's brother, he picked up the entire holy mountain and carried it back to Sri Lanka, scattering over 2000 healing plants across the width and breadth of India. After conquering King Ravana, for which King Rama rewarded Hanuman with the gift of perpetual life and youth, King Rama accused Queen Sita of being polluted by the evil demon king. Queen Sita swore that King Ravana had not touched her, but her husband was adamant. Broken-hearted, Queen Sita ordered a fire to be built and then threw herself upon it to prove to her husband how pure she was.

It was from this myth that the *suttee* ritual of widow burning developed. The logic of it escapes me. It's a bit like when the Europeans threw chain-laden women into the river believing if they floated they were witches and if they drowned they weren't.

All the male actors in this television melodrama had flashing black eyes, long dark eyelashes, turned-up moustaches and flowing black hair. The actresses all resembled the nubile sweeties in the *Kama Sutra*, with more jewelry if that was possible. The acting was dramatic with much singing even by the doomed Sita. The Indians lapped it up. So did I.

Next morning I rose very early and discovered that Umesh had not slept in the room that we'd paid for him to sleep in. He probably cashed it in and slept in the car. We had a lot to learn. Wanting to see the Ganges as dawn broke, I hurried down Urine Alley, around goats picking through last night's rubbish, over sewerage-filled gutters, past the very expensively built house of a successful guru, until I reached Lakshman Jhula Road and the swinging bridge.

I was not disappointed. It was wonderful. I stood in the middle of the bridge, staring down at the water with a Himalayan wind blowing through me while behind me the mountains glowed with an eldritch luminescence and the air tingled like chilled champagne. It was probably the freshest it would be all day as I was up before the manure patty fires were lit. Then along came the milkman.

He was riding a battered Vespa scooter with an aluminium milk-urn tied to each side. On reaching the middle of the bridge, he took a scoop of milk out of one urn and tossed it over the safety wire. For a moment, the milk hung like a silver arch, then it landed on the holy river's surface, spreading out in a long silver slick. It didn't mix with the flowing water and the milkman and I watched as his tribute floated away. It was one of those unforgettable moments and fitted in beautifully with a Hindu text that says, "In places without water, gods are not present."

Sally caught up with me in the restaurant where I was sipping a banana lassi (a delicious banana and curd drink) with Alex from Scotland. Alex was trekking to the Valley of the Flowers then to Gangotri, the birthplace of the Ganges, and then rafting back down the Ganges. He suggested we try the rafting. I did not tell him that I had once rafted down the Zambezi River past dead hippopotamuses that were polluting the water I was being dunked in, and that this had put me off rafting for life. Nor did

Sally mention that she couldn't swim, but if she could, nothing would get her into the Ganges.

Over an all-you-can-eat *thali* breakfast consisting of four breathtakingly hot curries served in dishes called *katori* that fitted into a metal platter, with pickles, curd and two chapattis to sop it up with, right hand only, I explained we were going to Haridwar, which didn't sound half as romantic as the Valley of the Flowers.

On the way back to our hotel, we found a sheet of corrugated tin blocking the entrance to the bridge. On it was a sign that we presumed said "no entry." But as everyone was climbing over the tin, including old widows in white saris who'd come to Rishikesh to die, we did the same.

At the far end were four workmen who clearly belonged to the Union of World Council Workers. Two, wearing dhotis, suit jackets and rust-colored turbans, were slowly levering up the slats with a crowbar, while two, wearing *lungis*, suit jackets and beige turbans, watched. Meanwhile everyone stepped around them, over the gap showing the river below, and over the piece of tin blocking off the other end of the bridge.

We found Umesh hovering around the car waiting to take us to the second most holy city in India.

Seeing the end of our four days in sight, Umesh was speeding along a straight road when Sally let out a shriek and I glanced up to see a red car hit a small boy. Up in the air he went like a piece of rolled-up carpet. Down he came, thump, on the hard tarmac. One leg flopping heavily, then he curled up and lay still. The red car swerved around him and sped on. Umesh would have swerved around the boy as well only for our shouts of "Stop." We were out of the car and running the instant he braked, with Sally screaming at two men who had appeared from nowhere and were trying to straighten the boy's leg. "Don't touch him, wait until the ambulance comes."

Now what planet was she living on? Here we were on a country road in the middle of nowhere. There would be no ambulance. Only another accident if we didn't move him. At first I thought he was dead because blood was coming from his mouth, then he opened his eyes, so I scooped him up and carried him to the roadside where I placed him on a carpet of grey dust and jacaranda blossoms. His friend or brother, a boy a few years older than himself, and the reason the younger one had darted out into the traffic, hugged him and called his name. Others, who kept arriving like flies around a fresh cow pat, tried to sit him up. A man with a scooter suggested he take him to a doctor. Horrified at the idea of trying to balance this boy on the front of a scooter, I said we would take him in the car.

Umesh had a fit. "He will get blood on the upholstery."

"Bugger the upholstery!"

I put the boy on Sally's lap in the back seat. Then as three men attempted to scramble in with her, I pointed to the older boy and one man, then told the rest, "No."

The hospital turned out to be a local chemist shop. Everyone except Umesh crowded inside, including the men who we had left behind and who must have all climbed aboard the lone scooter to get there. At the sight of his shop filling up so rapidly, the chemist rushed out from behind his counter as Sally and I carried the boy in. The boy resembled a broken doll.

"I think he has concussion, broken ribs and a broken leg," I said. This was one gigantic "off the top of my head" diagnosis as I know nothing about medicine.

The chemist dabbed the boy's cut forehead with iodine. The boy did not complain. He appeared to be in shock. I wanted to leave him some money but if I gave it to him, he was so dazed that someone might steal it from him. If I gave it to the chemist, he may not use it for the boy. If I gave it to the man who'd come in the car with us, how did I know he wasn't a passer-by? And if I gave it openly to the older boy, the men from the accident scene might take it from him. So I folded up four hundred rupees as small as I could and slid it into the older boy's hand, then we left.

Later, when I calculated what I had given I discovered that my grand gesture added up to about twelve dollars. A piffling sum considering the boy's injuries. I wasn't yet used to the big amounts written on the Indian notes adding up to so little and I had miscalculated.

Arriving at Haridwar, we parked in a pee-smelling car park beside the river. Every twelve years Haridwar hosts the Kumbha Mela fair. During the last fair over thirty million marigold-garlanded Hindus, who had assembled to chant and bathe, rushed into the water at the given signal and thousands were crushed and drowned.

We made our way through the litter, around the water-sellers and the stalls of sugar-cane juice and fried samosas, to a pee-smelling bridge. On the bridge, crouched a crippled mother with a baby, a dirt-ingrained child selling stones, and a row of female money-changers with little towers of *paise* stacked up in front of them. Nine paise for one rupee, and they kept one. The paise and stones are thrown into the Ganges as an offering to the god. I bought a handful of stones to throw for the accident victim.

Below the bridge, men using pieces of glass as homemade diving masks and sticks waded against the current in search of paise and jewelry tossed in by rich Indians to rid themselves of sin. It looked like hard work.

"Why not give them the paise and jewelry and save them from becoming waterlogged?" I said.

"Because then the thrower would not receive the joy of giving to the Ganges and the finder would not receive the joy of receiving from the Ganges," explained an old man, who'd overheard me.

I smiled my thanks and *namasté*-d him. But lovely as his sentiments were, my guess was that a lot of gold nose-pins, earrings and bangles were never found. Property of the Ganges, I guess.

To reach Har ki Pairi, the holiest of Hindu temples with its scarlet nipple-tipped domes and its six-sided temples sporting red frills resembling clowns' collars, we had to cross a second bridge. This one contained two black cows with gilded horns sitting head to head like ebony bookends, three grey Brahman bulls wearing gold material cloaks and marigold *leis*, a row of squatting manure-patty-ash-covered sadhus and a row of Maharishi orange men with flowing white beards and metal amulets. All the men held sticks and tin billycans (utensils for boiling water). Sticks for prodding the holy bulls to move over and billycans for the money, tea or rice donated by devotees.

We left our shoes with a shoe-minder and joined the barefooted crowd walking across the black-and-white tiles to the *ghats* which were covered in hundreds of neat piles of clothing belonging to the bathers. Closer to the water, beneath large white umbrellas, little boys' heads were being ritually shaved. Their long black hair, uncut since birth, went into the river as an offering to the god.

Farther along, people, wearing necklaces of black thread containing Hindu charms, squatted in the water praying. Rich men, with flabby white tummies and grey cotton underpants floundered in the strong current. Poor men, with brown skin, washboard stomachs and wearing a strip of rag, slid into the water without effort. Flower-decked women stepped in wearing their beautiful saris and jewelry. Everyone came out with their clothes clinging to them. The Ganges left no secrets.

Farther on, dozens of prayer men in shirts and trousers, looking like businessmen, prepared prayer boats of lily leaves.

"Do you want one?" one asked us. "I know prayers in English. Krishna is a bilingual god, you know."

We handed over our rupees and sat down on a marigold-petal-strewn step to watch.

First he painted an ochre paste dot on our foreheads, then he poured a cup of coconut juice into a leaf basket followed by a handful of cooked rice and a small garland of marigolds. He then sprinkled the lot with a red powder and began muttering prayers at a rapid pace in Hindi. Prayers over, the leaf boat was launched onto the water on its journey across India to the Bay of Bengal. As it swirled off on its lengthy journey to Varanasi, our prayer man said two prayers in English. One was for us to have long and fruitful lives and the other for our sons to have long and wealthy lives.

"What about our lives being wealthy?" demanded Sally.

"If you are here, Madams, you are wealthy."

Then he was beckoning to an Indian family to take our place.

We collected our shoes and climbed higher to the Bara Bazaar where rows of ramshackle stalls fought for space with the hundreds of belching scooters. I bought glass bangles and a small marble Ganesh to place at my front door along with my Saint Francis from Mexico and my Buddha from Cambodia. Sally bought necklaces, scarves and another woven bag.

We stopped at a yogurt stall where the owner was pouring an arch of milk from a metal ladle into a metal cup, then back again by holding both cup and ladle at arms' length. He never spilled a drop and he certainly caught our attention. We ate our curd from two unfired clay bowls, then we threw them on the ground where they would be walked upon and crushed back into dust.

The journey back to Delhi was uneventful. We arrived at our hotel at 9 P.M. and were welcomed by an army of male reception-ists, causing me to wonder if there were any women employed in Indian hotels. The renovations looked no closer to comple-tion. In fact I'm sure I recognized the same workman polishing the same piece of marble he'd been polishing five days earlier. He gave me a toothless conspiratorial grin and I answered with a "workers of the world unite" salute.

It took three minutes for Sally to have her case brought down. Its lid was unzipped and flung open before the waiter was out of the room.

"Feed me, feed me," it seemed to beg as its lid bounced eagerly on the floor.

So Sally fed it. In went all the stuff she'd bought along with a pile of rainbow-colored plastic bags turned into large blowflies.

"Thank you, thank you," cried the case, as she squashed these items into its already over-stuffed corners.

"I think I am going mad," I muttered. "I thought I heard your case speak."

She threw me my copy of the *Kama Sutra*. "Read while I repack."

So I turned to the index. "What do you want to hear about? The art of the five senses or the life of a courtesan?"

"Both."

I turned to the page on the senses. "There are five senses. Hearing. Feeling. Seeing. Tasting and smell."

"Describe the picture?"

"There's a gold-roofed, bejeweled pavilion covered with jasmine and shaded by a mango tree dripping with ripe, luscious, bottom-shaped fruit. That would be tasting. In this pavilion is a blue-skinned Krishna, wearing jewelry and green boxer shorts. (I wonder if the Indians invented shorts?) He is gently caressing the right breast of a creamy-skinned fully dressed female. That would be feeling. Around their bed stand six women. One is fanning them, one is spraying perfume, one is playing music, one is preparing sweetmeats, and two are dancing. Which pretty much covers all the other senses."

"It sounds a bit too communal for me," said Sally. "What do the courtesans do?"

So I turned to the courtesan section.

"To be a courtesan is to have an elite profession which allows the accumulation of a fortune while obtaining pleasure."

"Go on."

"Should a courtesan fall in love, she should never sacrifice money to her lover. Instead she should present him with betel nut, perfume and her skill in giving enjoyment." I looked at Sally bent over her case. "I once knew a Parisian stripper who gave her lover a sports car which he drove away and neither were seen again."

"She should have stuck to betel nut and skill," said Sally.

# Chapter 7

## FOR THE LOVE OF MUMTAZ MAHAL

At six o'clock the next day, we set off for the Delhi train station to commence our 204 kilometer train journey to Agra. Miraculously, we boarded the right train. Our car was clean and full of middle-class Indians and we immediately fell into conversation with the two pretty women sitting opposite. During our talk we learned that they were sisters-in-law, and that although they had passed university with honors, they had never worked. While in university they had both worn Western clothing and refused to wear Indian jewelry, but since marrying the men their families had chosen for them, they found saris and Indian jewelry preferable.

"A husband must be able to give his wife jewelry," said the taller one. "And a wife's jewelry must be worn all at once. One cannot do that with western jewelry."

Sally and I, both wearing modest pierced earrings, agreed one couldn't.

"Don't you mind not using your talents?" asked Sally, who minded greatly that she had not attended college.

The women shook their heads. Both had married immediately after graduating and both had moved into their husbands' family home. The taller was the more important as she'd married the eldest son, but the shorter was happy as her husband had fathered three sons. Both were flattered that we had visited their holy towns of Rishikesh and Haridwar.

"Which did you prefer?" asked the taller woman.

"Rishikesh," I said without hesitation. Haridwar with its carnival atmosphere could not compete with my magical Himalayan milkman and his silver arch of milk.

"So tell us," said Sally, the prefacing of her question warning me that it was going to be tactless. "What do you think of suttee? Would you throw yourselves on your husband's burning pyre to prove that you'd loved him?"

Not a flicker of expression crossed their pretty faces as they fingered their black-beaded marriage necklaces. Finally, the shorter one spoke up while the other nodded in agreement.

"Our husbands' family does not believe in suttee so this sacrifice would not be expected. Nor are our husbands elderly or sick, for which we give thanks to Vishnu on a daily basis. So the question would not arise."

Unless they were in a car accident, I thought. Then would you shave your heads, wear a white sari, and stay with his family eating unspiced and tasteless food while living the shameful life of a widow who hadn't prayed hard enough to keep her husband alive? Or would you return to your families? If so, who got the grandsons? The idea that they, as widows, would branch out on their own was manifestly unheard of.

Then Sally, with fox-terrier determination, asked, "What about girl children?"

This time the taller woman answered so quickly I wondered if it wasn't a sore point. "Every woman prays for sons. This makes her invaluable to her husband and his family. But when a daughter is born," I thought I heard a soft sigh, "she is accepted. I have two daughters."

"I have a daughter," I told her.

"I have a son and a daughter," added Sally.

"And your husbands don't mind you traveling alone?"

"We are divorced," I explained.

"Our husbands have remarried," added Sally.

The women's faces fell in sympathy. There was no question as to whether we had remarried or would remarry. Hindu women don't. Which meant if they marry as virgins, which they must, then they only make love with one man for their whole life. Now there's a momentous thought. The women got off before Agra. As we waved good-bye, I wondered how their husbands made a living on the parched earth that stretched out on both sides of the rail track.

We arrived at Agra Cantonment train station and, after fighting off a multitude of rickshaw-wallahs, chose one to take us to the Hotel Sidhartha, which had been highly recommended by the sisters-in-law. On the way I saw a poster of Shri Mataji, a Sahaja Yoga guru whose posters I had once followed around Italy. Two years later, I arrived at the Moscow airport and wondered why there were so many rose-holding Russians milling around, two thousand to be exact, until I realized they were all wearing Sahaja Yoga badges. Now Shri Mataji was touring India.

"Shri Mataji has left," our English speaking rickshaw-wallah informed us. Then he went on to tell us how the tarmac road we were riding along was only finished yesterday in preparation for the President of America's visit to the Taj Mahal. That was when I saw the tiger. We were passing an imposing house with a sweeping driveway. Opposite the front door was a cage the size of a shower cubicle. Inside lay a full-grown tiger, its nose pressed against the bars. It could barely turn round in such a confined space. I told Sally what I'd seen. Big mistake.

All through being shown our room in our delightful one-story hotel; all through admiring the garden of sweet peas, snap-dragons and bougainvillea; all through showering and eating lunch, she took it in turns bemoaning the tiger's plight, and becoming indignant that the United States' President's entourage would be passing such a disgraceful situation the following day.

"It's not the President's fault. He probably doesn't even know there's a tiger there," I argued. And it is seldom I argue on behalf of an American President.

"But if he knew about it he would say something."

"Like what? Naughty Indians you should not cage tigers. No chance. I think he is here to speak about more important world-shattering events."

"A caged tiger is world shattering. I can't believe you don't see that!"

I did. But I didn't think the President would.

That afternoon we took a rickshaw to the Taj Mahal. This national treasure is built on the banks of the Yamuna River. The same river that flows close to Delhi's Red Fort. At Agra it is so polluted that nothing lives in it or along its banks. Agra is an industrial city.

At the tomb's entrance we were surrounded by store-keepers, storekeepers' shrieking children, and store-keepers' lackeys all demanding that we follow them and see what wonder-ful bargains they had. "It costs nothing to look," they cajoled. "We have tablecloths, marble swans, good-luck pieces of the Taj Mahal that will bring you a lover." Which anyone in their right mind would know was a lie on both accounts, but which I later found out were so numerous in Agra souvenir shops that one could built a duplicate Taj Mahal with them.

Tavernier, the jeweler who'd seen Shah Jahan's peacock throne, wrote that the Taj Mahal cost eleven lakhs (about five million pounds sterling); and that Shah Jahan intended building a black marble replica for himself on the opposite side of the river, along with a flying bridge to link the two mausoleums, but the Shah's son, Aurangzeb, halted this ambitious plan, and imprisoned his father for eight years until the old emperor died.

We bought our entrance tickets and declared to the handsome soldiers, with their automatic rifles slung casually over their shoulders, that we were not carrying food or weapons. We flirted for five minutes (flirting with Indian soldiers is almost compulsory), and then walked through the three-storied gatehouse.

Entrance to Mumtaz Mahal's mausoleum is along a pathway lined with lawns, orchards and flowerbeds of yellow and pink daisies. Here, for twenty-two years, lived a village of 20,000 workmen and master craftsmen. At the end of the path stands the second gatehouse, as wide and as tall as the first with four arched doorways, four towers topped with onion-shaped canopies and two rows of beehive domes. Framed in an arched doorway was the Taj Mahal shining pearly white in the afternoon sun, and looking as cold as sculptured ice.

The author Aldous Huxley did not like the Taj Mahal. He thought its minarets were too thin, too tapered and too incidental. They are thin, like a pianist's fingers, but not incidental. Islamic religious law insists there be four minarets per tomb. The interesting thing about these minarets is that their center of gravity is to their outer sides so if an earthquake occurs they will not fall on the dome. Smart builders those Hindus. So far there have been no earthquakes.

With at least one hundred other tourists, but not feeling the least bit crowded as the tomb is so large, we wandered along beside the reflection pool. At certain points the path is interrupted by lotus-filled fountains circled by walkways to allow loving couples to be photographed in front of the largest love symbol in the world. Others take the same photograph of the tomb and its mirrored image portrayed on postcards hawked outside by hundreds of small boys.

I was photographing four female gardeners wearing sepia-colored saris, cutting grass with what looked like nail scissors, evidently a lifetime job, when Sally, emitting a yell of joy, bounded off across the lawn. Leaping two "Don't walk on the grass" signs written in English, she reached two enormous white, hump-backed bullocks pulling a mowing machine around the flower-beds. I followed, years of experience having taught me that to not follow meant instant loss of a friend for hours.

This was how I discovered two identical red and white buildings hidden behind the trees, each facing the other with the Taj Mahal sandwiched between. These are the eastern mosque and the western palace guesthouse, both used by devotees who come to pray on the anniversary of Mumtaz Mahal's death. I turned to tell Sally and found her being led away by two guards for trespassing on the grass.

Ten minutes of sweet-talk later, a freed, but furious Sally and a grinning me climbed the stairs to the top of the tomb's platform from where we had the perfect view of the river. Knowing how polluted it was, we were surprised at its opaque blue water, the same color as a newborn baby's eyes, its sand banks of ash blonde, and, in the distance, the shimmering pink Agra Palace. It was a lovely view.

"So," said Sally, leaning on the marble wall. "Read to me."

Sitting on the wall beside her, I read, "The Taj Mahal was built by Shah Jahan in memory of his exquisitively beautiful and extremely intelligent queen whom he loved at first sight. Which was just as well as theirs was a politically arranged marriage. Although only nineteen years old, Mumtaz Mahal became Keeper of the Royal Seal and no affair of state was decided without her opinion. The couple were inseparable, which is why she died at the age of thirty-nine. While eight months pregnant, Mumtaz Mahal went with her husband to another town to attend to court business and there she died while giving birth to their fourteenth child, or fourteenth 'blessing' as Shah Jahan called them."

"Fourteen blessings in twenty years," groaned Sally. "She must have barely stopped breastfeeding one before she was pregnant with the next."

I nodded while trying to recall the overwhelming, toe-tingling feeling of romance I'd felt a minute earlier when looking at the tomb.

"So he built this mausoleum fifteen years after she died to show how much he loved her," she continued. Her scathing tone caused any lingering thoughts of romance to wither away.

"I don't believe it was for love!" she continued. "He was addicted to building. He'd built the Agra Fort, the Red Fort, and the Great Mosque. All in Mogul style to stuff it up the nostrils of the conquered Hindus, so a tomb was next on his list."

She turned and gave the huge building a searing look. Then she frowned. "Does that dome look like a bosom to you?"

"It is said to be the shape of Mumtaz's left breast, and Sally, you're spoiling the romance."

"Romance is highly overrated."

Well, who could argue with that? Not me with my broken heart.

With this in mind, I stepped through a doorway into the mausoleum of the most famously loved woman in the world, and into one of the most beautiful of rooms I have ever seen. The walls, inset with different colored marbles, portrayed a garden of lilies, irises, daisies, roses and daffodils, all outlined in gold. The double marble dome gave everything a light and airy feel, while the dancing honeycomb shapes of sunlight filtering through the fretted marble window screens spotlit a beautiful filigreed marble screen. Behind the screen lay Mumtaz Mahal's mock tomb inscribed with the ninety-nine names of Allah.

Around the tomb's base is a carpet of flowers made from lapis lazuli, jasper, carnelian and chrysolite. It is ultra-impressive.

Standing within this cocoon of tranquility, it is not hard to understand why women flock here to pray to Mumtaz Mahal, begging her to send them a husband as loving as her own. A lover who will never remarry and who will promise his dying wife that he'll build her a tomb of such proportions that her name will live on in perpetuity. Not hard to imagine a desperate woman begging Queen Mumtaz Mahal's spirit to intercede with Allah to allow her to give birth to a son to warm the frosty heart of an unkind husband, one who is already looking round for a new wife who didn't produce girls.

The mausoleum is so. full of female wishes, dreams and prayers that it is all the more surprising to discover Shah Jahan's mock tomb shoved in a corner, without one name of Allah engraved on it, by Aurangzeb, his rupee-pinching son.

Sally had wandered off again so I crossed the wide expanse of white marble and red sandstone to the guest palace. Inside was a long vaulted corridor with a floor made of black-and-white marble tiles the size of prayer mats all facing Mecca.

Suddenly I felt a cool breath on my neck, smelled a whiff of spicy sandalwood perfume, and heard the soft tinkling of bracelet bells.˙ So close was the woman that as I swung round I thought I would knock her off balance. But I was alone in that shadowy place with only a sunlit archway the width of the building away.

Then I saw her. A tall, slim woman wearing a gold-edged, midnight blue tight-waisted jacket with long slim sleeves, and a full transparent skirt over tight blue trousers. Her fingers and toes were covered in rings with chains of bells connected to her wrists and ankles. It was these that had heralded her presence.

Her face was regal and her hair plaited with golden thread but it was her eyes that held me. They were large and prune black, made darker by kohl and the shine of unshed tears. That she was here to petition Queen Mumtaz Mahal I was in no doubt.

However, I also had the feeling that she wanted to talk to me so I stepped towards her, and in an instant she was gone.

I hurried over to where she'd stood. There was no doorway that she could have slipped through. She had simply disappeared. When Sally and I met up outside the guest's mosque, I didn't mention her.

Back in our motel, we decided to go to the exclusive Taj View Hotel to watch the sunset, so I went for a shower and discovered that the English people in the next room could be heard as clearly as if they were in the bathroom with me.

I heard the tearful voice of a mother, the patient voice of a father, and the whining of a daughter called Evelyn. Evelyn was accusing them of bringing her to India (no doubt forcibly, bound hand and foot, drugged and gagged, onto the plane) to break off a relationship with her boyfriend. Her father was insisting that the relationship was already over, and the mother said they had hoped the trip would buck her up. A door slammed and the argument stopped. I went to see if Sally was ready. She wasn't. So I arranged to meet her at the hotel.

On the way I stopped at a chemist to buy a roll of film and saw an advertisement for Kama Sutra condoms. I bought a packet for my nephew who saves different types of condom packets. The young chemist was embarrassed at my purchase. He turned his back to put them in the paper bag and refused to raise his eyes when I handed him my rupees. Women do not buy condoms in India. They should. AIDS is rife.

I was giggling over the blushing youth when I was almost plowed into the dirt verge by two dusty ships of the desert with colorful woolen pompoms attached to their nose pegs and large brass bangles clanging around their ankles. They were pulling a wagon that was so high the driver could see into the second story windows of the buildings he passed. This was a magical moment for me. My first Indian camel!

As they reached me, they raised their aristocratic noses and snorted. These snorts and the look in their false eyelashed eyes told me that they were not happy. They did not want to work twelve hours a day pulling a wagon with airplane wheels. They wanted to gallop across the desert like Lawrence of Arabia. They wanted fame, fortune and freedom, but mostly fame. It's been said by many Arabian poets that there are no happy camels. Happiness is not in their genes. As for galloping, they're not mad keen on that either, which was why those painful nose pegs were invented. Alas, like many others on this earth, animal or human, camels live in a dream world of extraordinary deeds and extravagant rewards without a great amount of effort. Join the queue, camels.

At the Taj View Hotel, I was confronted with an army of security men—smiling Indian heavies in short-sleeved shirts, and hot and sweaty American heavies in black suits looking like *Men in Black* film extras. The friendly waiters' brigade told me that the security men were in force because the President was lunching there the following day. Then they sold me a beer.

I was lying on the top of the man-made hill sipping this beer and chatting with some Germans and an English couple who happened to have a daughter called Evelyn who was not present, when Sally appeared. Storming up the hill, her cloth bags and long skirt flapping, she flung herself down beside me, announcing that the waiters had charged her thirty rupees to see a perfectly free sunset and demanding to know if I had paid the same.

"If you buy a bottle of beer, you don't get charged for the sunset," I told her.

"I hate beer," she snapped. Which ended my offering her half of mine.

So with Sally glowering at everyone, the soft chatter of the Germans, and Evelyn's father telling me about his job which was collecting chickens at an organic chicken farm, and how he had to crawl inside the cages, hook four hens per hand, then crawl out again, I sipped my beer and watched the sun fall without a splash into the Yamuna River. It was perfect; well, it would have been if Evelyn's father hadn't gone on about chicken poo.

On the walk home, I told Sally that the President was lunching at the Taj View the next day, so why didn't she write him a letter about the tiger?

Next morning I got up early and went to see the Taj Mahal alone. This time it was only the gardeners and me as it was too early for the Delhi train's daytrippers. Of course I looked for my lady in blue and of course she wasn't there. But I met a lovely Indian gentleman of about eighty who told me how the Taj Mahal was almost torn down and sold off as scrap marble by a British governor-general. The absurdity of it made us laugh. "How would the English feel if some conquering power decided to sell off their Victoria Memorial's marble? Marble that most likely came from the vast quarries of Rajputana?" he asked.

I took a wild guess. "It would cause a revolution."

This pleased him, and we parted friends.

I returned to Sally with my mind full of midnight blue saris and marble quarries. She told me that she'd delivered her petition to the President's security men and that she was sure on reading it the President would have the tiger set free.

"To go where?" I asked. "This is not exactly tiger country."

Sally rolled her eyes at me and then ignored me.

While waiting for her to un-ignore me, I read about the six Great Moguls.

I already knew about Babur the first, an expert swordsman, archer and landscape gardener, who, in 1526, conquered three million Hindus with 12,000 Muslims. Now I read about his son, Humayun, and how when Humayun fell sick, Babur offered his life to Allah in exchange for his son's life. Allah must have been listening, because Babur died and Humayun the second lived to build his floating palace.

After Humayun died from falling down his library steps, his son, Ali Akbar the third, took the throne at the ripe old age of thirteen. A contemporary of Queen Elizabeth I, Ali Akbar ruled for forty-nine years. He became so powerful that when he married a Hindu princess, the orthodox Mohammedan court could do nothing about it, other than to predict that this was the start of the watering down of pure Mogul blood that stretched all the way back to Genghis Khan. They were right.

Next came the half Muslim, half Hindu Jahangir the fourth, who was thirty-seven years old when his father, Ali Akbar, died. Although not a pure Mogul, Jahangir often visited Kashmir to lay out his famous gardens much as his great-grandfather Babur had. Handsome, hedonistic and romantic, Jahangir fell in love as a child and remained in love with the same woman all his life. Unfortunately, her father married her to another, so when Jahangir became emperor he did a "David and Bathsheba." He had his beloved's husband killed during a battle. Even so, their marriage did not immediately follow because the widow didn't talk to Jahangir for three years, and only then, because she saw him sickening for the love of her.

Next came my favorite, Shah Jahan the fifth, builder of the Taj Mahal, and my least favorite, Shah Jahan's nasty son, Aurangzeb the sixth. Aurangzeb was the last of the Great Moguls. Although there were emperors of a sort right up until 1803 when Delhi was captured by the British, the glory of Agra and Delhi vanished like a puff of desert wind, after Aurangzeb's reign.

By 1803 the Moguls' marvelous palaces were covered in bird poo and bat droppings, their bubbling baths and cooling canals were choked with leaves, and their ornate fountains blocked with dust. The last emperor, Bahadur Shah II, died in exile, a bewildered old man smoking an opium-laced hookah while wondering to whom he had handed over Humayun the second's sword. It was to Major Hodson at Humayun's tomb in Delhi.

At last Sally was ready and we caught a rickshaw to Agra Palace. On the way we were almost skittled by a puffball-truck. Puffball is the name we have given these trucks because of the burlap bags attached to them that bulged over their sides, rear ends and hoods, almost hiding the drivers' cabs and their view of the road ahead, but doubling the capacity of their wheat or rice loads. These trucks, with their "Horn blow please" signs painted on their back bumper bars, take up three-quarters of the road and are capable of knocking flat any rickshaw driver or passenger.

On arriving at Agra Fort, our driver doubled his price due to the danger he had undergone while trying to pass the puffball-trucks. I paid him the original agreed price then I asked him if he thought we looked particularly stupid. He graciously said no but that it had been worth a try.

Ali Akbar the third Mogul commenced building Agra Fort in 1565. Although it was to be a functioning military structure, Akbar loved beauty so much that he imported builders and architects from Bengal and Gujarat, and artists from Persia to enhance it. The result is 500 beautiful buildings protected by a two-kilometer, seventy-foot high sandstone wall.

"Agra's Halls of Public Audience and Private Audience are similar to those of Delhi's Red Fort and the inlaid marble is similar to the Taj Mahal," announced a nearby Indian guide to his group of American women tourists. "It was from Agra Fort that the famous peacock throne was taken to Delhi by Aurangzeb and later stolen from there. Had it remained here we would be looking at it today.

"Only two of Akbar's buildings survive. After Akbar's death, his son Jahangir had the other 498 buildings destroyed so that he could rebuild them in his own elaborate style. Jahangir Court is the only remaining example of that half-Muslim half-Hindu style. Please note how every surface is carved with motifs depicting Indian waterpots, Hindu wheels of life and lotus flowers which are the traditional symbol surmounting all Hindu temples. It is said that this court shows Jahangir's Hindu blood.

"Jahangir's son, Shah Jahan, replaced all his father's buildings except for the Jahangir Court. The reason, it is said, was because Shah Jahan preferred a more refined Mogul style. But my personal opinion is that Shah Jahan was angry at being forced to hide in Udaipur while in revolt against his father. I ask you, ladies, what better way to punish an emperor's ghost than to knock down his beloved palace buildings?"

"Why was Shah Jahan in revolt against his father?" asked one of the ladies.

The guide's eyebrows rose knowingly. "Emperor Jahangir's hot Hindu blood made him a romantic poet and lover, but his cold Mogul blood kept him practical. So when his eldest son attempted to usurp the throne, Jahangir had this son's army impaled on stakes, then, before blinding his son, he bound him to an elephant and paraded him in front of his squirming soldiers. The blinded son was Shah Jahan's older brother."

"First sons had a short shelf life," I whispered to Sally, and received a glare from one of the "paying" ladies.

We left the group as it entered a small Gem Mosque but we could still hear the guide explaining. "It was through here that Akbar disguised in female clothing joined the women of his zenana while they shopped in the ladies-only bazaar.

"Why would he do that?" asked Sally.

"To spy on his wives," I suggested.

The group disappeared as we reached the terrace where the eighty-year-old Shah Jahan had been imprisoned. Through a row of delicately carved arches there was a wonderful view of the Taj Mahal.

"I once read that the last Shah of Iran, the one buried in a Cairo mosque so that rebels couldn't desecrate his body, made love to his first wife, Soraya, in the Taj Mahal during full moon in the hope of having an heir," I told Sally.

"Did it work?"

"No. He eventually divorced her for being barren and married another."

"Did that one give birth?"

"Yes. But it didn't do the dynasty much good because the Shah of Iran was kicked out by the Ayatollah."

"Served him right for being so fickle."

While Sally photographed two gilded Bengali-roofed pavilions, I followed some Indian women into a small windowless chamber with thousands of tiny pieces of mirror inlaid in its walls and ceiling. A harem wife or daughter was expected to be vain, there being little else for a well-bred begum to do. So one or two mirrors could be expected, but a room full! That was something else. It had to be a love tryst room?

How easy it was to imagine a bemused male being smuggled into the ladies bazaar dressed as a market woman, then being led away to this twinkling Milky Way place where, resting on a pile of scented cushions, he was enticed to give his all to a veiled woman whose eyes shone as brightly as the thousands of mirror shards surrounding them. How delightful was her exotic perfume. How soft and pliable was her milk-white skin, how strong her plump white thighs. True, he would never know her name, see her face, hear her voice. Yet she would haunt him through an arranged marriage to an ugly woman, through a dull, over-worked, unrewarded life, through countless children, alive and dead, and years of growing too old too fast. Then, when he died, his family would puzzle over the tiny fragment of mirror they found wrapped in a scrap of cloth. The same fragment he had picked free from a wall with his little finger as the ravishing beauty covered his body with hers; the same handkerchief she gave him, wet with her tears, as they parted.

I found Sally in the Anguri Bagh or Grape Garden. Beneath these vines, planted in earth brought from Kashmir, on fine spring nights when the jasmine was in bloom, each of the four emperors had attended their full moon festivities. During these audiences the begums, dressed in white to match the moon's rays, danced among the white violets. It is also here that Jahangir drank too much alcohol and partook of too much opium which eventually killed him.

The gardens are no longer full of white flowers; instead there is a mishmash of pink and white petunias, blood red azaleas and dwarf banana trees. Like the Moguls, Ali Akbar's elegant Mogul gardens have been watered down by foreign imports.

After another rest, much needed because of the heat, we went to find the shaft cut into the rock into which the Maharajah of Jodhpur had been tossed alive. This maharajah had murdered an important court official then, while trying to escape, he'd jumped his horse off the walls of Agra Fort, killing the horse but not himself. We found the shaft. It was a long drop to the river.

"Bloodthirsty lot, these Moguls," I said.

"He deserved it after cruelly killing a horse that way," announced Sally.

"Bloodthirsty lot, these animal lovers."

That night, while Sally was working out the possibility of an emperor visiting 5000 wives (one visit per wife every fourteen years or three visits between the age of fourteen and forty-eight), I flicked through the *Kama Sutra*.

"It says here that a man must only seduce one woman at a time, but after he has enjoyed congress with her he can keep her affections by giving her presents while commencing to seduce another woman. Seducees can be the following: wives of other men, especially if the woman is of a higher caste; wives who rule their husbands; daughters of wives one has already seduced. Seducers can also, after congress, kill the wife's husband to obtain the husband's riches; if she is a widow he can obtain her riches; or ... oh you'll love this one .... if the woman he had congress with brings him the virgin he truly wants to have congress with."

"Charming!" snarled Sally, punching her pillow.

"On the other hand, when a courtesan finds her lover changing towards her, be he husband of another or not, she should get possession of all his things. After which, if he is rich she should continue to treat him with respect, but if he is poor she should leave him. There follows a list of ways of doing this. Want to know them?"

"Will I need my pillow?"

"Only if you are breaking up with it."

"I'm thinking about it. So read."

"Sneering during congress. Speaking on subjects of which he is not acquainted. Seeking the company of men who are his superior. Asking for things he cannot grant you. Criticizing his ability to connect. (I'd say that that's sure guarantee to deflation). Refusing to kiss him on the lips. Showing a dislike for wounds made by his nails or teeth. Keeping one's limbs unresponsive. Demanding affection when he is tired. And refusing to participate in traditional postures of connection that require a degree of yogi expertise."

"Do you hear that, pillow?" shouted Sally, throwing it against the wall. "I refuse to do yoga with you."

"That should do it," I told her.

# *Chapter 8*

## FATEHPUR SİKRİ

Two days later, we took the deluxe bus to Fatehpur Sikri, a ghostly playground older than the Taj Mahal. By the bus's battered sides, smooth tires, bent fender and lack of windows I guessed that it had not been deluxe for more than a century. The seats were so small that Sally and I, plus Sal's four bags (mine was jammed under our feet), took up three places. No one minded. Everyone was friendly. There was no surprise shown at seeing a tall redhead festooned with bags and a plump blonde with purple sunglasses squashed into their local bus. Tourists have been coming to India since Alexander the Great. Behind us, or to use Indian English, at our backside, sat three teenage women wearing their best saris and the same cherry-red lipstick and red bindis. Crammed in with them were a nine-year-old girl and two baby boys wearing crocheted bonnets that flopped over their tiny brown faces.

As the bus fought its way through congested Agra, I made the little girl an origami fortune-telling game from a page of my diary, then I held one of the babies for the rest of the trip. The dear little thing didn't complain at being handed over to a white-faced, green-eyed stranger who talked and sang to it in a foreign tongue.

Forty kilometers later, and fortunately without us having seen any of the bear-wallahs and their dancing bears for which this part of the road was famous, we alighted at the village of Fatehpur Sikri. A quick wave good-bye to the women, girl and babies, and we headed for a cafe and a loo. The loo door started at our knees which meant when squatting over the hole, one's everything was brought below door level and on an eye level with the cooks working in the sunken kitchen. A bit of a shock that! We negotiated with the owner to leave our bags in his kitchen then set off to explore.

The entrance to Fatehpur Sikri palace was up a steep track that meandered across the town's rubbish tip. The tip stank horrendously. We held our noses and raced across it, scattering dozens of rats frolicking among the plastic.

Rats are the only animal in India that Sally hasn't gone gaga over. Instead, she went gaga over two black-and-white goats being dragged along by two small boys. The goats' flanks and rumps were decorated with henna patterns because they were to be sacrificed to the goddess Kali, wife of Shiva the Destroyer. The boys were barefooted and incredibly skinny.

"Poor little goaties!" wailed Sally. "Goats are pets in England," she announced to all the Indian tourists galloping behind us across the rubbish tip. "We don't sacrifice animals for gain."

I waited for the Indians to reply but they were too well-mannered to do so, so I, who have eaten Jamaica's national dish of curried goat and loved it, and who was full of pity for the two boys, did it for them. "What about mad cow disease caused by feeding cows junk they weren't meant to eat? If that isn't a sacrifice to the god of Mammon then what is?"

Sally ignored me. Mad cow disease and sacrificed goats are two different things as far as she's concerned.

Fatehpur Sikri palace, which became my favorite palace, was built in 1570 by Ali Akbar. After living in it fifteen years, Ali Akbar abandoned it, and abandoned it remained for the next 350 years, so we had expected to find it a rat-infested, plastic-covered, monkey-ruled ruin. We were wrong. There wasn't a plastic bag, bottle, errant leaf, adventurous squirrel or a whirly-wind in sight. Fatehpur Sikri palace is eerily immaculate, breathtakingly beautiful and unearthly still. Plus it resembles the palace Aladdin wished for when he wanted to impress the princess.

"Some say it is haunted," explained a handsome middle-aged Indian wearing startling white *kurta* pajamas and a startling white grin to match. "People won't come here at night. They say they see things."

"Like what?" I asked, falling straight into his "catchem tourist lady" ploy.

"Slave girls dancing in the moonlight."

Moving closer, our informant introduced himself as Mr. Harry Shobha, a telephone salesman from Mumbai, on his way to visit his mother.

I smiled a "how do you do" and moved on. Mr. Shobha followed.

"The city was built by Bengali architects," he offered.

I thanked him and did a swift right turn up a flight of steps leading to a row of buttressed terraces overlooking the village.

"Want me to read from the tourist guide?" said Sally.

"Yes, please."

"Fatehpur Sikri is built in a sharp-edged geometrical style with many terraced walkways from which the emperor flew kites and fed his flocks of white pigeons and pet green parrots. In the evenings the emperor and his nobles strolled along the terraces followed by court musicians playing finger cymbals, sitars and hautboys, which is an ancient oboe much loved by the emperor."

She turned from the buttresses and pointed into a court-yard. "This is the Pachisi Courtyard. It once housed a lawn and marble game-board. Ali Akbar liked to watch the living pachisi game-pieces being moved about especially when they were female slaves chosen for their beauty. My guess is that it was his way of choosing the lucky girl for the night."

"Keep reading and walking. He is still following us."

"The palace contained many courtyards. Some were used for wild animal fights; another was used to prove the guilt of convicts. The convict was hurled into the courtyard in which a killer elephant was tethered. If they were trampled they were guilty, if they were ignored, they were innocent. Ali Akbar loved to tame wild elephants. Which is similar to training a horse, only more dangerous as an elephant's trunk can drag a rider from its back before trampling or gouging him to death with its tusks. Why should an elephant be tamed anyway?"

"No reason," I agreed. I did not want to get onto the plight of elephants. Not after the Agra tiger and the rubbish tip goats. But the taming of elephants made sense to me, especially if they were to be used in war or to carry people from one place to the other.

"In the *Akbarnama* which is the history of Ali Akbar," continued Sally, "there is an illustration showing the emperor mounted on a war-elephant chasing other war-elephants across a bridge. The bridge is collapsing. Onlookers are diving off it into the river. Everyone except Ali Akbar is in a state of panic as the elephants with their heavy howdahs hit the water. Ali Akbar's face is alight with the glory of war. I bet the elephants drowned."

"Elephants can swim for three kilometers."

"Not with war howdahs strapped to their backs."

She won.

Already hot from a mere hour's stroll but having lost Mr. Shobha, we sat on a parapet overlooking the village and studied the palace map. There was so much to see. Temples, pavilions, audience halls, formal gardens, orchards, elephant stables, fountains, bathing pools, a polo ground where night polo was once played within a circle of a thousand burning torches, and a lake, dry now, but in times past used for boat trips and boat battles. Although where the water came from is anyone's guess.

Having to start somewhere, we chose the Palace of Jodh Bai where we bumped into the lurking Mr. Shobha.

"This was where Emperor Akbar came to eat," he announced. "He was a vegetarian who ate once a day but no one knew when so the royal kitchens were never closed. Also, to avoid being poisoned, his food arrived on golden plates tied up in red muslin and sealed by the kitchens' head chef. The seal was broken by one of his 500 favorite wives and a food-taster tasted each dish before he ate. Which is why he lasted for forty-nine years."

"Who would want to poison him?" I asked. I can't help it. I love history and I love storytellers.

"One of his 500 jealous wives," answered Sally, while photographing a beautiful marble wall of carved roses and pomegranates.

Mr. Shobha shook his head. "Why would they? Where would they go if he were dead? They would be unwanted widows, used women. Used wives. No, it was the orthodox Muslims who wanted Ali Akbar dead. He was too tolerant of other religions. Too apt to take the side of the Hindus. Especially after he married the Hindu Princess of Amber. The orthodox Muslims even plotted to put Akbar's younger brother on the throne. Only Akbar let his brother know that should he contemplate this, his head would be placed on a stake outside the palace gates. It was very effective."

"I bet," I said, looking round for Sally. She'd vanished.

"Over here is the Palace of the Winds from where the begums watched what was going on below." Mr. Shobha's right hand gestured to a small room built of marble latticework while his left hand pinched my upper arm, an action considered very familiar by Indians. I backed away fast, then turned and ran. I caught up with Sally in the House of Dreams.

"How's Mr. Shobha?"

"He's an arm-pincher. I felt like a peach being checked out for how ripe I am."

"Maybe he's a descendent of Ali Akbar, husband of three 'most favored' wives, 500 favorite wives, and 5000 'once if you are lucky' concubines. Each one visited on a rotating basis."

"How do you know he didn't have help?"

"His zenana was guarded by African women warriors whose swords could remove a marauding male's equipment with one swipe. Which must have left a lot of unchaste and unchased women who would have loved to have had their arms pinched by Mr. Shobha."

I gave her a snake-eyed look guaranteed to paralyze any living creature. It washed over her.

"The odd thing about having all those wives," she continued, "was that Ali Akbar only had three children, and then only after he'd visited a holy man which is the reason why he built Fatehpur Sikri in the first place, to be near the holy man's cave. Rumor also has it that none of the three children resembled their father."

From the House of Dreams we followed a passageway to the pachisi court and the palaces of Ali Akbar's three most favored wives. For his Persian wife he'd built an intricately decorated pavilion with fifty-six differently carved columns on top of which was balanced a second palace called the Panch Mahal. This filigreed wedding cake creation consisting of five open platforms topped by a small marble kiosk was where this devout Persian princess fasted during Ramadan.

For his second wife, the Goan Catholic princess, Akbar designed a gilded pavilion called the Golden Mahal. It no longer exists; neither does the chapel built by three visiting Jesuit priests, where she prayed daily.

For his third wife, Miriam, the Princess of Amber, who it is rumored fell in love with his reputation as an elephant fighter long before she met him, Akbar built a Rajput-style palace. This whimsical piece of flummery with its fairytale cupolas, delicate fretwork balconies, marble pavilions and ornate fountains is as lovely now as it was when he gave it to her as a gift for having given birth to his first son, Jahangir, the Mogul who fell in love for life and who blinded his first son. I reckon the princess deserved the palace.

Leaving the palaces of love, we walked through a garden of lawns and herbaceous borders kept weeded and watered by an old woman in a blue sari. Everything was so quiet and still that we had the uncanny feeling we were surrounded by ancient ghosts stretching out their hennaed fingers to touch our T-shirts, our sunglasses, our red and blonde hair. Suddenly there was a flutter of wings as a grey-beaked crane took flight, and we entered the Hall of Private Audience at a run.

In the center of this amazing room stands a six-meter high octagonal pillar supporting a red stone capital on which Akbar placed his throne. High above his courtier's heads, he listened to readings by scholars, debating by philosophers, and reciting by poets. From this throne, he challenged the orthodox Muslims to defend their Prophet against the beliefs of the Brahman, the Jain, the Zoroastrians and the Jesuit fathers. No wonder they wanted him dead. In the end, tiring of the orthodox Muslims' head shaking and finger pointing, Ali Akbar founded his own religion, which incorporated all known faiths. He did this around the same time as the Spanish Inquisition was burning and torturing non-believers in Europe, which showed what a wise man he was.

What puzzled me was why he'd abandoned Fatehpur Sikri with its 100 elephants, 30,000 horses, 1400 tame deer and its zoo of leopards, tigers, buffalo, etc. Was it the lack of water? Was it the fear of being overthrown by the orthodox Muslims? The isolation? What happened to make Ali Akbar return to Agra for the remaining thirty-three years of his reign, never to return to Fatehpur Sikri? Did it have to do with the birth of his son?

Having seen as much as the heat would allow, we decided to visit the tomb of Shaikh Salim Chishti, the saint who predicted that Akbar's wife would give birth. The tomb is in the Grand Mosque, which is outside the palace so we left through the impressive Buland Darwaza Victory Gate. On this gate, among the Koran inscriptions, there is supposedly a quote from Jesus which goes, "The world is a bridge. Cross it but build no house upon it. He who hopes for an hour—hopes for eternity."

I think it gained in the translation. What Jesus probably said was, "In my father's house there are many rooms, so you won't need this big palace in Heaven, as it is easier for a camel to pass through the eye of a needle than it is for a rich man to enter the Kingdom of Heaven."

Or something like that.

The moment we left the security of the palace we were dived upon by hordes of trinket sellers. The noise of their bargain chatter was unbearable so we raced for the mosque with the trinket sellers fast on our heels, shouting "Madam, buy from me," "You will save my life if you buy," "Madam, fixed price—no bargaining."

Who were they kidding?

"No," I shouted, as bracelets, anklets and carved statues were shoved in my face.

"No," shouted Sally. "Oh ... show me that again."

In the end, we bought ankle bracelets, not realizing that this implied to all the other bracelet sellers that we were vulnerable. Within seconds, every bracelet seller inside the State of Uttar Pradesh descended upon us. In panic, we took flight into the dimly lit cemetery, a long-columned, covered-over courtyard full of ancient, lopsided tomb-stones, which we leaped over, dodged around and galloped between, with twenty salesmen in hot pursuit, dropping their prices with every lap.

It was a miracle that our one detour led us into Shaikh Salim Chishti's tomb where women go to pray for sons and where males are forbidden to go. In a pretty inlaid marble room the size of a bathroom, and as cool as one, we did as all the other women were doing, and tied a piece of pink string around a twisted toffee-shaped column and made a wish. Mine was not for a son. But I did have a murder mystery manuscript I was trying to sell.

While we watched the women make their wishes, I couldn't help wondering why they wanted babies so much. Surely, with one-sixth of the world's population unemployed and India's billionth child just born, babies were the last thing they needed. But if the wives gave birth to a son they wouldn't be replaced by another wife, so I suppose it made sense.

Half an hour later, we rushed out of Shaikh Salim Chishti's tomb through the waiting trinket sellers and across the bazaar area with the cheering men in hot pursuit (I think it is all a game to them to relieve their boredom), and through the Buland Darwaza Victory Gate where I discovered I'd outrun Sally. In fact, she was nowhere in sight.

I was wondering what to do when Mr. Shobha appeared. "Are you looking for your friend?"

"Yes."

Turning to a nearby stall holder, he spoke to him for a few minutes, then he informed me that a red-haired woman in a long skirt and many bags had gone into the bazaar to shop.

"You're kidding!"

"I am not kidding," answered Mr. Shobha seriously. "I am

never kidding. If you accompany me, we will seek her out."

So I accompanied him, knowing it was a stupid idea, knowing I was being conned, but not knowing what else to do.

There followed thirty minutes of being accidentally brushed against and frequently pinched in about twenty marble-carving shops, and upper-arm-felt, up and down ten cobbled alleyways. In the end, I lost my cool. "Do you have to manhandle me?"

Mr. Harry Shobha stared at me most innocently. So I told him I was going back to the cafe.

"But you will become lost," he cried, in what could have been mistaken as true distress if I hadn't known he'd gotten me lost in the first place so he could pinch me.

"I shall keep going up until I reach the palace."

"I will help you."

My look of "one-step-closer-and-you're-dead" did it. With the wounded eyes of a kicked puppy, he backed off.

I found the palace. The rubbish tip. The cafe. I collected our bags. Paid their rent and placed them close to the bus stop. The four o'clock bus came and went. Still no Sally! I was really worried and so angry at her that I could have eaten dust, or beheaded her with my penknife and stuck her head on a stake.

She arrived at five, skipping blithely across the rubbish tip like Tinkerbell. "You'll never guess what I got," she trilled.

"We missed the bus to Bharatpur."

"Ooops!" A tiny flash of guilt. "Never mind. When's the next one?"

"Four o'clock tomorrow."

"Oh." Slight hesitation while registering this unpleasant fact. "I am a silly, aren't I? Want to see what I bought?"

"No." My voice would have frozen the balls off a ferret moving at the speed of light. It did nothing to Sally.

She waggled a marble egg with two swans carved inside it. It was exactly the same as those the trinket sellers had been trying to sell us in the mosque.

"So what are we going to do?" she asked.

"The village does not have a hotel but the cafe owner will rent us a room. Only there is no shower and the only toilet is the one beside the kitchen which we know is not view-proof."

At last, the enormity of our problem hit her. Sally goes to the loo four times a night. I could just see her going down the stairs in the pitch black. Especially as it looked as if the stairs were where the kitchen left its saucepans to dry and where the kitchen staff slept.

We sat dejectedly on our baggage, watching what looked like the death-throes of a frothing-at-the-mouth water buffalo that had fallen to its knees between the shafts of an overloaded cart. I was holding Sally back from going over and telling the owner what she thought of him, when who should appear, but the fastest-hands-in-India, Mr. Shobha.

"Ladies. The cafe owner says that you have missed your bus so as I am driving to Bharatpur I am offering you a lift."

"You're driving to Bharatpur?" repeated Sally, dragging her gaze off the buffalo that had miraculously staggered to its feet. Then she grinned at me as if all our problems were solved. Which was fine for her because she wouldn't be sitting in the front seat with Mr. Speedy Fingers.

During all our years of hitchhiking through Europe it was always me who sat in the front. Why? Because I didn't panic when my knee was patted, or when the driver's hand slipped off the gear stick onto my thigh, or when he drove with one hand while the other slid along the back of the seat and accidentally dropped onto my left boob.

"You've saved our lives," she told him.

As predicted, Mr. Shobha packed Sally and our bags in the back seat of his Morris Oxford look-alike and opened the front door for me. So I sat beside him with a bunch of maps in my hand, ready to slap him with them should his fingers stray.

Amazingly, they didn't. Even more amazing was that Mr. Shobha was a bird lover. There was nothing he didn't know about the open-bill stork, the painter stork, the silver grey egret, the white ibis, the spoonbill heron, the sarus crane and the snake-bird. All of which he promised we would see at Ghana Jeel Lake. Sally was ecstatic.

"You know, ladies," he said, slipping into storytelling mode. "When the British ruled India, Ghana Jeel Lake was the most popular place for the annual Imperial Duck Shoot. King Edward the Eighth bagged 2222 birds in one day."

"That's disgusting!" cried Sally.

"What did he do with them?" said I.

"Had them photographed heaped up in front of himself and the maharajah then divided them among the villagers. Although, as you know, many Hindus do not eat bird meat."

We nodded as if we had known this, which, along with King Edward the Eighth's shooting spree, we hadn't.

"Hunting was a big thing with the maharajahs," he continued. "It was not uncommon for a maharajah to kill thousands of tigers in his lifetime, or hundreds of buffalo, rhinoceroses and leopards during one week's hunting. It was considered good sport. I think this was why the maharajahs preferred the sporty British to the trading Portuguese."

"What about the British East India Company which practically ruled Indian trade for over a hundred years?" I asked.

"True," mused Mr. Shobha swerving around a camel wagon and coming face to face with a puffball-truck which refused to move over so we had to bump down into a ditch in an effort to miss it. "But you know, without the British we wouldn't have such a wonderful civil service and a workable system of law."

"And a load of Anglo-Indian government clerks to make both work," added Sally.

Mr. Shobha nodded enthusiastically as we bumped out of the ditch. "And an efficient lot they are too."

# Chapter 9

## BİRD SANCTUARY

On reaching Bharatpur, Mr. Shobha dropped us off at a guesthouse that had once been a royal hunting lodge. He thanked us for our company and we thanked him for the lift. He'd been a charming and informative host and hadn't pinched my arm once, which made me feel guilty for being so cool in the beginning. But that's the trouble with men. The minute you like them they do something you don't like. Then when you don't like them they do something charming, such as Mr. Shobha inviting us to dinner to meet his mother that evening. Of course we accepted.

Although it was late afternoon and Mr. Shobha would be returning in a few hours, Sally couldn't wait to see the birds. We were no sooner shown our room, which contained two gigantic carved double beds encased in voluminous mosquito nets and a bathroom large enough to hold a party of a hundred in, than she was organizing a rickshaw.

Our rickshaw guide was a Sikh and a refugee from Muslim Pakistan.

"In 1947 when the British divided India to stop the Hindus and the Muslims from killing each other, my family were forced to flee," he informed us as he pedalled furiously. "My parents were destitute until they reached Bharatpur where they found Sikhs to help them."

"So you were born in Bharatpur," I said.

"Yes, Madam. But in India one can be a refugee for generations."

"What do you know about the bird sanctuary?" asked Sally, completely untouched by his sad story.

He handed her his binoculars. "It is my living, Madam. There are over 350 species of bird in Keoladeo park."

"How many do you think I will see?"

"Three hundred and forty-nine, Madam. The Caspian stork has not yet arrived."

The entrance to the Keoladeo Bird Sanctuary was a cluster of falling-down houses inhabited by hundreds of lethargic, bum-scratching monkeys. We didn't stop. Sally doesn't like monkeys anymore. Our guide pedalled down a long road flanked by grey-colored canals full of khaki-colored frogs and yellow marsh grass. Stopping beside a lake, surrounded by half-submerged acacia trees, he commenced his lecture.

"Before the Maharajah of Bharatpur took charge, Ghana Jeel lake dried up every year. After the enterprising Maharajah diverted the water from the adjoining farms, the birds began to arrive. Look, Madams," he pointed at a skinny pink bird balancing on one leg, "that is a red-billed Siberian crane. Its nest is in that black-trunked tree over there. Look."

I looked, Sally photographed.

"Duck shooting was very popular until 1963," he continued, pedalling in slow motion. "On one day alone, one of your lords bagged 4273 ducks."

It was lucky Sally hadn't heard the mention of the bird massacres. She would have had a fit. Instead her attention was caught up in the camera and binocular straps that were twisted as she alternated between looking at the crane and kingfisher.

"So what happened to the farms?" I asked.

"They did not have enough water, Madam. Look, a sambar deer."

"Sally," I whispered, as a rusty brown doe stepped so close I could see the whites of her almond-shaped eyes.

"Sssshhhh, I'm watching a pelican."

The sambar disappeared with a disdainful flick of her fluffy white tail.

"That is a Dalmatian pelican," said our guide.

Sally's eyes glazed over with happiness. A Dalmatian pelican! What bliss. She told him to stop so she could look more closely and was soon ankle deep in swamp water and wading in deeper.

"Are there crocodiles?" I asked.

"No, Madam."

"Water snakes, eels, quicksand?"

"There are pythons but if one bites Madam, the Indian government will give her money. But I suggest you call Madam back. People disappear now and then."

"While they're being watched?"

"It has been known."

I kept my eyes on Sally and asked, "Who or what disappears them?"

"Madam will think me foolish."

"Never. So what is out there lurking in the murky depths?"

"Spirits, Madam."

"Oh! Is that all! I come from a country full of spirits. What are your spirits like?"

"Female and naked, Madam. They entice you into the water until it is too deep, or they upset your boat, and they drown you."

Compared to Australian bunyips and English fairies, Indian spirits sound far more exciting. "Are there naked men spirits to entice women?"

"Definitely not! Only women spirits, who are jealous of real women! Please call Madam back. I can no longer see her."

Neither could I. For a split second, I visualized inheriting the monster case.

"Sally!" I yelled, causing a pair of purple herons to take to the indigo sky with squawks of fright.

Five minutes later, Sally appeared with her pants rolled up and her sandals sodden. "I think I saw a rare bird."

"Did it look like a naked female?"

"What?"

"India has 1244 species of bird, 350 species of mammal, 408 species of reptile, 65,000 species of fauna and 15,000 flowering plants," recited our guide.

"Amazing," sighed Sally.

But it was becoming dark so we told him we had better go back to the guesthouse. Which he did gratefully. He had an eight-kilometer ride home after he left us and, he confessed, he hadn't done the shopping.

"Why doesn't your wife do the shopping?" I asked.

"Oh no, Madam. A wife's place is in the home. Also, I would not like my wife to speak to those rascal shopkeepers. It would be immodest of her. Truly, Madams, she has enough to do. She must collect water, which is a good distance from our house. She must walk the cow to find grass and collect the cow dung to make patties for burning. She must clean the house, tend the four children and the baby, and she must cook the chapattis. She is quite occupied."

"I bet," said Sally.

"Chapatti cooking is not easy," he continued, getting into his stride now we were on the homeward stretch. "Especially if I cannot afford flour and must take back wheat which she must clean and grind by hand before she can cook it."

"While she breastfeeds the baby," added Sally.

He gave her a smile of approval that implied, at last, a foreigner who understood.

"And if she fails in any of these wifely duties you are allowed to beat her," continued Sally, even though I almost nudged her out of the rickshaw to shut her up.

"It is a possibility," he answered seriously. "But my wife never disappoints me."

We gave him a large tip so that he would not have to buy wheat. As he pedalled away, I said, "Do you realize that it is very likely that his wife has never held a coin in her hand?"

"Never had to worry about what to buy for school lunches," added Sally.

"Never had the problem of too much to choose from at the supermarket."

"Or what to buy when guests are coming."

"I'd say it was a great load off her mind. Any woman would swap places with her."

"Immediately," Sally agreed. "Except for the cow manure patty making. I wonder if you can make goat manure patties or camel manure patties or even elephant manure patties?"

"Goats, no! Camel and elephant, yes!" I said, with all the authority of a non-manure patty maker, and grateful for it too.

The Shobha residence was the smallest art deco house I have ever seen. Squatting on a dusty block of land fenced with thorn bushes, its tiny cream-painted porch and four rooms looked as if it had been built as a child's playhouse. After leaving our sandals and Mr. Shobha's Western shoes at the door,

Mr. Shobha, "Harry" now, because we were friends, proudly showed us his lounge-dining room which boasted of a small two-seater lounge and coffee table both covered with lace doilies; his bedroom, the largest room in the house, festooned with frilly curtains, bedspread, silk cushions and many pictures of Krishna; his mother's bedroom, small, dark and incense smelling with a large collection of sandals lined up along one wall; and his pride and joy, the kitchen.

At first glance it looked like a modern kitchen. Only the refrigerator didn't work because the electricity wasn't strong enough, the shiny new taps weren't attached to water pipes so the sink was never used, and the cupboards below the marble workbench were false panels made to look like cupboard doors. "My mother prefers to cook outside," he said.

Mrs. Shobha was in the backyard, squatting in front of her coal-burning, drum-shaped cooking stove surrounded by aluminium pots. She was dressed in widow white, which answered where Mr. Shobha senior was, and had a sweet face and the most adoring black eyes. Adoring of her son that is. He was her lifeline and while he supported her and there was no wife, she was of use. She spoke no English but when I gestured that I would like to make roti, she handed me a ball of millet flour and a rolling pin the size of the inside of a toilet roll. Gesturing to me to squat beside her, she proceeded to demonstrate how to jam a thumb loaded with ghee inside the ball, how to roll it out, flip it over, roll again, flip again, until it was the right size to be stuck to the hot interior of her terracotta stove.

After my roti-making effort, which wasn't at all bad, Harry whisked us away to drink an overly sweet non-alcoholic cordial and to talk about world affairs and philosophy, so I didn't get to find out how Mrs. Shobha cooked everything else. But I did have a long philosophical conversation. Although philosophy, like cooking, is a subject I know nothing about.

Once we were seated on the carpet around the coffee table, a bare-footed, bent-double Mrs. Shobha, her sari tucked up so she wouldn't trip, entered the lounge-dining room carrying a steam-ing bowl of dhal soup smelling of ginger and garlic. Next came dishes of vegetable garam masala, sweet pickles, spicy tamarind chutney, chickpea curry, samosas stuffed with mouth-searing chili and smelling of fried ghee, *pakoras* stuffed with chickpeas, lentils fried in ghee and fluffy rice flavored with turmeric and other spices unknown to us.

Mrs. Shobha did not sit with us although we invited her to do so. Later, on my way to the outside toilet, I saw her squatting in the middle of the modern kitchen floor eating from the alu-minium pots.

Our animated conversation over dinner covered every-thing from the delicious basmati rice we were eating, which Mr. Shobha said he had bought especially for us as it came from the Himalayan rice paddies and was the best in the world; the President of America's whirlwind visit and what good it would do India; whether Kashmir should belong to India or Pakistan; Britain's unfair colonial salt tax and Ghandi's salt march across India to protest against it; the Dalai Lama living in northern India; and why Harry was no longer married.

His young wife had died in childbirth, he explained, and as he had truly loved her he was in no hurry to replace her. Not only that, his business was doing well so he had no need of a wife's dowry and there was his mother to consider. A wife might not get along with her, so he would not remarry until she died.

"What if you are fifty or sixty years old?" asked Sally.

"I am a well-off man, it will be no problem," replied Harry.

At ten o'clock, Harry drove us back to our hotel where we found that our room had been taken over by plump pink geckos with near-transparent bodies. They scurried across our ceiling on their suction padded feet, making a loud cricket-like sound. Sally didn't like them so she wrapped herself in her mosquito net in case any dropped on her. But mosquito nets give me claus-trophobia. Shrouded beds make me think of vampires. Not only that, I think geckos are cute.

The next day at the crack of dawn, we returned to the bird sanctuary to lie in the long cream grass to watch arrowheads of squawking geese flying south, blue-winged teals skimming over khaki mirrored water, and to marvel over many, many more birds that Sally recognized and I didn't. I lost count after two hundred. It was a wonderfully lazy day.

That evening, we ate at our guesthouse. First we drank banana *lassis* in the polished wooden-floored lounge room, lying back in overstuffed lounge chairs that had been placed around a fireplace full of sesame twigs in preparation for winter. Beside us was a blond veneer radiogram (radio-stereo combo) with shelves full of an ancient *Encyclopedia Britannica*, and behind us stood a glass case holding silver plates, a Kashmir shawl, and a royal Bharatpur servant's outfit of a yellow turban and tight green jacket with crest and diamond buttons.

The tour de force was a highly polished veneer coffee table covered with dozens of silver-framed photographs of the maharajah's ancestors riding white horses, plus a pamphlet telling the history of the House of Bharatpur that included gossipy incidentals. Such as how one maharajah always booked a plane seat for his Krishna statue. How the Shah of Iran's first wife Soraya had shot three tigers. And how it was the Maharajah of Bharatpur who assisted her husband, the Shah of Persia, in arranging that famous night of love in the Taj Mahal. How in the village of Bharatpur there remained a fort which had withstood an 1805 British attack, and a widow's sanctuary with blood-marked walls where grieving widows, wishing to move on to another reincarnation, repeatedly hit their heads.

Sally wandered off to look at some stuffed birds.

I read on.

Before de-recognition of the maharajahs, the Maharajah of Bharatpur owned fifteen Rolls-Royce Phantom II Tourers. He acquired these after a Mayfair Rolls Royce salesman had insulted him by not recognizing him and salaaming low enough. To show how rich he was, the piqued maharajah bought the contents of the showroom on the condition that the salesman accompanied the cars to Bharatpur. On their arrival, the maharajah informed the salesman that the vehicles would be used to collect the municipal rubbish. This broke the salesman's heart—as it would have broken mine since I have a passion for antique cars. And to think of all those beautiful cars paid for with taxes gleaned from the poverty-stricken Bharatpur farmers being treated like that just because of piqued pride.

Although the state of Bharatpur, consisting of only 1982 square miles, was small bucks in the maharajah stakes, this did not stop the Maharajah of Bharatpur from objecting virulently when in 1972 the traitorous (as he saw it) Indian government forced the 277 maharajahs to give up over two-fifths of India. Overnight the maharajahs were stripped of their titles, privy purses (some received more than a million rupees a year), and their royal privileges such as free water, electricity, medicine, armed guards, police escorts, personal flags, their own red State number plates, the importing of unlimited bottles of duty-free alcohol, immunity from legal action and the right to be buried with military honors without having served in the Indian army.

Gone were the halcyon days of virgin swapping, drinking pearls in champagne and hunting tigers from the backs of elephants, the one animal a tiger will not attack. Gone were the nights of dining on partridge livers, roast doves in white wine and honey, and lemon soufflés served on Wedgwood while drinking Napoleon brandy from imported Belgian crystal. No more sleeping in solid silver beds, no more French champagne-filled swimming pools to celebrate the birth of an heir. Or in the youthful Maharajah of Bharatpur's case, no more frolicking in a fountain filled with lotus blossoms and forty naked girls. Modern India could no longer afford such frivolities.

Forewarned, the royal Houses of Jodhpur and Udaipur turned their opulent palaces into expensive hotels. Others, who hadn't seen the writing on the wall and if they had wouldn't have read it, panicked and sold their Fabergé clocks,

Rembrandts, Cartier jewelry and gold bath plugs, and were robbed with each transaction as selling was not something maharajahs were accustomed to doing. Hurt to their royal marrow, they retrieved their sons from their English prep schools and withdrew to their summer palaces until their money ran out, which it did very quickly, economizing being another thing maharajahs knew little about.

Back to their villages went the thousands of servants, without pay or pension, each bemoaning that there would be no more standing at attention during their Highnesses' gun salutes; no more stroking their Highnesses' feet; no more sleeping outside their Highnesses' door in case their Highnesses needed their backs scratched. Their Highnesses had to economize. Long live their Highnesses.

Houses such as the royal hunting lodge we were staying in were sold off or left to rot. But not this one! Its proximity to the Keoladeo Bird Sanctuary saved it. It became a money earner for someone who had never earned anything in his life.

I found Sally in the dining room, a grand salon with French windows, matching mahogany sideboards set with gold plate, and rows of stuffed animal heads hanging on its walls. As neither of us fancied all those glass-eyed tigers, snow leopards and spotted deer gazing down at us while we ate, we decided to dine in the garden where the sitar players were performing.

Indian nights are special. The perfume of the gardens is heady, the night sky resembles velvet, the stars are so big and hang so low that they resemble unearthly fruit, and the music is haunting and hypnotic. We had no sooner sat at our table than we were wafted back to maharajah days. Feeling very royal indeed, we ordered banana lassis and omelettes, which is the best bet when not ordering vegetable thali. Sally is still refusing to eat thali.

Halfway through dinner, Sally complained of feeling sick. This was a worry as I had recently read about a scam where some hotel staff fed travelers urine-contaminated food so they could share in the doctor's fee. Sally went to bed groaning and moaning. Finally, I asked the hotel receptionist to ring for a doctor.

The doctor was a dapper chappie with a well-pressed suit, a black leather bag full of pills and needles, and a kindly smile. He was indeed a very handsome doctor. He gave Sally an injection in her bottom and some anti-nausea pills, which cost her $40. Which is a small fortune in India, and was no doubt shared out generously.

She was well enough the next morning to set off into the pre-dawn mist on a rented bicycle with the head-waiter's binoculars slung around her neck for her last look at the birds, while I walked into town to look for the widows' sanctuary. I never found it. No one understood a word I said, and my pantomiming of a widow, which consisted of my weeping over a body (me again, with my hands crossed over my chest), didn't work. In fact, it had those villagers for whom I performed it backing off at an incredible speed.

The next morning we caught the local bus to Jaipur. As Jaipur was 174 kilometers away, I had calculated that the trip would take three hours. It took the entire day.

The inside of the bus was sticky hot. Outside the bus it was boiling hot, dusty and excruciatingly noisy, as trucks and tractors fought our bus for road space. Their weapons were the blasting of their horns. Ours was our driver's musical horn. Everyone was deafened. No one won. Within a few kilometers the bus was packed. People and children stood in the aisle and mountains of luggage took up the back seats. It didn't seem possible that the overladen vehicle could hold another body, yet as it chugged west the driver picked up, packed in, put on the roof any passenger who hailed him. From empty crossroads, men with waxed moustaches and pumpkin-shaped turbans climbed on for a two-hour ride then climbed off again at another empty crossroad. Three women carrying babies stood in the aisle, hips jutting forward, earrings swinging cheekily, their arrogant jet-black eyes challenging everyone. Their skirts, tops and scarves were brightly patterned and their wrists, ankles and toes covered in heavy silver jewelry. All their colors clashed and their clamoring children (the first we'd heard complain) were filthy. They had the same narrow, ratty faces of the gypsies of Europe and the other passengers edged away from them. They got off an hour later, stepping from the bus onto a roadside verge covered in yellow poppies, their bare feet and silver bracelets disappearing into the golden carpet, another color to add to their many.

"Perhaps they were Rabari or Raika," I said. "You know, the nomads who take their camels and sheep on long treks towards Pakistan in search of fodder."

"So why didn't the other women like them?"

"Because the Rabari and Raika are more independent. They control their husband's money and have more freedom than the village women. And because the Rabari and Raika graze their herds on other peoples' land."

After hours of heat-induced languor, there was a moment of excitement. A camel train of wheat-laden carts filled the road, forcing our bus to skid on the stony verge and tilt dangerously as it veered past at top speed with its horn blasting and its back-seat luggage sliding to the low side of the bus. The bus swerved back and the luggage slid to the other side, and there in front of us were two mange-riddled dogs pawing at a road kill with three vultures hovering just beyond the dogs' snapping teeth. The bus roared straight at them. Sally hid her face. The vultures and dogs scattered and the road kill was indented with more tire marks as four shepherd boys jumped up from the roadside shouting a greeting.

The bus stopped at a market place opposite a whisky shop appropriately called The Bagpipe Shop. We watched as men pushed their money through one slot and were handed their purchase in a brown paper bag through another. No bright window displays here. Not a lot of choice either. But then Hindus and Muslims are not supposed to drink alcohol. I wonder how the shopkeepers get away with selling it. In a way, India is one of the most democratic of countries.

Everyone alighted except us, as we weren't sure how long the bus would stop there. Within minutes, our windows were surrounded with boys carrying trays of lemons, pickles, pawpaw, tomatoes, onions, sugar cane, limes, cucumbers, green tomatoes and peanuts. Where did all this fresh produce come from? Surely not from the dry, grassless plain we'd just crossed. Sellers of ice cream or platters of hot *parathas* fried in ghee held up their wares for us to smell their enticing aromas. I bought two parathas on the premise that any germ fried in ghee was truly dead. Sally bought grapes. A man entered the bus selling a concoction of seeds, spice, nuts and chili mixed to the buyer's choice on a sheet of newspaper and eaten from a cone of the same. He offered me a taste. It resembled an instant non-cooked curry. I bought a cone. The bus filled up again and we were off rattling through the town at a speed guaranteed to have anyone crossing the road in front of us skittling for the verges.

Ten kilometers on, we began passing pyramids of pink marble. Were the slabs brought by camel wagon to the closest main road so they could be transported by truck to somewhere else? Did builders drive along the highway choosing marble at their leisure? If so, where were the salesmen? There had to be salesmen.

"If an Indian has two match sticks, he is a businessman because he can sell one," I was told by a London Indian. This answered my next question, which was, why were Indians the convenience shop owners of New York, England, Jamaica and Kenya, and the petrol (gas) station owners of Australia. Because they are businessmen.

We approached a second town with horn blaring. Above us hung a ruined fort the color of dry cow dung, below it white and scarlet bougainvillea covered the roofs of a string of shanties. This time we parked opposite a row of beach umbrellas. Music blared through loudspeakers. Women in long, full skirts and tight jackets (no bare midriffs here) haggled over plastic jewelry. Five chillum-smoking men in bright saffron and orange turbans squatted on top of a bicycle-wheeled stall, sharing it with piles of roti and samosa. Others, in long white shirts worn over baggy trousers, sipped chai in a corrugated-tin chai house. Behind them on a dusty oval three small boys played cricket. One bowler. One batter. One fielder. A group of men carrying red triangular flags decorated with gold fringes and stars marched across the cricket pitch beating drums, and the three young cricketers came to attention and saluted.

"A political meeting," explained a young man who had sat down beside me in the empty bus. "Do you like cricket?"

Not to know the rules of cricket, or not to love the game of cricket is a sin in India. But as it has only been men who have discussed the game with us, perhaps Indian women, like Sally and I, don't care one way or the other. I did not tell the young man this. I simply smiled.

He then proceeded to tell me his life's story. He was his mother's only son; he lived in London, and was on his way to his village for a month's holiday. As he talked, he waved his hands about beautifully. His wrists were covered in brassy bangles; his fingers in cheap rings, and his two overly long thumbnails were painted with turquoise nail polish. His colorful conversation covered AIDS, war, God and homosexuality. He asked me what I thought of all four. I have noticed that Indian men don't care much for small talk. They want to get into the deep and meaningful instantly, and they have no fear about speaking what they call the truth. Not waiting for me to answer, my Londoner said that the Hindu goddesses were the strongest of all goddesses; even in love they were the strongest. I assured him I thought him right. He continued with, did I know that Shiva and his consort Parvati made love for one hundred god years during which time Shiva's sperm never once dried up? He did not elaborate on what this had to do with the strength of goddesses.

"No, I didn't know that," I answered, as if discussing Shiva's sperm with strangers on a bus was a commonplace occurrence. "But if goddesses are so wonderful, why do Indian men treat women so poorly? Why are there so many fatal kerosene stove burnings just so their husbands can remarry some other unfortunate woman and receive a second dowry of a television or a scooter? Then when that dowry is used up, there is a second kerosene stove accident and a third wife and dowry, and so on."

His answer, which ignored the dowry burnings, floored me. Apparently a diet of steak and kidney is boring so a man needs to try something new. I said I thought his explanation trite, and anyway, weren't Hindus forbidden to eat beef? Plus women were not steak and kidney, they were human beings equal to any male. That ended our conversation.

When he got off, his entourage of equally bejeweled young men swaggered across the road behind him. I wondered if his mother or theirs knew what they were up to.

# Chapter 10

## Jaipur and Elephants

On alighting at the Jaipur bus station, we were grabbed by the closest auto-rickshaw driver. We shouted the name of our hotel over all the other noise and he nodded vigorously. Ten minutes later, we discovered that he was a great nodder, and that he didn't speak a word of English and that he didn't know where we were going. We were lost for half an hour and saw a lot of Jaipur before putt-putting through an enormous pink archway covered in lacy pink and white patterns; around a disgusting vomit-smelling intersection where cows, pigs, goats and dogs snuffled noisily through a mountain of discarded vegetables; and up the circular driveway to the Hotel Bissau Palace, once the abode of a Jaipurian noble, now a medium-priced tourist hotel. After an instant unpack, we hurried out to explore.

Jaipur, City of Jewels, is a planned city unlike higgledy-piggledy Agra and modern, old and ancient Delhi. The reason being that when Aurangzeb the sixth died 272 years ago, and a revolution broke out all over Mogul-ruled India, it did not touch Rajasthan. Rajasthan had miraculously remained independent of the Moguls so with Aurangzeb's armies no longer a threat, Maharajah Jai Singh II decided to quit his over-crowded aerie fortress and descend to the Jaipurian plains, to partake in the princely hobby of city building.

"My new city will have European-style boulevards," he announced to his courtiers. "It will have fountain-cooled parks and tree-lined places for public gatherings, areas designated for each caste and function. But most of all, it will be able to expand."

Unfortunately, since the 1972 de-recognition of the maharajahs, the pink-and-white city of Jaipur has been mostly ignored. Although, due to the President of the United States' visit, the Chandpol Gate and the shopfronts of Chandpol Bazaar, Tripolia Bazaar and Ramganj Bazaar had been tizzied up with gallons of pink and white paint. Maharajah Ram Singh started this custom—which resembles stencilling over paper-doilies—in 1876 when the Prince of Wales visited Jaipur. The effect is pretty, if one is speeding by, and the President, who has only a week to see the whole of India, will be speeding by.

Meanwhile we, who have all the time we like, dawdled along enjoying the three colorful bazaars that stretch along the main street. The spicy food, and glowing jewelry, Western clothing and shoe shops were doing a brisk trade. The rickshaw owners were not. Perhaps shoppers were not ready to go home yet.

Begging children roamed everywhere, annoying everyone until seeing us they made a beeline, through the flow of ramshackle togas pulled by starving ponies, to where we walked along the road because the pavement had been taken over by extended shopfronts. I bought ice creams for three grubby little girls. They gobbled them fast, but not before a boy tried to grab one and was only stopped by my indignant shouts.

During our walk, we saw the largest and busiest round-abouts I have ever seen in the world, and that is saying something after one has been to Cairo. Getting around a Jaipur roundabout meant joining a reckless rush with whichever four-footed creature or rickshaw was going in the same direction.

We passed more Shri Mataji posters (so she was in Jaipur now), a cow dining on washing on the roof of a shop porch, three goats cavorting with a group of children along a row of third-floor balconies, and a herd of Brahman bulls heading for the night cow hostel. But what astonished us the most was on our return journey home past Swine Corner every piece of rotting vegetable and every plastic bag had been removed and there wasn't an animal in sight.

That night we shared our hotel table with a most delightful Indian couple. He was a retired history teacher. She, a never-to-retire housewife. Both had saved all their working lives to have their second honeymoon in Rajasthan. Together we watch a papier-mâché puppet show about a princess being kidnapped by the sword-wielding prince of her dreams, and a snake charmer who hypnotized his cobra with the swaying movement of his gourd-shaped pipe until it almost stood on its tail.

We were surprised at how many Indian tourists photographed the snake charmer and dropped a coin in his basket, including the couple at our table. Snake charmers are good luck, they told us, so Sally and I gave him twenty rupees.

Over coffee, the retired teacher talked about the maharajahs. Especially his favorite, the Maharani Gayatri Devi. When he spoke of this beautiful princess, his eyes lit up as if she were a long lost love. His wife smiled at him indulgently.

"Madho Singh I, the ancestor of the present maharajah, was very fat and quite unfit. Oh yes, quite unfit. He was married o three princesses whom he never visited. He had been warned by a soothsayer that he would die if he sired a legitimate heir so he adopted Sawai Man Singh, a village boy of the right caste, naturally."

"Naturally," we echoed.

"When Sawai Man Singh was ten years old, the Royal Houses of Amber and Jodhpur arranged his engagement to two Jodhpur princesses. One the same age as himself, the other a twenty-two-year-old. Marriage to the older princess followed immediately."

"When he was ten years old," exclaimed Sally.

The teacher nodded. "They had been married five years, and he was fifteen and she twenty-seven when she gave birth to a daughter. But Sawai Man Singh persevered and in 1931 an heir nicknamed Bubbles was born. Having done his duty for his kingdom, Sawai Man Singh sailed off to England to indulge in the life of a visiting prince. He played world-class polo, you know."

We didn't know.

"In 1932 he married the younger princess and although she bobbed her hair and wore nail varnish, as was the fashion, she still lived and slept in the zenana with the other women. She continued to wear purdah and being a strict Muslim, when she fell pregnant, she insisted on being diagnosed from the next room."

Here the history teacher shrugged. "So although she produced two sons, she was ignored by the modern-thinking maharajah. Then he met the thirteen-year-old Gayatri Devi, Princess of Cooch Behar. They fell instantly in love. Although Gayatri Devi's mother, Ma Cooch, a beauty in her own right, made them wait until Gayatri was twenty-one before they could marry."

Here the teacher paused for a breath, and his wife took over. "Life in Jaipur did not suit this liberated princess who had shot her first tiger at twelve, raced elephants around the Cooch Behar palace gardens at thirteen, and at fourteen sailed to England to be educated. What did she have in common with the two wives in purdah?"

"Not a thing!" answered her husband. "The 400 palace servants were too serious for her. Jaipur court life was too formal. The zenana women spoke Hindi of which she spoke little. They were boring and she was homesick."

The teacher sighed, his wife pouted, and we waited. Finally the wife spoke up.

"So she demanded an apartment adjoining her husband's and a trip around the world, after which they became inseparable."

"Sawai Man Singh was besotted with her," continued her husband. "He could refuse her nothing. So when she entered politics in 1961 as a right-wing candidate he backed her all the way. What a strange sight it must have been for those illiterate peasant women hiding behind their screens to see this modern-day woman driving her 1948 Buick into their mud-walled villages. How astounding to have her garlanded with marigolds, sitting on a mat in the head-man's hut, waving her manicured fingers or fingering her jewelry as she talked. How amazing that the men listened."

We agreed.

"What she said won over their naive hearts and in turn she won her parliamentary seat with the highest majority of any democratic election in the world. Then with the help of the raj-matas (dowager queens) of Jodhpur, Gwalior and Bikaner, she managed to shout down, ever so decorously while wearing expensive French scent, all of Mrs. Gandhi's congress's plans for a democratic India."

"Which would have enhanced the lives of the very females who had voted her in," concluded Sally.

"Exactly," said the teacher's wife. "They actually voted to stay in poverty."

We finished our coffee, said goodnight to the lovely couple, and went to look outside the hotel gates to where a crowd of men were dancing and singing around four drummers. This celebration of a groom-to-be went on all night, much like any bucks' night anywhere else.

Due to the drumming which stopped the entire hotel from sleeping, I read the *Kama Sutra*.

"Want to know about the ideal match?" I asked.

"Like Sawai Man Singh and Gayatri Devi."

"Like the history teacher and his wife."

"Go on then."

"Man is divided into three classes—hare, bull and horse. Women are divided into three classes—deer, mare or elephant. There are three equal unions and six unequal unions. There are also nine kinds of union according to the three forces of passion and nine kinds of union according to time taken during congress. This makes eighteen successful unions and eighteen unsuccessful unions."

"One would need a computer to work it out," complained Sally. "What about finger-tip-tingling romance? What about eyes meeting across a crowded room? What about ... being unable to look at them because you care so much and ..."

"It's all here," I said, tapping the *Kama Sutra*. "I just have to find it."

"Forget it. The last time I felt like that was when I looked at George Clooney."

"What about your boyfriend?"

"What about him?"

"Is he hare, bull or horse?"

"Mind your own business!"

Next morning, weary from lack of sleep and ready to lynch the bucks' night drummers who were still drumming, we breakfasted on omelettes, then walked the length of Chandni Chowk to the Hawa Mahal, the famous pink Palace of the Winds. This palace of a thousand windows is not as big as I'd expected it to be. From its photographs, which are in every Indian tourist brochure in the world, it looked enormous. It isn't. Nor am I sure why it is called a palace. Because what it is is a beautiful, rose-pink sandstone façade in the shape of a step-pyramid, full of delicately worked lattice-covered windows beneath half cupolas. Originally built to allow the court ladies to spy on the everyday happenings of the city, its five floors can be climbed for a splendid view of Jaipur. I would have loved to have climbed it but our bus was leaving.

The bus ride to the ancient capital of Amber took half an hour. On the way we saw an exquisitely designed white palace floating like a mirage in the middle of a crystal-clear lake. Although there were water buffalo feeding around the lake's edge, the woman beside me said that the palace had not been occupied for years. What a waste, I thought. Still, isolated like that it will be preserved and one day, like Fatehpur Sikri, it will be opened up to the amazement of all. I named it the Palace of Loneliness.

The bus terminated opposite Amber Palace Lake where two elephant-wallahs were scrubbing their pets. The elephants splashed, tumbled and squirted each other like gigantic rubber toys while their keepers waded between them, wielding scrubbing brushes on long sticks and exhibiting no fear of being rolled upon and squashed. Sally and I rushed to take photographs and saw what we thought were bodies among the lake's debris. These turned out to be life-sized string and straw figures lying in uncannily life-like poses. The elephant-wallahs said they were effigies that had been drowned to free their owners from an evil spell. Sally poo-pooed the idea of evil spells, but I, who have an Irish mother, am well acquainted with spells, and have even put the cut-out figure of a neighbor in my ice-tray to stop him from building his garage higher than my fence. We patted the elephant's trunks, photographed their flower-painted faces, and crossed a bridge to where other elephants wearing red-and-blue gold-fringed tablecloths waited to earn money for their owner, the Maharajah of Jaipur.

Behind the elephant station, outside a row of mahout's houses, squatted six black lumps. Wives in purdah with eye slits in their tents to allow them to watch the crazy behavior of the foreign tourists, which is probably as good as watching television, a habit much frowned upon by orthodox Muslims.

The Maharajah of Jaipur owns Amber village, the elephants, Tiger Fort, Amber Fort, Rambagh Palace Hotel and the City Palace. Each is a paying concern and the elephant rides to Amber Fort are expensive. The alternative is to climb the steep road, only it is crowded with elephant traffic. Not to mention great globs of poo and the danger of being showered with hot yellow pee. We chose to ride.

Climbing onto an irritated, bored, it's-time-I-had-my-bath elephant is not easy. Once again I chose the back seat, mainly because at the same time I was negotiating the buying of a hat. Suddenly the elephant lurched forward, and the salesman, seeing his meal ticket disappearing from the designated area of sale (salesmen are not allowed on the maharajah's private road), threw the hat to me and I threw down the agreed price.

"Madam, Madam, one more dollar, please."

"I don't have dollars." (They always mean U.S. dollars.)

"But Madam, I am a poor man."

Poverty is relative, I wanted to shout. For instance, after buying my elephant ticket; paying to enter the seventeenth-century Amber Fort (some say that it was a city 800 years ago); paying to enter the eighteenth-century City Palace, and buying tickets to see its miniature paintings and famous observatory, thus assisting to support the maharajah in the manner he was accustomed to when his father received 90,000 rupees a year, I too would be considerably poorer. Not only that, but the hat wasn't worth that much.

On the slow trek upwards, I read of how the Amber Palace had been built by a Rajput commander in Ali Akbar's army, hence its strategic situation on the edge of a gorge overlooking a lake giving it both height and water, two essential ingredients to outlast a siege. Above it, perched on a sheer ridge and accessible only by a zigzagging pathway, is the palace's last retreat, the Nahargarh or Tiger Fort which protects the Jaipur family treasure. Tradition dictates that each maharajah must choose one item from the treasure and that this item will predict the type of ruler he will become. So far the present day maharajah has been hesitant to choose.

On reaching the palace gate, our elephant swayed through an archway high enough to allow a gold-and-crystal howdah covered by a fringed parasol carried by a turbaned mahout to pass through with ease. Inside was a large square where the maharajah's military had once camped. It was now an elephant station.

To reach the palace proper we had to climb an imposing staircase guarded by a tribe of wispy grey-haired monkeys with bad-tempered frowns, elongated arms and slim musicians' fingers. Two of these fought over Sally's breakfast. She has forgiven the monkey clan but now threw her toast at them. At the top of the staircase is the Drum Hall and an imposing hanging gallery from where we could either spy on the many courtyards, gaze over the stony Rajasthan landscape, or look down on the road we had just come up and its trundling toy-sized elephants.

The maharajah's apartments were off a terrace of carved marble windows so delicate that one dared not lean against them for fear of falling through and plummeting into the lake, thus destroying the palace's much photographed reflection with one mighty splash. All the rooms had walls and ceilings inlaid with precious gems depicting flowers and fruit.

My favorite was the Ganesh room named after the little black elephant-headed god statue inside it. Ganesh is my favorite Hindu god. Not only because I am a writer but because of the story of how he got his elephant head. The Lord of Beginnings, Remover of Obstacles and Patron of Scribes was once asked by his mother Parvati to guard the door while she had a bath. Ganesh tried to do this, even against Shiva, who, in a fit of rage, cut off his son's head. On hearing the lamentations of Ganesh's mother, the father god immediately promised to replace the head with the first living creature passing their door. This happened to be an elephant. The walls of the Ganesh room were covered in daintily carved plaster niches and its white-ribbed ceiling was filled with lace-like gesso studded with pieces of mirror. The effect was one of spider webs in the rain, and was exactly how I imagined the room where the beautiful Princess Scheherazade had made up her magical stories to entertain her bored sultan so that he wouldn't chop off her head as he had his hundreds of other unwanted wives.

Feeling all palaced out and having lost Sally again, I retired to a shaded terrace where I sat on a wall, drank chai and gazed up at the Tiger Fort trying to imagine battalions of turbaned warriors defending it. The saddest thing about the warriors of these two forts is that after hundreds of years of successfully repulsing the Mogul hordes, it wasn't a superior army that subdued them, it was the British Empire with its tantalizing offers of an extravagant lifestyle far beyond any mountain prince's dreams.

So, like the Moguls before them, these handsome moustached heirs gave up their battle-scarred forts, their pastel-pink palaces, their white war-horses and golden-tusked elephants, and succumbed to the "good" life of Savile Row tailors, Ferragamo of Florence shoes, European mistresses, Parisian nightclubs, polo tournaments, the royal sport of racing, and the occupying of entire floors of exclusive Paris, London and New York hotels. No longer clear-eyed warriors defending their kingdom, these dethroned princes drank themselves to death from swimming pools filled with champagne while their people became the most poverty-stricken of India.

Sally found me and excitedly told me that she had discovered where the present day maharajah worshipped. I followed her to a small marble temple behind the palace. Pushing open its silver doors, I stepped inside and stopped short with shock. The stone floor was sticky with recently spilled goat's blood. The sweet smell of it made me gag. Around the red silk-covered walls stood statues of black-faced, crooked-legged Kali looking exactly like the Mexican mother goddess Quetzalcoatl with the same blood-covered tongue and hands, the same skirt of serpents and necklace of human skulls. How had these two countries, which were so far apart, come up with the same frightening goddess?

Hindus believe that Kali, who is also prayed to as Durga the Terrible, rules over epidemics, earthquakes, floods and storms. With her holy scissors she pitilessly cuts the threads of her worshippers' lives, and appeased her blood lust with human sacrifices until the British forbade it in the nineteenth century. She is powerful and much loved. But I wouldn't want to come across her in a dark alley.

Back in Jaipur, after a color-coordinated curry lunch in the coolest place we could find, a Tripolia Bazaar cafe, with loaves of flat bread that hung over each side of our plates, we returned to our hotel for a well-earned siesta. We awoke at 6 a.m. the next morning.

Completely reinvigorated, we decided to tackle the City Palace. Back past the Palace of the Winds we went, stopping to dig through a box of carved wooden stamps. The stamps were for stamping designs on material. A young Indian man showed us what they looked like by stamping them up our arms. We arrived at the City Palace entrance covered in tattoos of elephants, fish and camels and with three carved stamps each.

Jaipur City Palace is really a cluster of palaces, or a village of palaces, each one built at a different time by the last six maharajahs. Altogether they contain 1500 oleander-pink and white rooms (which would take getting used to if you hated pink), all with gold ceilings; hundreds of Baccarat crystal chandeliers cleaned regularly by 400 servants; 300-year-old carpets of rose and gold silk that the toilet-cleaning Untouchables had to edge around as they were not allowed to walk on them and if they did so in the past they would suffer death; thousands of pieces of inlaid ivory furniture, kilometers of Benares brocade curtains, bedspreads and seat covers; plus a private museum of miniatures and a well-equipped observatory. Just reading about the place made me tired.

We started with the Welcome Palace, famous for its little silver bicycles used by parrots trained to ride them by one maharajah; a gold tongue-scraper used after a night on the town in London or Paris; photos of the diamond-and-ruby encrusted turtle that one maharani took to the Monaco casino to bring her luck (as if she needed it); and a voluminous quilted cloak of Benares brocade belonging to Maharajah Madho Singh I, who weighed 250 kilos and was almost as wide as he was tall.

"When Maharajah Madho Singh I dressed for a festive occasion," so the palace guard told us, most proudly, "he was held up by two gentlemen-in-waiting because of the weight of his pearl crown and his emerald-and-ruby necklaces which covered his stomach."

"Which was massive," whispered Sally.

"Was he the one who had the three unwanted teenage wives whom he refused to visit?" I asked.

The guard nodded, then continued with his spiel. "Although the present day maharajah is not as wealthy as Madho Singh I, he is still expected to wear nine different jewels every day. Nor is he allowed to wear the same jewel twice in a year."

"That's over 3000 jewels a year," gasped Sally.

The guard nodded.

We were suitably impressed. Well, more than suitably. We were gobsmacked.

We moved on to the hall containing silver-embroidered shawls made from Kashmir goats' beards. There is something magical about being able to pull a shawl through a wedding ring, as if something enchanting should happen, such as a puff of smoke and the appearance of a genie.

Our next stop was the Diwan-i-Am Hall, the hall where the maharajah gave audience to his subjects. This hall is full of ancient Persian and Sanskrit manuscripts, paintings of maharajahs cuddling their leopard cubs, photographs of the royal couple going to the cinema (her in a slinky, long, ashes-of-roses Parisian gown, him in tails), and group photos of the family clustered around an Indian Father Christmas, each baby prince with his nanny and each older prince with his tennis coach.

We moved on to the Diwan-i-Khas Hall or private audience hall. Outside this hall stand two enormous silver water pots once filled with holy Ganges water. These had accompanied a Hindu maharajah on his journey to England and back as he did not trust the Thames water, and that was before the Londoners began reusing it. He traveled by steamer and the lifting of the pots into the hold must have been a sight to see, not to mention an engineering success.

Madho Singh I's private apartments had no steps, only ramps. Being so fat, he had to be pulled around in a lacquered wood cart by four male servants except when he visited the zenana. During those times, six strong women pulled him around. In the zenana there is a sloping bed invented by an English engineer to assist the overweight Madho Singh I to connect with his concubines.

Across yet another courtyard is the royal weapons palace and the royal coach-house, which housed fifty carriages and coaches. One enormous camel coach has holes in its sides for twelve purdah-wearing women to look out of while traveling from one city to another. Another coach, built to carry British royalty, is upholstered in gold and silver brocade with silver fittings. The stables that accommodated the maharajah's horses and camels are big enough to house an Olympic village.

Completely overwhelmed by so much wealth, we rested in the shade and read about Gayatri Devi, the maharani our teacher friend had such an enormous crush on. Gayatri Devi had lived in the City Palace until her husband died, then as rajmata, she'd moved to the Rambagh Palace Hotel. Now Maharajah Bubbles and his Hindu wife and daughter live in one of the palaces, the seven-storied Moon Palace, famous for its 200 varieties of roses and its moon garden of dark cypress and white violets. It is rumored that the two Jodhpur wives that came before Gayatri Devi, one the mother of Bubbles, died of loneliness or broken hearts.

Outside the palace all was quiet except for the buzzing vibrations of cicadas. Where was the traffic noise that we'd become so used to shouting over? Where were the crowds of teeming people? The wandering cows? All taking a siesta by the looks of the reclining rickshaw pedallers. One pedaller slowly unwound himself and cycled over. He told us that he was married to an English girl and asked if we wanted to meet her, as she would love to meet us.

English Celia was not at all embarrassed by us arriving on her doorstep or at having two strangers sitting on her double bed, there being no chairs in her one-room apartment. This room had once been the servant's room of the private house next door. It was painted blue and furnished with an iron-framed bed and cloth mattress covered with a printed sheet, and had a window overlooking the lake. Their toilet and place to wash and cook were outside.

Celia told us that she had wandered around India for three years before falling in love. After a courtship that included poems and love songs, and her husband following her from town to town professing his infinite love, they were married in a Hindu ceremony with her wearing a borrowed red sari and fake gold jewelry. Her family accepted her wish to remain in India and had already been to India to see baby, Aliesha. She added that she had always been one of those "If Allah wills" women. Although as her husband was Hindu, she was probably an "If Vishnu wills" woman now.

After our visit, Celia's husband pedalled us back to our hotel. We wanted to give him money for the baby but didn't know how to do it politely so we overpaid him for the ride.

Back at the hotel we were greeted by our Indian couple who excitedly told us that they'd arranged to take us to a concert. But did we mind departing immediately? We didn't mind at all.

The concert was held in an ancient building with a sagging façade, wooden benches and a large, noisy audience. The performance had already started. As we squeezed into our seats a double-jointed child, holding a lamp between her teeth, was turning herself inside out. What followed next for two hours was an amazing collection of performers, starting with ten Nepalese women performing a harvest festival dance to finger cymbals, followed by a man wearing a pyramid-shaped headdress and a hooped skirt both covered in lighted candles while he held two blazing candelabra aloft and danced.

We'd barely caught our breath at these incredible feats when out somersaulted a troop of acrobatic drummers followed by two elaborately dressed gods, one wearing the feathers of at least ten peacocks attached to his headdress, the other dressed as Krishna with a painted blue face.

They somersaulted off and twelve men in long white dresses and turbans ran on playing pipes. In front of them swayed a row of brightly dressed women with scimitars between their teeth, three water bowls balanced on their heads with plates of marigolds on top of the highest bowl, while they swung lengths of string attached to balls.

No sooner was the last swinging ball out of sight than on leaped eight Udaipur men in gold and red costumes and heavy silver belts covered in bells. Lunging at each other, they performed a sword, shield and bell-jangling dance that left us exhausted from just watching.

Next came a troop of women wearing felt skirts covered in sequins with large snakes draped over their shoulders. While the women and snakes whirled and a man in a dhoti put straws through his cheeks, our teacher leaned over, and whispered that he was pleased to see that the snakes' mouths were not stitched shut.

Agog with the idea of sticking kebab skewers through our cheeks or sewing up a snake's lips, especially a python which kills by crushing and not biting, we watched as the snake dancers swayed off stage and a team of black-faced Kali dancers holding flaming torches whirled on. Following them pranced a grotesque Kali with her necklace of skulls.

Then ... without any bowing of performers or applause from the audience, the concert was over, leaving us positive that we would never see such sights again.

After Sally had gone to bed, I sat in our hotel garden thinking about Celia's love for her rickshaw-wallah and the three cloistered wives of Madho Singh I, married off to an unattractive youth before they turned thirteen. Had these high-caste virgins ever experienced love such as accepting Celia had? Had their hearts beaten wildly at the sight of a handsome guard glimpsed from their zenana window? Had their dark eyes filled with tears at the words of a poem sung by a sad-eyed musician or spoken by a honey-tongued storyteller? Celia's eyes had. Mine had, for a short time. It's a heady experience.

Had one of the princesses become infatuated by a court noble glimpsed from behind the Palace of the Wind's lace-work windows? Was there a scented billet-doux delivered to him by a bribed servant? Did the brave recipient respond? Did he follow a soft-footed servant to a special mirrored room? Was a secret child born? A beautiful doe-eyed daughter called Aliesha? Or had the three virgins dried up like golden leaves and died for the want of affection like the two Jodhpur wives? What an amazing place India was! How easy it was to understand the enchanted web that had captured Celia and kept her here. How easy to understand the great romances of Haji Begum and Emperor Humayun, or of Mumtaz Mahal and Shah Jahan.

The next morning, after a night full of romantic dreams about lovers which I daren't tell Sally about otherwise she would have said something berating, I read an interesting item in the newspaper. The item emphasized the trouble that had been brewing ever since the Indian government insisted that twenty-seven per cent of the Untouchables be given civil service jobs.

"Kambalapalli village, which consists of three hundred Dalits and three hundred Reddys, has a Reddy-operated well which the Reddys refuse to share, causing the lower-caste Dalits to walk two kilometers to fetch water. Last night enraged Reddys set fire to two Dalit houses, killing seven Dalits in retaliation for the death of a Reddy well guard. This is the first time a Reddy has been killed by a Dalit, although Dalits are regularly killed by the high-caste Reddys.

"In Rajasthan, a Dalit woman is raped every three days, Dalit property is attacked every five days, and one Dalit is murdered every nine days. The conviction rate of attackers and rapists is low due to the police taking money from the higher castes to arrest the Dalit victims for slander. Should a Dalit persevere, they must pay a 225 rupee fee to enter the police station and much more if they want the police to move on their complaint. For example, a Dalit recently sought the return of 150 rupees that he had been forced to loan to an upper-caste Gujjar. Enraged by his request, a gang of Gujjars pierced his nose, put a rope through his nostrils, and then paraded him through the village. The victim is now too terrified to take the case farther."

I put down the newspaper. "I think we should start each day with a prayer that goes, thank you God for not making me one of the 170 million Dalits condemned to a live of scavenging, carcass disposal and cleaning of public toilets."

"Done," said Sally.

After breakfast, we packed for our 2 P.M. train then set off for the Jaipur Spice Market. Five minutes after we turned away from the incredibly busy and noisy Chandpol Bazaar, we were lost. Not a spice shop in sight, only streets of sculpture shops. The sculptures were mostly of Hanuman the monkey god, hero of the Ramayana, best friend of King Rama, and after Ganesh, my favorite Hindu god. Hanuman can whistle up a cloud to fly him anywhere and he can take any shape he likes. The shape most popular in India is that of a human-size monkey warrior holding a club in one hand and his tail in the other. There were plenty of these statues in all the shops.

All sculptured out, and on the premise that we would be hungry the minute we got on the train, we stopped at a cafe to have yet another curry, this time with a side dish of parathas stuffed with potato and garnished with chili and egg pickle, finished with *paan*, a perfumed seed chewed after dinner to sweeten the breath.

This lunch made me wonder if McDonald's would ever make inroads into India as they have in China. For instance, beef burgers wouldn't sell because Hindus don't eat meat and definitely not beef. Muslims might buy them, only they wouldn't eat the buns unless they were sure they hadn't been made with pork fat. Vegetable burgers might sell, but Hindus would want to check the saucepans first to make sure they had never been used for the cooking of meat. Chicken burgers might be popular, but Muslims won't eat chicken unless it was halal killed and Hindus aren't fond of eating birds. Fish and chips would need refrigeration, which would entail more overloading of electricity wires that are already overloaded beyond belief. So I can't see the "golden arches" springing up over India. But then again, India does tend to consume and swallow up so many different cultures, changing them just enough to make them India's own.

# Chapter 11

## Holi Holi and an Indian's Delight

On boarding the train for the small town of Jhunjhunu, we chose the wrong car. This one was crowded with third class betel-chewing and spitting, feet-tucked-under saris or skirts, non-English speaking Indians with dark wrinkled skins and black inquiring eyes, all showing immense surprise when we sat among them. It looked as if it was going to be an interesting ride until the ticket inspector brusquely informed us that we were in the wrong seats. His high-handed gabbled-off information made little sense, but as our sitting there offended him, we waved good-bye to our fellow passengers and moved on.

When we finally found our padded seats, they were occupied by a family who were in no mood to move. Eventually after much smiling and showing of our tickets (they appeared to have none), they moved their children and parcels and we gained our window seats which we stared out of in embarrassment for being so much richer than everyone else in the compartment.

Our fellow passengers' resentment soon disappeared when a student who wanted to practice his already perfect English began asking us questions. Such as "How old are you?" "Are you married?" "How many sons do you have?" and "How do divorced women live in England and Australia?"

"Happily," I answered.

All our answers were translated to the overflowing car while it rattled and shook its way across the semi-desert of Shekhawati. Shekhawati, what a fabulous word. I rolled it around on my tongue for a good ten minutes enjoying the sound and taste of it.

The area of Shekhawati is bound by Delhi, Jaipur and Bikaner. Not a lot survives there. I looked out of the window and was surprised that anything at all survived there. Then I saw a group of men herding what looked like a moving hill which proved to be several hundred sheep. The shepherds wore white, the sheep were white and when the sun shone on them, they all disappeared.

I returned to reading my guidebook. Sometime between the fourteenth and fifteenth centuries, the few Shekhawati families that had miraculously survived were thrilled to find that their wells were on the Gujarat caravan route. It must have been like winning the lottery. One morning they woke up, stuck their heads out of their manure-walled lean-tos, and saw hundreds of laden camels trudging by. "Satjayit!" shouted Mom.

"Go, fetch the manure so we can make manure patties to cook rice and curry. We're opening a restaurant."

Overnight the rural town of Jhunjhunu became a toll-collecting center and trading post. By the eighteenth century, Jhunjhunu's merchants were so wealthy that to display this wealth they had their six-storied *havelis*, their mansions, covered in murals inside and out. The largest havelis had six courtyards, one opening into the other, where the merchants' many women folk idled away their time in the cool shade.

Our train stopped frequently. Each time heads popped out of windows to summon food vendors or to shriek last minute requests to those departing. Those who mysteriously knew how long the train stayed at the station jumped off to fill their water bottles at the Hindus' tap, the Muslims' tap, or farther down the platform, the Untouchables' tap. I wondered if I should want to fill my water bottle, which tap I would go to. Not the Hindus' tap otherwise they would never use it again. So would the Muslims mind sharing water with an infidel? Or was it down the platform to the Untouchables for me?

There was little to see at these desert stations other than a raised siding with an invisible name and a few black plastic humpies belonging to Outcasts whose soot-covered children raced barefoot alongside the trains the minute they started off. Jumping up, they tapped on our windows begging for food, which, on seeing our faces, became "bucks." We wondered why they couldn't beg while the train was in the station? Was there a caste rule that stopped them?

At last we arrived at Jhunjhunu and but for our trusty floor-sitters would have missed the stop. Setting up a deafening hubbub, they pushed us towards the exit and we landed on the platform with barely enough time to wave a thank you to those who'd grabbed our treasured window seats.

As we were the only people to alight, we were soon speeding along a dusty, plastic-rimmed road in a brand new rickshaw with red wheel hubs and a red-fringed top. On each side of the road grew trees as high as four-story buildings full of screeching peacocks. Their disturbing cries sounded like women in pain. I have never cared for peacocks. My mother, who knows all about such things, says their feathers bring bad luck and are often used in making bad spells. She would know.

The Hotel Shiv Shekhawati was a joy to behold. On our arrival at its large doors we were greeted with music from a man, wife and son team. She, wearing an orange, black and silver *orni* (a long scarf) that hid her face, wailed at us in a high-pitched voice sounding a little like the peacocks, while her twelve-year-old son, in cool dude sunglasses, jeans and striped shirt, thumb-tapped a *timila*, an hourglass-shaped drum, and her husband, in a white dhoti, long shirt, pineapple-yellow turban and matching pointy-toed *joolis* (flat shoes with pointy toes), strummed a sitar. Next came the always-welcome banana lassis, a marigold garland each, and a handshake from the handsome Mr. Laxshmi who informed us that he owned the rickshaw with the red-fringed top and another hotel around the corner. It had a swimming pool, he told us proudly.

After a wonderful tikka chicken masala dinner, the best we'd had so far, we were enticed by the laughter, beeping of scooter horns and honking of car horns outside our hotel to walk into town. This upset Mr. Laxshmi mightily as he thought it dangerous.

Our walk was perfectly safe and not very exciting. There was no lighting except from the "males only" cafes scattered along the route and the headlights of scooters that rocketed by with three or four men laughingly clinging to each other while throwing colored powder at us. On our return, Mr. Laxshmi looked relieved. I suppose it's the way he was brought up. Men protect women by keeping them imprisoned for their own good.

Next morning Mr. Laxshmi appeared with the request that we play with his wives.

"What do you mean play?" we asked.

"Holi! Holi!" he said, handing us packets of colored powder.

Out we went to the back of his hotel where his wife and daughters lived and where we were all soon covered in brilliant lime green, scarlet, emerald, saffron and purple dust.

Holi Holi is a religious festival heralding spring and the burning of the Hindu cupid, Kama, by the fire in Krishna's eye. Mr. Laxshmi told me the reason why later. It goes like this: Commanded by Indra to fire his arrow of desire at Krishna in order to inflame him with love for the goddess Parvati, Kama did so and in return he received the full impact of Krishna's third eye reducing him to cinders. (Krishna was in his Shiva the Destroyer form, wearing his tiger skin and snake twined round his neck, at the time.) In a later birth, Kama succeeded in piercing the heart of Shiva and filling it with love for Sati (a married woman), which much relieved the god Brahma, who was concerned that Krishna/Shiva's lack of romance would bring the universe to a standstill.

Back to Holi Holi. During this festival, everyone is allowed to throw colored water called *gulal* and colored powder called *kumkum* at everyone else regardless of caste. So if you had a grudge against someone, Holi Holi is a good time to get even. I think it is a sort of safety valve thing to stop revolutions. Holi Holi is also, so Mr. Laxshmi said, a time when people were allowed to touch. I wasn't sure if this meant men touch men, or women touch women. It certainly couldn't have meant men touch women. Not in India! Although Mr. Laxshmi then proceeded to chase me around the garden, trying to get dust down the neck of my T-shirt.

After a frustrating half hour, he complained that I was running too fast.

"On the contrary," I told him. "I am running just fast enough."

He giggled at this and told me I was a very naughty woman.

To which I replied that he was a very naughty man. More giggles.

It was all a bit of fun. Especially when he gathered up the Europeans from his two hotels and marched us around to the Governor's bungalow where tidbits, sweets and saucers of colored powder set out on tables on the lawn were awaiting us. Once again, all females were ushered through to the back of the house where we were pelted with powder by eight sari-clad women with no understanding of what they shrieked at us when we pelted them back. We then pelted the Governor in his white Nehru suit. Although I was not sure if women were allowed to pelt men, he took it all in good humor.

I asked Mr. Laxshmi how many suits he thought the Governor changed into throughout Holi Holi morning? And he told me that a tactful man would change often so that each group thought they were first to spoil his suit and so get the most satisfaction. See what I mean about a safety valve?

Next we visited the Inspector of Police's bungalow where a large family and servants were waiting to throw powder at us. No hiding in the back of the house for these sari-clad ladies. The Inspector of Police, dressed in white and wearing new white *joolis*, greeted us and was answered with a cloud of powder, and once again Mr. Laxshmi chased me around the garden.

We visited three more officials' homes before Mr. Laxshmi led us, multi-colored from head to toe, to his second hotel. Here he informed us that Holi Holi was over and that we must jump fully dressed into his swimming pool. Which we did, turning it from transparent turquoise to opaque lavender. Some of the others started urging Mr. Laxshmi to join us. Needing no further bidding, he stripped off his trousers and white shirt and in his grey baggys leaped into the pool and headed straight for me. Next minute I was being bounced around the pool. "Bouncy, bouncy, Trisha." I have not played bouncy, bouncy since I was a teenager when the customary way a boy showed that he liked a girl was to pick her up and dump her in the Bondi surf. Imagining that I looked somewhat whale-like (photographs later proved my assumptions to be entirely correct), I yelled that I did not want to play bouncy, bouncy. Finally, struggling out of his arms, I took refuge at the deep end where, being a non-swimmer, he could not follow.

Later, as we lay around the pool drying off, a dressed Mr. Laxshmi invited me to see his special rooms.

"Love to," I said, grabbing Sally.

The rooms he showed us were covered in copies of the murals painted in the eighteenth-century havelis. One wall contained a bride and bridegroom on a swing and another dancing women, sword-wielding warriors, bowls of roses and fruit, men carrying a weighing scale, and lovers picnicking on carpets. Over the doorway was Krishna riding a white horse and on the domed ceilings were writings from the Vedas scriptures. So proud was Mr. Laxshmi of these exclusive hotel rooms that he immediately launched into the history of the havelis and offered to show them to us the following day.

That night, Sally grabbed the *Kama Sutra* first. I believe she had been waiting all afternoon and evening to do this.

"There has to be something about bouncy, bouncy," she said. "Ah! Here it is. When a man under pretext touches a woman's body with his own, it is called the 'touching' embrace. When a woman stands behind a man and accidentally touches him, it is called the 'piercing' embrace. When a woman clings to a man as a creeper, then bends his head down to hers with the desire of kissing him, this is called the 'twining creeper' embrace. Do you think that covers bouncy, bouncy?"

"I did not twine. Whine was more like it. And why didn't you come to my rescue?"

"And spoil his day? Oh! I like this." She flashed a picture of a couple standing under a golden pavilion, and then she read, "When a woman places one foot on her lover's foot and the other on his thigh, passes her arms around his neck and wishes as if to climb up him, it is called 'climbing a tree' embrace. I reckon that's what Mr. Laxshmi had in mind when he invited you to see his special rooms?"

"He did not! He was just being nice."

"Then why did you need me along?"

Next morning we set off in Mr. Laxshmi's car to see the town of Jhunjhunu, in the daylight this time. We discovered it to be an unpainted, unlovely and half-empty village with cracked wooden doors, hanging plaster fretwork, stained walls, and small footpath shops full of pottery, aluminium and brass water pots. These shops were tended by indolent youths with transistor radios held to their ears like gigantic beetles eating out their brains.

Apart from the transistor radios, nothing has changed in Jhunjhunu for hundreds of years. I would not have been surprised to see fifty heavily laden camels swaying through its narrow streets followed by men in long white dresses, mustard turbans and red-and-black scarves, while beside them, herding their goats, ran their women with their colorful ornis tucked into their long skirts. How marvelously exciting those caravan days must have been. How this forgotten backwater, and Mr. Laxshmi with his near empty hotels, must wish for them to return.

Mr. Laxshmi's first stop was to show us an interesting biblical stepped well with staircases going down six levels and only ever used by the women. The collecting of water was not a man's job.

"What if a man isn't married?" asked Sally.

"His mother will collect it."

"What if his mother is dead?"

"His sister or female cousin will collect it."

"What if he has no sister or female cousin?"

Mr. Laxshmi stared at her as if she was mad. "All Indian men have sisters and female cousins."

Next stop was a 200-year-old haveli where the *chowkidar* (caretaker) opened up a studded wooden outer-door then an embossed silver inner-door to let us in. What an amazing place this haveli was with its outside walls, outer and inner courtyard walls and cool hidden rooms, all covered in murals portraying mythology, history and eroticism. There were ceilings of Shiva, Parvati and Krishna with haloes, panels of green-turbaned warriors on elephants and brown-turbaned warriors on camels. There was even a border depicting a steam train with cars carrying Europeans followed by marching British soldiers wearing bowler hats and pith helmets. Mr. Laxshmi explained that the British army had been stationed in Jhunjhunu to control the Dacoit (armed-robber) bands that preferred to attack the silk caravans rather than set up cafes like everyone else.

"Why would the British care?" I asked.

"They collected taxes."

"Aaaahhh."

"There are other havelis," continued Mr. Laxshmi. "Some are closed because the owners preferred Delhi. Others are lived in but are in disrepair because the owners do not have an income. The town is no longer on the trade route, you see."

By my calculations it hadn't been on the trade route for a century or more.

Our next stop was Shri Ranisatiji Mandir Temple. This magnificent temple with its six-storied, bay-windowed gateway and Romeo and Juliet balcony was built in memory of a brutal murder. A rich man and his wife had gone on a journey. On the way they were attacked by Muslim bandits and the husband was killed. The wife burned her husband's body then, before throwing herself onto the pyre, she told her family to put their ashes onto his horse and where it stopped they must build a Hindu temple. Which they did.

Inside the temple's immense gateway stand twelve white Sati Chowk towers leading to the main hall which has a mosaic ceiling depicting the husband riding a horse and the wife following in her wagon which is being driven by a servant.

Above them floats a haloed Krishna, an elephant-headed Ganesh and a seductively smiling Parvati. Below, set out on a huge white sheet in front of the altar was a feast of sweets, cakes, Cadbury chocolate and rice dishes. These were the offerings of a local businessman brought to honor the gods, and feed the pilgrims who can reside free in the temple guesthouse for ten days.

"What happened to the servant when the bandits killed the husband?" asked Sally.

"Why would you want to know about him?" asked Mr. Laxshmi.

Back at the car a widow in white accosted us. She pushed her too tall, too plain daughter forward and although I didn't understand her words I knew exactly what she was saying.

"Sir, you are rich and when your daughters marry you will provide a dowry worthy of them. But I am poor and my daughter must wed before I die. So please, here within the gaze of Krishna, donate something towards her dowry."

Mr. Lashmi gave her ten rupees. I wanted to give her more but it would have made him lose face, so I gave her ten as well. On the way back to the hotel, I asked him how long it would take her to beg a dowry. He said it was possible that they had the dowry money already but that begging was their way of staying together because once the girl was married her mother would have to live and beg alone until she died. He also said that he would go into debt to borrow sufficient dowry money for his daughters as he was determined they would marry well. Which was interesting because apart from the government officials, I'd say Mr. Laxshmi was the richest man in town, so I asked him, "Where will your lovely daughters find a wealthy husband?"

He then explained that they would pray to Gauri, an incarnation of Parvati, to find one. We were, at this moment, in the eighteen days of the Gangaur festival when all women pray to Gauri. The married women prayed for the long lives of their husbands (considering the alternative was the life of an unwanted begging widow, I bet they pray hard), and the maidens pray for the husband of their dreams. A healthy, long-living husband, no doubt.

"So Trisha, will you be praying tonight for a husband of your dreams?" he fished.

I sighed loud and long and batted my eyelids seductively as the *Kama Sutra* had told me to do. "It's so sad, Mr. Laxshmi, but the husband of my dreams is already married and lives in a different country than my own."

He looked immensely pleased at this.

# Chapter 12

## BELLES OF BIKANER AND RAT TEMPLE

After resting in Jhunjhunu for a few more days, swimming in Mr. Laxshmi's pool, and talking to his wives and daughters by using our hands and drawing pictures, we set off for Bikaner. The Bikaner bus was to pick us up outside the hotel. When it arrived, there was such a rush of passengers from the neighboring houses that we were pushed into the bus and ended up sitting in the aisle again. Our prepaid seats could have been under any two of about seventy people. We decided not to bother.

Crossing the Thar Desert took four hot, no-toilet-stopping hours. Halfway there, I got a seat between two men. They were so embarrassed that I could feel waves of it flowing from them as they stared fixedly out of the bus windows. As there was nothing I could do about my thighs and hips touching theirs, or almost landing on their laps every time the bus hit a bump, I stared fixedly ahead.

The Thar Desert is the home of the Raika or Rabari. The local villagers call them *bhoot* which means ghosts. I would have liked to have seen these elusive nomads who live on camel milk, chew sticky black opium, and who bury their gold, their profit from selling sheep or smuggling guns and opium, somewhere in the desert. But I saw no bhoot. Not even the shadow of one, shadows being in short supply. All I saw were their dead campfires, sooty circles of charcoal frosted with beige dust surrounded by bleached camel poo, left as a message for the next Raika or Rabari. "Come brother, sister, light your fire upon this spot as we have lit ours, and, although we have not yet met, we will become as one." A nice thought, but unlikely as each Raika or Rabari tribe is highly suspicious of the other.

Arriving at the Bikaner bus station, Sally discovered that she'd mislaid one of her four bags. She immediately went into panic mode. I immediately went into I-am-not-with-this-hysterical-red-haired-woman mode.

"It has my pamphlets, maps, tourist information, postcards, newspaper cuttings and diary in it. Someone has stolen it."

"Why would they? It's not exactly full of essentials for Indian living," I yelled back.

"My diary is very important!"

"Your diary is empty."

"I won't go until I find that bag!"

I stayed outside guarding our bags while she, looking more and more dishevelled, appeared above the seats, or at an open window to inform me that it matched her long skirt and that it was her favorite Peruvian bag. Sally has never been to Peru.

"I'll buy you another," I promised. Anything to get us away

from the hot bus station and the growing crowd of curious bystanders.

She reached the back seat and with a whoop of delight, waggled the bag from the rear window. "Must have slid all the way down," she yelled.

"Must have," I replied, while privately believing that the thief had seen the rubbish inside and ditched it.

We caught an auto-rickshaw to the Hotel Harasar Haveli, which was too modern for our liking but the owner, nicknamed "Bubbles" after the Maharajah of Jaipur, wore beautiful purple joolis which we could not resist. He also promised to take us to his farmhouse to see village dancing, so we stayed.

After a shower and a quick read about Bikaner, which told us that the city had been settled 500 years ago by Prince Rao Bika of Jodhpur, and how its situation on the Gujarat trade route had made it so rich that a seven-kilometer wall had to be built around it to protect it, we caught a bicycle rickshaw to Kem Road and the main Bikaner bazaar. This rickshaw had a flat tire, causing it to lean so much to one side that Sally had to hang on to me to stop from sliding off onto the road. A fact that did not deter our pedaller from pedalling furiously while leaning almost horizontally in the opposite direction to balance the rickshaw.

Kem Road is the main "fix it" road of Bikaner. Spilling out onto the tarmac are mechanics' shops where old rickshaws go to be mended or die (if a dying rickshaw is allowed in "waste-not want-not" India) and dozens of bicycle menders with hundreds of precariously balanced bicycles leaning against each other, waiting to be repaired. Kem Road was probably where the lopsided rickshaw pedaller was going to when we hailed him.

Stepping around two goats with turmeric paste painted on their foreheads and an "I know I'm going to be sacrificed to Kali" look in their devil-eyes, we entered the bazaar. Each shop was two arms' width wide with poles sticking out, draped with gold-bordered saris, tie-dyed ornis and lengths of brilliantly patterned cloth. The floors of these don't-turn-round-fast-or-you'll-knock-down-all-the-bolts-of-material shops were bottom high so that a buyer could sit down, slip off her sandals, swivel round and sit cross-legged on the material-covered floor, while the owner, who need not move from his sitting position to reach all his wares, could show them to her.

Buying material is the main occupation of middle-class Bikaner women. We stopped to photograph two. The mother wore a matching pink chiffon skirt and orni trimmed with pink lace to match her pink glass bangles and pink nail polish. Her daughter wore a yellow short-sleeved top, green skirt, and orange and gold orni. She also wore a silver ball on her head kept there by a silver thread tied around her perfume-oiled hair, a red bindi, a silver nose-ring, silver earrings, a green and orange beaded necklace, a black and gold necklet, a gold choker, and three gold bracelets above each elbow to match her gold nail polish. They were so happy to have their photographs taken that they preened like male peacocks. After we moved on, I wondered if the younger woman might have been a new wife being shown off by the shop owner, who, in his white pajamas, lounged back against his bolts of cloth, watching her with immense pride.

My next photograph was of a silk shop so crowded with women that the salesman was having problems unrolling his material. All the women wore red, orange or pink saris that showed off their bare bellies and bangle-covered bare arms. Outside stood a Muslim servant in a blue skirt, long sleeved cerise over-dress and purple orni over her hair. She showed no bare skin and wore no jewelry.

As we wandered from one colorful alleyway to the next, what became apparent was that the women of Bikaner were not interested in hiding their faces, their delicious brown bellies or their shiny jewelry. The belles of Bikaner expected to be admired. In fact, they demanded it.

It was hot in the bazaar so we decided to search for a lassi shop in the old part of town. We entered medieval Bikaner through one of its five gates and were somewhere in the middle when we saw a most wonderful sight. Parked behind the iron gates of a rose-pink mansion was an antique 1927 Buick with its silver dragon-shaped horn and its emerald-green chrome polished to a mirror shine. It was too beautiful to pass, so we walked into the forecourt for a closer look and discovered the wonderful Hotel Bhanwar Niwas. This hidden-away gem, with its two floors of carved stone balconies overlooking a Mogul garden and fountain, was exactly what we needed. Forget the lassis, we wanted a good cup of English tea.

"All the apartments have their own treasures," explained the male receptionist, when we asked about afternoon tea. "Would you like a tour?" Of course we would.

Each apartment was furnished with different-patterned inlaid or carved wardrobes, different-colored silk and ribboned sofas, carved bedsteads, silver lamps, brocade footstools, silver flower containers, and Persian-style paintings. Each had a lounge room, bathroom, reading room, study, and maids' and butlers' rooms, and all were full of fresh flowers.

"Who stays here?" I asked.

"Americans."

"Who used to stay here a hundred years ago?"

"The owner of the palace and visiting princes, princesses and the British Raj."

"Of course."

As we had shown suitable adoration for the hotel, we were then shown its large lounge room. A magnificent room with green and gold walls, curved-legged gold-leaf tables, throne-like chairs, peacock-shaped lamps, gold-framed mirrors, and crystal cabinets full of French porcelain. After we'd had cheese on toast and tea on the terrace, Sally and I creeped down and took photographs of each other sitting on the gold thrones. We felt very regal.

Refreshed and revived, we left our dream hotel wishing we hadn't paid for the other, purple joolis or no purple joolis.

Outside, a boy accosted us. He informed us that he was a Muslim and a student, that he did not want money, all he wanted was to practice his English (which is what all hopeful Indian guides say).

"Did we want to see the Jain temples?" he asked.

We did.

Ali, who looked about twelve but was probably closer to sixteen, led us along a complicated route of alleyways and narrow streets guaranteed to make it look as if the famous fifteenth-century Jain Bhandeshwar temples were farther from the hotel than they were. At the top of the temple steps, we were greeted by a chubby, grey-haired, grey-bearded caretaker wearing a startling white T-shirt and dhoti. But before this caretaker could begin to tell us about his temple, Ali interrupted him and, in Bikaner language, fiercely told him to go find his own fish to fry.

The caretaker backed off but the love of his temple was too great, he could not contain himself, he had to tell us about it and how he had been photographed by *Vogue* magazine and put on a calendar for all the world to see. So off he rushed to fetch a battered calendar that he graciously presented to me. Sure enough, there he was sitting on the floor of his temple beside a beautiful model wearing an emerald-green and gold creation.

"This temple is built on a hill," he announced grandly, which we already knew as we had just climbed it.

Then taking hold of my elbow, he led me away from Ali. "It has three floors and a view. But first ... a story."

He stooped and ran his fingers over the black, orange and white tiled floor. When he held them up, they were covered in grease. "In the years that this temple was built, Bikaner had no water, so the builders used ghee. That is why every hot day ghee oozes up between tiles and why the columns are sinking."

He pointed to a white-and-gold column leaning dangerously among a forest of similarly leaning columns. The columns were decorated with statues of bare-breasted women in dancing poses. "Deities," he explained with a nonchalant flick of his fingers. As if being surrounded by half-naked women, in a country where women were so modest, meant nothing to him.

We climbed to the second floor where the statues of the dancing women wore red bikini tops, transparent trousers, and sexy hipster belts. Ignoring these delightful nymphets, the caretaker told us about the wall paintings. "This is of Devananda, the mother of Mahavira, the founder of Jainism. She is dreaming of the fourteen auspicious objects that predicted her son would be a holy man. This is Ali Baba up a tree hunting for honey. The rats are eating the tree, the snakes are under the tree, and the elephant is shaking the tree. Is Ali Baba afraid? No, he is not. See, God is in the clouds protecting Ali Baba. Come, we will go to the top."

From the roof of the temple, we could see all of walled Bikaner and the surrounding desert.

"Mahavira was the first of twenty-four *tirthankars*, makers of the river-crossing," explained our guide while Ali glowered behind him. "A tirthankar is superior to the gods and untouched by the eternal change of time. Do you understand my English?"

We nodded. He smiled.

"Jainists believe that the universe is a giant human figure."

"Male or female?" asked Sally.

Our guide shrugged, showing that whichever it was, it wasn't important.

"Jainism is India's third religion. It has three million followers and was founded in 500 b.c. by Mahavira, a contemporary of Buddha. Mahavira preached that to reach purity of soul one must merely rid oneself of material goods, meditate in lonely places, fast, and avoid violent thoughts and actions, war and sex. Mahavira ..."

"What about the sexy statues downstairs?" interrupted Sally.

Our two guides looked at us with uncomprehending eyes. So I pointed downstairs and did one of the poses of the dancers. The caretaker nodded enthusiastically.

"Which could mean, yes, you have the figure of a dancing girl. Yes, you can dance for me tonight. Or ... come up the minaret, honey," said Sally.

"Wrong religion."

"Some Jainists go naked using their hands as begging bowls," continued our guide, determined to earn his tip. "Others sweep the path before them to avoid stepping on living things and wear a cloth over their mouths so as not to breathe in insects and kill them."

"Seems a bit excessive," said Sally.

Our guide nodded, although whether he agreed or not, his nod didn't say, and then he switched subjects completely. "Sand comes tonight," he pointed to a sandstorm far off on the horizon. "Keep your mouth and eyes closed."

We said we would.

On leaving the temple, Ali suggested we give the caretaker fifty rupees which we did while wondering if the wily lad would return and demand half of it. Promising to send the caretaker the photographs we'd taken of him, we caught a rickshaw back to Kem Road, dropping Ali off outside the Hotel Bhanwar Niwas with a hundred rupees. He said it was not enough. Sally reminded him of how much English practice he'd had.

That night there was a sandstorm. Ancient sand from as far away as the Gobi Desert blew in between the hotel door- and window-frames that had never met, not even when first constructed. It coated the washbasin that drenched our feet every time we turned on the tap. It blew into the toilet that only worked if one had an engineer's degree, and it blew through the filthy air conditioner which we'd turned off for fear of catching Legionnaires' disease.

Tiny grains of thousand-year-old grit creeped in under our sheets, into the corners of our mouths, and under our eyelashes. We woke at dawn to find a fine layer of it over everything and our mouths tasting as if we'd eaten a bucket of Bondi beach.

Why did we wake at dawn? Because our hotel was on a truck route and as all Indians know, it is a trucker's god-given right to sound his horn continuously when leaving a city. So we got up and in the coolest part of the day, which wasn't that cool, set off by taxi to see the government-run camel farm which was eight kilometers out of town. On the way, we saw a camel train incongruously carrying enormous cement electricity pylons into the desert, and a herd of cows led by a proud white king bull and followed by a moth-eaten camel suffering an identity crisis.

The notice outside the camel farm said that it was the only government-run institution for camel breeding and research in Asia. I boasted to Sally that due to isolation Australian camels had fewer diseases and were in great demand as breeding camels for Asia and Arabia. She was unimpressed. Camels once used by Afghani tinkers to carry their needles, thread and bolts of material across Australian deserts are not as romantic as camels used by Lawrence of Arabia during World War I.

The camel farm wardens explained how they had 250 camels and three different breeds. How one enclosure contained the in-heat females, another the one-year-old raring-to-go males, a third the pregnant females, and a fourth the mothers and babies. This was the enclosure we saw first. All the mothers were pushing to get to a feeding trough while all the babies were shoving against their mother's knobbly knees and pushing up at their mother's teats. I fell in love with the newly born, woolly, beige calves. I loved their stick-legs, pom-pom knees and eyes too big for their "Look, Mom, I'm born" surprised faces. There were twin albinos that had adopted the warden because their mother had died giving birth. He fed them from huge bottles and slipped them cubes of sugar while they trotted and lurched after him bleating "Mama, Mama."

Next we saw the bull camel stables. I was admiring the walls, painted blood red to keep the male camels sexy, when I discovered that camels have long, revoltingly slimy, fat tongues that fall out of their mouths and dangle purple and slug-like over their rubbery lips. They also gurgle, grumble and rumble in their throat crops, sounding like broken drains, while ruminating so sloppily that a pale greenish drool dribbles between their yellow teeth and drips to the ground. I was unimpressed even though their rear ends were painted with the most attractive patterns that apparently female camels find irresistible.

The warden told us about Bikaner's famous January camel festival.

This reminded Sally and myself of when we hitched to Erfoud in the Sahara Desert to attend the Fête des Dattes, and how we'd seen amazing feats such as racing camels turning on coins while their Blue Souk riders, swinging their swords above their heads and screaming bloodthirstily, bore down upon us, the only two infidels in town.

"I'd like to come back here in January," whispered Sally.

"Me too."

With more photographs of baby camels than anyone would ever need, we returned to Bikaner, visiting the impregnable Junagarh fort on the way.

Of all the forts we'd seen in India so far, this one was the most formidable. Built in the sixteenth century by General Raja Rai Singh Ji, the sixth ruler of the Rathore dynasty of Bikaner, its sandstone walls are protected by a moat (although one wondered how in this desert a moat was kept full or how General Raja Rai Singh knew about moats). Behind the moat is a sloping ramp easily defended from the five-floored rampart towering above. No wonder Junagarh fort was never breached.

Inside the Sun Gate we were told that the present day maharajah had donated the fort to the town and that no one could enter it without a free guide. It sounded good but within seconds it was clear that our guide wanted to get home. Soon as he could see no tips forthcoming from us in our travel-stained cotton, or from two elderly Sikh gentlemen with their bushy white moustaches, blue turbans and large curved daggers worn in decorated slings over their shoulders, he set up such a pace that we saw everything as a blur. When we didn't keep up, we were treated like recalcitrant daughters and hurried along by the elderly Sikhs while our guide threw snippets of information at us in English between whatever language he was using to explain the fort's history to them.

In this fashion we learned that the magnificently ornate Har Mandir Temple built within the fort was where the royal family worshipped their gods and goddesses. That the Rang Mahal (Palace of Pleasure) was where the late maharajah played his favorite games of blindman's buff and let's jump into the fountain naked. That the Chandra Mahal (Moon Palace) with its exquisite paintings on lime plaster was where the royal family danced beneath a full moon to the palace's eight-piece orchestra. And that the Phool Mahal (Flower Palace) was where the maharajahs and their princesses cavorted upon beds strewn with rose petals.

"I think he is making it up," whispered Sally.

The guide threw a daggered look at her and began walking faster and speaking faster. "When the Prince of Udaipur married the Princess of Bikaner, fourteen princes with their entourages of over 5600 retainers attended the wedding in their private trains." How these trains, furnished with looped velvet curtains, silk sofas, beds, cocktail bars and fresh flowers, jammed the Bikaner station. And how the bridegroom sitting in a gold howdah was carried to the wedding on the back of an elephant adorned with silver and how the guests ate from solid gold plates which were sold off after the Indian government stopped giving the Maharajah of Bikaner his generous pension.

"How did the Princess of Bikaner get to the wedding?" I asked.

"She did not go to the wedding, Madam. She had her ceremony elsewhere."

"Where did they live after the marriage? Bikaner or Udaipur?" asked Sally.

"Udaipur, Madam. It is cooler."

"Was it a successful marriage?"

"All Indian marriages are successful, Madam."

Then he was off at sprinter pace describing the present-day maharajah's hunting lodge which was full of antique mahogany furniture, brass carriage lamps, four-poster beds and stuffed animal heads, and had a resplendent view of Gajner Lake.

"During the legendary annual imperial sand grouse shoot the sand grouse came to Gajner Lake to drink. It was a poor morning if less than 4000 woodcock, golden pheasant, mallard, teal, pintail, widgeon and red-crested shoveller were not bagged."

"It shouldn't have been allowed," said Sally, who was thoroughly fed up with chasing after this little man.

"Maharajahs are allowed to do anything," he answered, snootily.

"Not anymore they're not," she answered, equally as snootily.

The guide halted his stride, swung round, pulled himself up to his full height, which was to Sally's shoulder, and announced grandly, "The Maharajah of Bikaner attended the famous Mayo College where each prince had his own house, his own garage to house his own Bentleys and Jaguars, his own stables, chefs, jeweler, tailor, barber, water-carriers, cleaners, secretaries, accountants and his own gun carriers."

"Really," retorted Sally, gazing haughtily down at him. "So that's where he learned to shoot 4000 birds at forty paces and call it sport?"

At this point, the two elderly Sikhs and I stepped between them.

Outside the Sun Fort, while catching our breaths, and no he did not get a tip, we decided to forgo visiting Lalgarh Palace which was famous for its hundreds of stuffed animal heads shot by the Olympic shooter; its rooms filled with clocks from the Tsar of Russia, framed letters from King George V and Queen Mary, and hundreds of photographs of tiny princes in miniature turbans wearing patent leather Christopher Robin boots and sea otter fur-collared overcoats. We'd had enough of luxury gone crazy, we wanted Kem Road and some local food. At least I did.

The sweet shop owner fell immediately under my Lady Lakshmi spell and insisted on handfeeding me tidbits of this and that, while asking me about my marital status and if I'd consider marrying an Indian. I answered as best I could with a mouth full of coconut-covered green jelly squares, and boat-shaped glutinous bits of sweet stuff that could have been animal, mineral or vegetable. "Yes, I would consider marrying an Indian, if I fell in love with one, and if he would live in Australia where I worked." The shopkeeper was ecstatic.

I bought a bag of green jelly squares and was following Sally out of the shop when we saw a dog bowled over by a car. Sally let out a bloodcurdling scream as I grabbed her, spilling my green squares in my attempt to stop her from rushing into the middle of the road and picking up the pitiful flea-ridden mute.

So began another dog argument.

"No. You can't take it back to our room for medication. Not even if you find a sack to wrap it in. Not even if you find a rickshaw driver to take it to the hotel. No. No. No."

"You are heartless, cruel and unfeeling."

"Oh, I do not think so," interrupted the shopkeeper who was glued to my right elbow. "Madam, please come back into my shop and I will give you some more sweeties."

To him, "No thank you." To her, "Do you think for one second that Bubbles would let that dog into his hotel?"

"He definitely would not," said the shopkeeper.

To me, Sally hissed, "He doesn't have to know." To the shop-keeper, "Mind your own business."

"You'd really take that flea-riddled dog to our room?" I demanded.

"Oh no, Madam, no!" exclaimed the shopkeeper.

To me, Sally nodded, "Yes." To him, "Will you shut up?"

"Then you'd be sleeping in it alone," I yelled. "That dog is diseased. It has dog AIDS."

"And many fleas," added the shopkeeper from his doorway, where he had retreated for safety in case the fiery red-haired creature, who appeared bent on strangling her very nice blonde friend, turned on him.

"It's one of God's creatures," retaliated Sally.

Now there's a remark to stop one in their tracks. I just wished that I had a bag of go-to-sleep-forever injections so that I could put to sleep all of God's unloved, unwanted, miserable-eyed Indian dogs. But I didn't tell Sally that.

We arrived back at our hotel with five minutes to change before heading off to Bubble's village. Off we went in four jeeps along a road leading straight to the Punjab and Pakistan.

"This military road was built by our maharajah," boasted Bubbles. "The maharajahs of Bikaner have always been enlightened. They even tried to stamp out suttee."

I was trying to work out how a military road added up to enlightenment when Sally asked, "Did they stamp it out?"

Bubbles turned to one of the men and asked him if he liked cricket. So I guessed they didn't.

The jeeps stopped at a crossroads where four camel wagons waited. This was how I discovered how hellish camel wagons are to climb up onto if one is short of stature and wearing pants that are too tight; how camel wagons stink and are full of splinters; and most of all, how the average camel does not appreciate pulling a wagon load of tourists and isn't slow to bellow so.

Sally was in seventh heaven. She had talked our wagon driver into letting her ride our camel, a bad-tempered, buck-toothed, grunting prima-donna with four clothes-pin legs and a string of continuous complaints which, when translated, were all about how she was one of the original descendants of Noah's ark and destined for better things.

Bubble's farmhouse was the manor house of the area. It had an inside toilet full of plastic bottles waiting to be filled from the well and sold to unsuspecting tourists as pure imported water, and an outside patio where Bubble's laborers thrashed the wheat. At one end of the patio were a row of chairs, at the other end sat four men playing the hand organ, click-clacks, pipe and drums.

Bubbles bowed us in. As we took our chairs, little boys appeared carrying trays of whisky, rum, gin and a methylated spirit-smelling liquid, all in unlabelled bottles. With the alcohol came the village children sneaking up to lie on their stomachs at the edge of the thrashing floor. Next came the women squatting behind them. Finally, as the lamps were lit, the men arrived carrying their chairs.

The hand organs groaned, the clackers clacked, the pipe wailed, and Bubbles gave a speech about how donations for the village school could be handed to him. Then as the villagers watched us drink and we watched them watching us drink, I wondered if Bubbles had charged them a rupee each to see the foreigners get drunk.

More unlabelled alcohol arrived. Sally and I drank Indian beer from labelled unopened bottles. Then a dancing girl in a red skirt, short top and swirling orni danced into the middle of the patio. With seductive hip movements she flashed her kohl-rimmed eyes, gyrated her jeweled belly button and pursed her rouged lips. It was ten minutes before anyone realized she was a he.

It is common for Indian transvestites to be employed to dance at weddings and celebrations but I had hoped to see some authentic village dancing. But why should these women dance for us? They were not performers. They were Bubble's field hands, and when they danced they did so for themselves and their holy days. We were tourists brought there for Bubble's profit and apart from the band, who we paid for, the villagers did not benefit from us sitting around their thrashing floor. So let Master Bubbles pay for a dancer and let it be a man if no female would dance.

Next came four different identically tasting curries served by the same small boys who hung around like mosquitoes, filling our plates whenever it looked as if we'd managed to swallow a peel-the-skin-off-the-inside-of-your-mouth spoonful.

The music, dancing and alcohol continued until eleven when Bubbles collected the bill, the jeeps arrived, and with good-bye waves to the villagers, we were driven back to the hotel.

The next day we slept very late, visited the silk bazaar again to marvel at the colors, textures and shoppers, had afternoon tea at the wonderful Hotel Bhanwar Niwas without seeing Ali, and went to bed early. The next morning we caught a taxi to the Karni Mata rat temple where thousands of holy rats have been worshipped ever since there was a rat plague in 1934.

"The rats are called Kavas, they carry the souls of future holy men. It is considered auspicious to see a white Kavas," explained our taxi driver guide as we neared the town.

Sally made a face. She hates rats.

"The temple is always floodlit," continued our taxi driver.

"Only so the villagers will know if the rats decide to leave the temple and invade the village," whispered Sally.

The driver heard her and paid her back by saying, "It is auspicious to let the rats run over your feet."

"Forget it," shrieked Sally. "I'm not going!"

I read from our guidebook. "Prince Rio Bike of Jodhpur, the founder of Bikaner, was blessed by the goddess Karni Mata, who is an incarnation of the goddess Durga. Ever since then the maharajahs of Bikaner have worshipped at this temple."

Sally shuddered so strongly the taxi rocked. "I bet the maharajah doesn't let the rats run over his feet. I bet he doesn't take his silk socks off."

"They are all God's creatures, Sally," I said, and got a punch in the arm for my effort.

The entrance to the rat temple consisted of a huge arch set into a beautifully carved white façade with one side depicting three elephants, two Dr. Seuss type-trees, and three huge elephant eggs. On the opposite side stood the goddess Karni Mata surrounded by what looked like Italian Renaissance angels.

Realizing that our admiration of the huge silver-embossed doors flanked by black elephants was only putting off our entering the temple we took off our sandals and stepped inside. There were rats everywhere. Rats with stringy tails running across the beams, rats with hairless pink tails and extended bellies huddled in corners gorging corn, rats with bitten-off tails fornicating on the cornices, in the niches, in cracks, and rats with vicious-looking teeth running straight at us.

"Keep going," hissed Sally, keeping behind me.

We high-stepped across a floor covered in corn and feces to where there were more rats. Thousands of them! Some so bloated they could barely waddle, others so diseased their next reincarnation looked imminent, many dead. Around us worshippers placed platters of food on the floor and prayed.

Passing through various rat-filled courtyards, we arrived at the inner sanctum where in a gold and marble alcove sat the goddess Karni Mata, beloved of Prince Rio Bike. In front of her squatted a priest with dozens of rats playing with his toes. Between them sat a large padlocked moneybox where worshippers placed money to feed the already stuffed rats. The priest shooed us away, telling us not to take photographs, something we had forgotten to do in our fear of having a rat run up our trouser legs.

We bolted.

Opposite our taxi sat three middle-aged women wearing washed-out cotton skirts, long sleeved tops, and grubby ornis drooped nonchalantly over their heads. What was interesting was their casual sitting position, with one foot on the bus-stop seat and one leg dangling down, showed us the first bit of female thigh we'd seen so far.

"Men," said our driver.

"All three?"

He nodded. "They live on a farm inherited from their father."

"Which answers the question of where transvestite dancers go when they are too old to dance," said Sally.

"But not why three men would choose to be three women in a society that doesn't value women," I argued.

"They are landowners," answered the driver. As if that answered everything. Which it did. Peasant women cannot be landowners, transvestites can.

On our way back to the bazaar, I tried to reconcile the modern-day rat worshippers with the fact that Indians were using geometry, algebra and astronomy while Europeans were living in caves. That 3000 years before Christ this area sustained a civilization equivalent to those of the Nile, Euphrates and Yangtze. And more recently, in 1873, how Indian doctors helped discover fingerprinting. The disparity between it all made no sense.

Leaving the taxi at Kem Road, we were making our way through the hundreds of propped-up bikes outside a bike shop when I accidentally bumped one. It was a mere tip of my finger but it upset the bike which fell against the next one, and in one horrifying slow-motion moment that I could not stop, the entire block of bicycles toppled over. There was a hushed silence at the final crash, then the owner of the bike shop smiled sweetly at me. I apologized profusely. He told me that it was karma. That if the bikes were meant to fall, they were meant to fall. My causing what looked like utter devastation to his bicycle mending business was karma so I must not be distressed. What a graceful way of letting me off the hook. I could imagine what niceties an Australian bicycle mender would have yelled at me. I could feel myself falling in love with India.

I thanked him and we made a swift escape into the bazaar where, miracle of miracles, I found an e-mail shop. Alas, after I had paid, I was told it wasn't working because the phone lines were busy. It had been the same in every town we'd been to. I don't think the World Wide Web is connected with India yet. I think they're just pretending.

# Chapter 13

## JAISALMER, QUEEN OF THE DESERT

Jaisalmer is a seven-hour bus ride from Bikaner and as we did not want to sit in the aisle again, we booked our seats and arrived early. Opposite us sat four village women. Two with nose rings the size of gold buttons and heavy silver bracelets embedded with red gemstones that must have weighed half a kilo each, and two with silver balls dangling from their ears and with their arms covered in bone bracelets from their wrists to their shoulders. The bone-bracelet women were arguing over a parcel that was being pounded as each gave her loud point of view. It was the first time we'd heard Indian women being assertive and the clash of at least a hundred bracelets was awe-inspiring. I decided to barrack for the one on the right. Sally took the one on the left. My woman won.

She later told me that her bone bracelets were put on at her marriage and could not be removed until her husband died, when they would be ceremonially smashed. I asked her how hard it was to sleep, eat and bathe in them. She said that she was used to them, but that if she wasn't interested in sex, a good slap with an arm covered in bone bracelets got the message across. More assertion. Could it be the cooler weather?

Behind us, the other women on the bus wore gold-trimmed ornis and long tunics over full skirts. There were no bare midriffs. We were moving out of Hindu country into Muslim country. The men wore bunched-up skirts, long jackets, large hooped gypsy earrings and loosely coiled turbans. Their skin was lighter, their moustaches bushier and their hooked noses more prominent.

The view from the bus was uninspiring yet over 300 million years ago the Thar Desert was a marsh that sustained hundreds of dinosaurs and more recently, forests where herds of blackbuck and *chinkara* and a myriad of bird-life flourished. But the forests have been cut down for fuel or by logging companies for profit. Now, there was only an oasis here and there where a wild ass might survive and plenty of bones to show when they didn't. This was also the desert that the Indian government used for experimenting with nuclear weapons.

The bus stopped once and the passengers spread out quickly. Less fussy than before, we went behind the chai shop in among the desert lilac, a beautiful plant with a purple flower that thrives on nuclear-contaminated urine. Then it was into the shop for a quick chai in throwaway pottery cups and back onto the bus.

Hours evaporated. Unable to read, I fell into a reverie about how it must have been for the English in India. Being the last in a long line of conquerors such as the Aryans, Persians, Greeks, Bactrians, Scythians, Afghans and Moguls, who all stayed to become part of India, the British (who did not) were unwelcome, and when Indians don't want you around they can be very stubborn and most unhelpful. It is my belief that Indians invented passive resistance. Then there was the fact that the English were coming from a cold climate to a hot one with no medicines to speak of, no knowledge about boiling water to kill cholera bugs, no knowledge about rats causing typhoid and mosquitoes bringing malaria. It's a miracle any of them survived.

Of course there were benefits. Even the lowest of government clerks lived like lords of the manor. For a pittance a fellow could employ fifty household servants to keep his bungalow clean, his punkahs operational, and his grass-screens moist. Then there was the excitement of an imperial tiger and rhinoceros hunt, of attending a grand ball at the viceroy's palace, of the nightly visits of the sloe-eyed servant girls who slipped so willingly beneath their master's mosquito nets. Who wouldn't have gambled with heat, disease and leprosy if the alternative was a bicycle ride to work in the drizzling rain, two rented rooms in Clapham, and a cold pork pie for tea?

Returning to Britain must have been very staid indeed, if not utterly painful. No wonder so many East India Company retirees took their hookahs home. An afternoon puff of the old bubble pipe and a 78 rpm/12-inch LP record of Indian music on the old gramophone, and one could imagine oneself back in good old India. Wot!

Sally elbowed me sharply. "I just saw a long-legged bustard."

"A long-legged what?" I repeated vaguely.

"It's Rajasthan's state bird. Dying out everywhere else, it thrives in the Thar Desert. I wonder what it lives on?"

"Sheep killed by nuclear fallout."

More hours passed and I was beginning to think that we were caught in a time warp when I saw, shimmering ahead of us in the heat haze, beautiful, golden Jaisalmer, Queen of the Desert. Lit from behind by the setting sun, this tinsel-tipped fort with its lavender-colored city swirling around it like a ballerina's tutu, was the loveliest place I had so far seen in India. Even lovelier than Fatehpur Sikri, the abandoned city of romance that I had fallen in love with.

The bus dropped us off at the bottom of Trikuta Hill. Our hotel was at the top. The walk, first through two massive gates, then up a cobbled road to an arched entrance, was bewitching. Each step took us back a century as we climbed past gypsy women selling bell-encrusted bracelets, men selling tie-dyed scarves, and donkey water carts struggling up hairpin turns. On each side of the road carved into the rock were shops exhibiting dhurrie rugs and appliquéd quilts decorated with netting, organza, shot silk and velvet sewn with gold and silver thread. Each was a work of art and I wondered whether I could carry one for the rest of the trip and if I did where in my flat I would hang it.

Passing through a third gate, we stepped into a square. On the right was the former maharajah's palace. In front was a bakery. Beside it was the Hotel Paradise. We staggered inside calling for two chilled lassis.

The Hotel Paradise is built along the top of and inside the fort's walls. Our room had a balcony hanging over the ramparts, giving us a view of lower Jaisalmer, the local rubbish dump, and a cow enclosure, which doubled as an open-air urinal. It had a monastic feel about it, with its vaulted ceiling, white-washed walls, two hard single beds, nails in the walls for the hanging of clothes, and a toilet that when flushed sounded as if the plumbing went through the rock to ground level. Which it did. Modern plumbing is Jaisalmer's biggest problem, as it is expected that one day the city will subside from being water-logged, much like a big sandcastle.

That evening, we ate mutton curry at the 8th of July Cafe which was ten knee-high steps above the bakery, which was twenty knee-high steps down from our hotel. The cafe was crowded with travelers from all over the world listening to the haunting music of flutes and drums, discussing their next adventure, passing on information about work or cheap trips, and flirting with the opposite sex. Jaisalmer is the backpackers' Mecca of Rajasthan.

That night we could not sleep. Probably because of the magic seeping through the walls. So I read the *Kama Sutra.*

"Want to know how to show your lover how much you love him?" I asked.

Sally grunted. "What lover?"

She was in a bad mood because we weren't eighteen and traveling the world for the first time. I knew the feeling.

"It's called the passionate pressing of love places."

"Go on then."

"The passionate pressing of nails, along with biting, is only practiced with those who find it agreeable. Places for nail pressing are the armpit, throat, breasts and thighs. Although, if passion is excessive, other places can be considered. Without marks to remind one of one's lover, the love is diminished. When a woman sees the marks on her body her love becomes fresh again."

"Rubbish," snapped Sally. "I hate marks on my body."

I agreed with her. And brown skin scars dark so I wouldn't have thought that Indian women would care for it either.

"Oh, here's a list of love positions. Interested?" There was no answer, so I continued. "When a woman's body refuses to release her lover's body it is called the mare's position. This is learned by much practice and is chiefly found among the women of the horse-owning tribes of Andhra. I wonder where Andhra is?"

"I bet all the men know," muttered Sally.

"When the woman places one leg on her lover's shoulder and stretches the other along his body, then alternates her legs, this is called the splitting bamboo position."

"How can she remember to switch legs if she is in the middle of a biting-and-scratching passionate embrace?"

"Plus," I added, "making the sounds of the dove, cuckoo, pigeon, parrot, bee, sparrow, flamingo and quail."

"They'd have to be very, very young to do all that."

Deciding not to go down the "I want to be young again" route, I continued describing positions. "When one leg is placed on her lover's head and the other stretched out, it is called the fixing-of-the-nail-position. This position is learned by much practice."

"You surprise me!"

"If during congress the man turns around without leaving the woman and she embraces his knees and he embraces hers, this is called ..."

"Let me guess. Hands, knees and booms-a-daisy."

I gave up. If she wants to be that miserable she can be.

With only three days to see Jaisalmer before we galloped away on our ships of the desert, we set off early next morning to explore and were lost within minutes. Every alleyway twisted and turned like a dog's leg. Not one was wide enough for two people to pass without brushing against each other. This necessitated us walking up peoples' front steps or into shops, as one does not brush against strangers in India. Although there were at least two I wouldn't have minded brushing against. Jaisalmer men are exceedingly comely. I wonder if they'd be interested in my list of positions?

We had turned into an alleyway which had no side alleyways running off it, when we were unexpectedly confronted by a cow. With its rump jammed against one wall and its head resting against the other, it refused to move until a passing man showed us what to do. Grabbing the cow's tail, he twisted it sharply. With a moan of annoyance, the bovine goddess heaved herself up and moved on.

The second time this happened, Sally, who understands animals, approached the large cow lying across our path and after assuring it with baby talk that she was not going to hurt it, which was a lie, she clasped its tail and twisted. With a bellow that was heard all over Jaisalmer and into the depths of the Thar Desert, the animal lurched to its hoofs, revealing that it was not a cow but a well-endowed bull. Then it charged. I leaped up the steps of a nearby house into the arms of a watching man who backed off so fast I almost fell on top of him, thus adding to my list of love positions, the "throw yourself at him" position, which would have truly freaked him out. Sally had taken to her heels, with the bull after her.

Fortunately one is never alone in India. There is always someone cleaning their teeth over the gutter, washing their babies over the gutter, or as this time, a woman washing her dishes from her front step. She heaved Sally into her doorway. Then with peals of laughter, she shouted the joke to her neighbors, all the while patting Sally's shoulder and repeating "Krishna, Krishna," implying that the bull would not hurt us.

I'm sure she was right. Indian cows and bulls are the most indulged and spoiled of animals, but when one is galloping towards you with swinging testicles and freshly painted horns aimed at your middle regions one tends to forget this.

We thanked the woman, who had the most beautifully hennaed hands, and continued up the cobbled lane in search of the Jain temples, which we never found. Instead we found some magnificent seventeenth-century doorways with carved doors studded with huge spikes. I was once told in Zanzibar that these spikes were meant to stop war-elephants from using their foreheads to push the doors down. Supposing that war-elephants had been able to squash along Zanzibar's or Jaisalmer's tiny alleyways to get to the marble doorways in the first place.

The city of Jaisalmer, built in 1156 by Jaisala, a Rajput chieftain, has never been a dull place. First to do battle in this Ali Baba fortress of carved butter were the Rajput clans, each trying to outdo the other in proving which was the greater warrior caste. Then came the Muslims. While pillaging and plundering their way east, they lay siege to the city. This resulted in the fierce Bhatti Rajputs fighting to the death while their females and children leaped from the fort's ramparts.

Centuries of wealth followed as Jaisalmer became a vital caravanserai on the silk route between China and Europe, causing the House of Jaisalmer, which claims both Lord Krishna and the moon as their ancestors, to flourish. But alas, in a world becoming more modern by the second, there is always a cheaper, speedier way to do things, so when Bombay became a great shipping center the camel caravan became obsolete.

Next came the British, replacing the silk trade route with railway lines and the power of the maharajahs with the power of Queen Victoria, Empress of India. Soon Rajasthan maharajahs were being bought off with medals, privy purses, obligatory gun salutes on their golden coach arrival in Pall Mall (must keep the princes happy, Albert), and narrow-gauge railway lines, so they could visit each other in their private trains to have champagne picnics in the desert, or hunt tigers, or do whatever out-of-work maharajahs do. (But no broad-gauge railway lines, Albert. The Indians might use them to mobilize their armies.)

It was the combination of India's independence, the partitioning of Pakistan from India, and a water shortage that sealed Jaisalmer's fate—it became a ghost city. Then hostilities between Pakistan and India flared up and Jaisalmer was rediscovered as a military base. Which means if there is a war between these brother nations, this golden city will go up in a big puff of golden smoke. Then, Allah and Krishna be praised, around the same time as the hostilities along came tourism with its never-ending supply of foreigners willing to pay big bucks for a glimpse of a sunset behind a sand dune. Any sand dune as long as there is a picturesque camel nearby. No wonder, each day as the sun sets, Jaisalmerians can be seen gambolling along the tops of the sand dunes shouting, "Long live the camel."

Back at our hotel and after a reviving shower to add to Jaisalmer's soggy foundations, we looked at what Sally had bought. Which turned out to be one hell of a lot. When will she wear it all? She doesn't drive a car, she rides a bicycle, and it rains a lot in Scotland. Try as I might, I can't see her turning up to weed some mossy woodland dressed in her Wellingtons, her elephant-patterned skirt, mirrored jacket and cap, festooned in clinking, bell-jingling Indian jewelry.

Next morning, after a banana lassi breakfast (I had decided that two lassis are better than one omelette), we were off again. Leaving one quarter of Jaisalmer's population guarding the fort, we headed down to where the other three quarters live, sharing the road with a cartel of donkey carts that, having gotten up speed, careered downhill behind us without a lot of control. Through the three gateways we raced, donkeys in front and donkeys behind. Dodging a woman carrying a kerosene tin of water on her head and passing the leper brigade, I wondered, fleetingly because the donkeys were getting closer, why there were no female lepers begging from the gutters.

In the main market, where the streets were only minimally wider than those above in the fort, we discovered an enterprising cafe selling fresh pineapple juice. Beside it was the *bhang* shop. Bhang is a drink made from hashish and yogurt, a sort of pot lassi which one of the Americans in the 8th of July Cafe warned us would either send us blind, insane or stop our hearts. "But if it doesn't do those three, you are going to feel great."

That evening we ate on the second floor of a curry house situated over a city gate. The view of the city around us and the fort above us was spectacular, and the curry was great but we were tired, mainly from visiting every jewelry shop in the lower town. What we hadn't seen were any temples or mosques.

Back up the road we trundled to the top of the fort where I collapsed on my monastic-style bed while Sally packed her camel safari bag, then squashed everything else into her cloth bags which she intended leaving in the hotel's storage room.

The following morning sometime before dawn, a hammering on our door awoke us. We dressed, grabbed our luggage and headed for the square where we were to meet up with our camel group. Here, we were amazed to find the two Australians we'd met in Delhi, Liesha and Tanya, and the English couple and their daughter, Evelyn, among the twelve other tourists.

We were divided into four jeeps. Sally went with the Australians while I shared with the English couple and their glowering daughter Evelyn. Charlie told me in much detail, while Evelyn glared at him, how they'd suffered Bikaner belly sickness. She was emanating such hatred that it would not have surprised me if she had self-immolated.

We were heading either towards Khuri village or the Sam Sand Dunes national park because that was what we had paid for, but no one knew which including our driver.

"I follow him," he said, pointing to the jeep in front.

"Where's he going?"

"He follows the first jeep."

Our destination was clearly on a need-to-know basis and we didn't need to know, one sand dune being as good as the next to a tourist. Tundra flashed by spotted with bleached bones heaped like modern sculptures circled in mauve shadow. "Wagoned out of town as the cows died," said Charlie, tapping his guidebook. "There are deer here too. They could be deer bones." I wondered how the deer survived and if Hindus ate deer. I later discovered they didn't.

Finally we arrived at a given spot. Given to the jeep drivers, that is. We tourists were still guessing our destination by the position of the sun.

Twelve camel drivers raced forward in a flurry of long dresses and sandals to choose the tourist they thought would tip them the most. I was led away by my Omar Sharif look-alike wearing a cream turban, a blue *ghagra* pajama suit, and an orange scarf looped casually around his aristocratic neck. He took me to an ancient camel with a chewed tail, scabby knees, and an evil grin that let me know immediately who was boss. All the camels wore padded saddles on top of quilts strapped tightly around their bellies. The older the camel-owner, the younger the camel and the brighter the quilt, reins and saddle decorations. It reminded me of the older successful businessman in his red Porsche.

When we were all standing beside our camels, a command was shouted and the grunting, complaining animals sank to the sand as if their legs had turned to jelly. It was then made clear that we were expected to climb up onto this army of hairy beige mounds. Which I did ungracefully. Sitting was extremely uncomfortable: the saddle was hard; my thighs were stretched into a ballet position I hadn't practiced for decades; and there were no stirrups.

When everyone was seated, including the camel-wallahs on their own flash-looking camels decorated with multi-colored braids, pompoms and mirror-encrusted crocheted halters, the lead camel man shouted and all the hairy beige mounds rose as one. This mass rockathon was accompanied by gasps of pain, shrieks of incredulity, squeals of fear from the tourists, and grins of amusement from the wallahs.

My camel, who I named Agnes, rose in two movements. Kneeling on her front knees she unfolded her back legs, causing me to lunge forward and almost somersault over her bristling chin hairs. At the same time, my unsuspecting pelvic bone was slammed up against a wooden pommel doing it untold damage. Then, as I leaned back almost horizontal so I would not slide down her wrinkled neck, she unfolded her front legs, propping them up at the same time as her back legs seemed to give way beneath her. This rocking motion flung me back so far that it was only by hanging onto the single nose-rein (attached to nothing that would tell her which way to go) that saved me. Then, before I'd gained my balance, off she trotted with her powder-puff feet going plop, plop, plop, in unison with my bottom.

All the wallahs, except mine who thought I wanted to cross the Pakistani border in absolute solitude, hovered like flies around their tourists, waiting for them to fall off. No one did. But Charlie's and Tanya's camels galloped off in the opposite direction to eat a yellow flowering bush called a desert coral tree, and a Dutch woman's black-faced camel bumped into Sally's beige-faced camel, causing a camel confrontation. Sally was positively vitriolic when the black-faced camel refused to budge. Then it was touch and go with scowling Evelyn who had scored a camel which refused to move no matter how viciously she kicked its neck. Life has a way of balancing things.

Being the oldest, Agnes knew the ropes. The faster she got to the sand dune the sooner she got rid of me, so within minutes we'd left the rest of the group behind. An hour later, up galloped my Omar Sharif stand-in whose name was Daniel. Daniel, whose real name was probably Mustafa, spoke good English and as Agnes fell in behind his magnificently embellished bull camel, he swung round so that he was nonchalantly sitting side-saddle, once again reminding me of a sports car owner, and began telling me how Agnes was of second-hand vintage while his steed was a newer model; that all the camels were owned by the wallahs who rode beside them; and that all the wallahs lived in the villages that we were galloping past. When he said galloping, he meant galloping. Agnes was a good galloper.

"Muslim." Daniel pointed to a cluster of round thatched-roofed houses crowned with vultures hidden behind a yellow wall.

"Rah Rah," he shouted to a Muslim man standing outside.

"Hindu," he said, pointing to two turbaned men herding goats into the never never. "Namaste," he shouted.

"Namasté," they shouted back, along with something which translated probably went, "I see you have your crazy tourists with you again."

Everyone knew everyone else. It's a small desert.

Then Agnes smelled water and her galloping speed went up a notch, causing me much pain. My thighs throbbed. The blood had gone to my feet and would probably never come up again. The only way I could get relief was to link my ankles around the pommel and take the chance of being bounced off. Did Agnes care? Did Daniel notice? He probably thought this was the way all Australians rode their camels.

Coming to a skidding stop beside a water trough half a kilometer ahead of everyone else, Agnes collapsed. The reason for this, other than plain nastiness, was that camels do not drink with anyone on their backs. Seeing the earth coming up to greet me I camel-rocked like a professional. After all, I'd been on Agnes for three hours. I knew what it was all about. It was the getting of my numb leg over the pommel that was the problem. My legs had solidified.

The well had different troughs for camels, sheep and goats. It was also a kilometer from the closest village to stop pollution. Milling around it were at least fifty women with more trudging over the hill like a rainbow ribbon. All wore the brightest of saris, and most wore bone bracelets. One woman tried to take my earrings off me. I escaped but she sent her young son after me.

The goats and sheep wore tinkling bells. The boys watering the animals wore Western trousers and shirts and the little girls collecting water wore Western dresses. I wondered at what age the children change to turbans and saris?

Then I saw the most beautiful of women. She wore a butter-yellow sari and was carrying a pottery water jug on her head. With her full lips, finely arched eyebrows and aristocratic nose with its delicate nose-ring, she was of Miss World class, and there have been a plethora of Indian Miss Worlds. As I watched her, I suddenly had the thought that had the maharajahs still been in power, their emissaries would have spirited this desert rose off to the palace, either to become a favorite wife or, after a few nights of dillydallying, a concubine to languish unvisited in the zenana.

Which was best, I wondered: Faded beauty in a zenana. Or faded beauty under a pitiless sun? Unlimited boring luxury. Or unlimited tedious water carrying? Mother of a prince. Or mother of a dozen children, all sons if she were to be of value? As water carrying was not my idea of a fulfilling career, I opted for the zenana and the gamble of being a favorite wife.

While our camels drank, the women gracefully dipped their pots into the water, then while still gossiping, they balanced three pots on top of each other, lifted the lot onto their heads, and walked off barefooted along the dusty track. A line of radiant color melted into a landscape of beige sand dotted with carcasses of dead cows and one lone dog chewing on a leathery knee bone.

We remounted our camels. Me with reluctance, as my urge to gallop across the desert à la Lawrence had died within the first half hour. Sally seemed to be in a dream of contentment or was it acute pain? Either way, she was speechless. Off went Agnes with that special sand dune in mind. With heaving sides and heavy asthmatic breathing, she beat everyone to the camping spot. After she'd done her collapsing act, Daniel and I unpacked her and I discovered I was sleeping on her lumpy saddle quilt. What happened to the eight-sided striped tent with the mirror pieces sewn into the ceiling and the chiffon panels billowing in the desert wind that had been featured on the front of the tourist pamphlet? Clearly, another camel camping company.

With our mattresses spread out on the sand, our group quickly dispersed over the dunes to search for the arcanum of Rajasthan.

Far to the west the sun, looking like a huge apricot, slipped beneath the horizon. At its disappearance there was a pregnant pause, as if the whole world was holding its breath waiting for some empyrean god to catch it and throw it back. The stillness was so complete it made my ears twang. We sat like that for fifteen minutes, and then we heard the calls of those of our group, who had walked across the dunes until they were mere purple specks, and who, swallowed up in instant darkness, had only our shouts to guide them back.

Sally and I returned to the camp, via a stop behind a clump of wild cotton plants, to find that our Muslim wallahs had galloped home to dinner and a comfy bed, or to partake in their part-time job of smuggling cows over the border, and that our Hindu jeep drivers had produced a dinner of pappadums (thin wafer or flatbread), fried vegetables, rice, dhal and a vegetable curry. There was no meat because the jeep drivers were Brahmans and they would not allow meat in their vehicles.

By now, it was so dark we couldn't see the camels but we could hear them clearing their throats, gurgling, farting and complaining in a whining manner that was most unbecoming.

With dinner over, out came our driver's special singing costumes, long white dresses and red turbans. Sitting cross-legged around the fire, with one beating a double-sided drum called a *thavil* and two sawing at string instruments called *sarangs*, they sung a sentimental love ballad. With the sky spangled with stars, the bass snorting of camels in tune with the music, and the scarlet sparks from the fire lighting up the singers' faces, it was a beautiful moment destined not to last. Silent until then, Evelyn now began to wail like a demented wraith. Everyone stared across the fire at her. Her parents tried to hush her but she would not be hushed. She could not cope with the romance of the night and with the lovelorn serenade. Three weeks of being torn from the bosom of her loved one (whether he loved her or not) was more than she could bear. She wanted to go home. Now!

The singing petered out.

As Evelyn would not be placated, the obliging singers, who understand the cry of a broken heart, offered to take her back to Jaisalmer.

"Feel like a walk under the stars?" I suggested to a disgusted Sally.

Once away from the fire, the stars seemed larger, the salt-bush turned silver, and the moon lit up a milky path across the sand, enabling us to avoid the camel poo. It was lovely, but we both agreed that the Thar Desert wasn't a real desert. Not like the mighty orange Sahara or the cream-colored sand dunes of Egypt. The Thar Desert had too many thorn bushes and too many tourists. A real desert only had sand.

Back at our quilts and to the serenade of rumbling camels, we fell asleep in our clothes only to be awakened by the snoring of what we thought was one of the wallahs who had rolled himself up in his quilt a little too close to us for comfort.

"Prod him to stop him snoring?" hissed Sally.

"I can't. It's his country. He's allowed to snore in it."

But after half an hour and a few shuffles of the wallah so that he was practically snuggling up to my back, I rolled over and prodded him, and discovered I was poking the hump of a very small camel that was snuggling up because he was lonely.

"It's a baby camel," I whispered.

"Isn't that perfect?" sighed Sally.

Next morning we were up at dawn, breakfasted on porridge, chai and toast, and seated on our camels by six. The baby camel was nowhere in sight.

During this agonizingly long day while I communed with Agnes, the sand, the vultures, and the many piles of bones, Daniel, who would make any woman's heart flutter at twenty paces, instructed me on why a Rajasthan turban of nine meters is called a *safas* whereas a turban of twenty-five meters is called a *pagris*; how it took four weeks to train a camel to take a rider and how making a camel crawl was essential if it were to learn to obey commands. He told me about his house, his three wives, and his dog that he loved very much. I told him I had two dogs that I love very much. Staring deeply into my eyes, he told me we had a lot in common. I felt so too.

That night when we stopped to camp, Daniel showed me how to hobble Agnes. Without fear of her big yellow teeth that could snap like a bear trap, he picked up her right front leg, twisted a rope under the hock, and then looped the rope around her neck. The result was a very uncomfortable lopsided camel, who, unless she was good at three-legged races, wasn't going anywhere. This hobbling gave me great satisfaction and all the lamenting Agnes went on with during the night brought not one tear of sympathy to my eyes.

Three days later when the group turned towards Jaisalmer, when Agnes fell into last place in the camel line, and Daniel galloped up beside me to ask if there was work in Australia for a camel-wallah, I knew that if I ever again felt the uncontrollable urge to visit a sand dune I would do it in a jeep. And in another life, in a jeep with Daniel. If that could be arranged. True, he had three wives and six children back in his dung-colored, mud-walled village, but he was kind to his dog and I have two silkies. He also smuggled cows over the Pakistani border and who could resist an old-fashioned smuggler? Not I.

"Should you be here again, dear Madam," he whispered as he helped me off Agnes, "I would have great pleasure in showing you how the smuggling takes place."

Ah, thought I, under different circumstances I would have great pleasure in being shown. But as we have just galloped passed battalions of "Vietnamese jungle green" camouflaged anti-missile guns being trucked to the Indian–Pakistan border, and as it was reported that the Pakistanis were amassing similar equipment on the other side, and that the words "nuclear weapons" had been bandied about, I doubted if I would return. But who knows. It is said everyone who goes to India returns one day.

# Chapter 14

## Indigo Jodhpur and Saffron Lassis

We returned to Jaisalmer in our waiting jeeps, leaving behind our well-tipped camel-wallahs and our relieved camels, especially Agnes. After waving good-bye to Liesha, Tanya and the English couple, minus Evelyn, we decided to stay in the fort for a week, adding more shower water to its dodgy foundations, wandering its ramparts, eating in thatched-roof cafes and resting.

It was a wonderful week of lost time, book reading, chatting with locals who were beginning to recognize us, drinking countless banana lassis and browsing in shops. We even visited the Jaisalmer Palace museum, although we both agreed we were all palaced out.

Finally it came time to move on. After an uncomfortable night, because our overhead fan would not turn off and was so wobbly we were afraid it would fall and decapitate or de-leg one of us, we awoke with barely enough time to grab our bags and run.

Down the cobbled road we raced, neither of us thinking about sprained ankles or broken necks which would necessitate a visit to an Indian hospital, an event we'd been warned not to contemplate. Through the market area with a tail of little boys shouting "Do you want to see my brother's factory?" until we reached the Hotel Neeraj where the driver was revving the bus's engine as we flung ourselves up its sagging steps.

Within minutes of finding a seat we were tearing along a military road as if the entire Pakistani army was after us. Or after our tires which was more likely as tires are scarce in Pakistan. The drive south took us through the western desert which to our untrained eyes looked identical to the eastern and southern deserts except for the distant army pillboxes, lookout towers and passing trucks carrying anti-aircraft guns.

We stopped twice. Once to pick up the bumper bar that was wired back on by a passing multi-talented farmer. The second time at a cafe furnished with ancient carved chairs, sagging charboys and a huge stainless-steel pot of boiling chai.

After leaving urine spots in the dust, along with four Indian women, all of us pretending the others weren't there, we drank chai surrounded by men with turned-down moustaches and golden skin that matched their golden earrings worn looped over their ears. Where had the women from the bus gone?

"Why are the cafes full of men?" I asked a chai-sipping man.

He pointed to a herd of sheep milling around an STD telephone Internet box and said that the men were working. Shepherding sheep from a cafe chair I understood. But why would anyone here in Dustville need the Internet? For the price of sheep on the world market? I doubt it. Still no women in sight.

Chai over, the women appeared from behind the chai shop and the bus took off again with all the turbans nodding in time to music coming from a borrowed radio. This time when the bumper bar fell off, it was left behind.

With the sun straight overhead everything outside was mono-toned except for the golden whirly-whirlies that cork-screwed across the sand, scattering golden-tipped chaff over thorn bushes as brittle as fingernails. I craved a splash of color, a hint of movement. No wonder the women wear such bright clothes. I got my wish. Jodhpur is a cobalt-blue city. Blue walls, blue houses, blue paint everywhere, which would make going to the paint shop a non-event but a cheap one.

We arrived at our Jodhpur hotel to find that it was built opposite a large fetid drain. But it had a swimming pool that could be swum in as long as you kept your head above the non-blue water, and a restaurant that served the famous Jodhpur chicken.

Next morning our spluttering rickshaw had an engine-attack on the steep hill leading up to Jodhpur's Meherangarh Fort. With the first expression of anger that we had seen in India, our mechanically minded driver whacked his "money maker" with his screwdriver. When this highly skilled action did not miraculously cure the engine's ills, and with the picture in our heads of the three of us rolling backwards into the nearby ravine, we offered to walk the rest of the way. Our driver graciously pocketed the agreed amount of money, without refunding any for only having gotten us half way, then, with his useless screwdriver clenched between his teeth, he coasted downhill in search of a better mechanic, or two more gullible tourists.

Half an hour later, we arrived hot and tired at the fort's battle-scarred entrance gate where we bought our gold-embossed tickets.

"The building of Meherangarh Fort with its magnificent views of fiery sunsets and statuesque mosques was started on the 12 May 1459 a.d. by Rao Jodha the Seventeenth," I read from the back of my ticket. "Wonder how they knew it was the twelfth of May?"

"Indians had calendars long before anyone else," said Sally.

"Not only that!" I continued reading, "The most famous Jackie Kennedy thought Meherangarh Fort the eighth wonder of the world and British Rudyard Kipling thought it the work of angels, fairies and giants. Those two got around, didn't they?"

"It's what famous people did ... do."

At the Jayapol Gate, constructed in 1806, after the Maharajah of Jodhpur conquered the armies of the Maharajah of Bikaner, we leaned on a cannon to catch our breaths and admired the magnificent view of the statuesque mosques.

"Weren't the Maharajah of Jodhpur and the Maharajah of Bikaner related?" asked Sally, proving that she did listen when I read to her. "Wasn't it Rao Jodha of Jodhpur who started Bikaner?"

I nodded, while trying to find this piece of elusive information in my dog-eared guidebook.

"So what was the Maharajah of Bikaner doing coming all this way to Jodhpur?" I asked Sally. "Didn't he have enough desert of his own? Or was he coming to retrieve his favorite sister who had written to say she was unhappy and needed rescuing because she had not produced an heir and was about to be discarded? Or because she was being cruelly treated by the other wives in the zenana and thought she was being poisoned?"

Sally nodded. "Life would be tough for a non-son-producing-out-of-town princess." Then she pointed over the town. "What's that building way over?"

I knew this one because I'd looked it up earlier. "That's the Umaid Bhawan Palace Hotel owned by the present day Maharajah of Jodhpur who built it when he realized that the de-registration of the maharajahs would leave him rupee-less. It is very expensive and has made him the wealthiest maharajah in India, and I reckon we ought to have dinner there."

"Done."

At Ded Kangrapol Gate, renamed the Dead Kangaroo Gate by Sally, we rested again. Then we tackled the hairpin bend that brought us to Lohapol Gate. On the side of this gate are the handprints of the widows of Maharajah Man Singh.

I whipped out my guidebook. "On their husband's death, his fifteen devoted wives committed suttee, leaving behind these handprints which were once coated with silver but are now stained crimson. These handprints are still much worshipped." By whom I wondered? Who would pray to fifteen living torches? And for what? What would one ask fifteen burned widows for? "In the 1830s the British outlawed suttee although the practice didn't stop until much later."

"Wasn't Maharajah Man Singh the one who beat the Maharajah of Bikaner in battle?" asked Sally.

"Correct."

"So that means the Bikaner princess wasn't saved by her brother?"

"I made her up, Sally."

"I don't care. I bet there was one. I bet she was one of those widows."

On we trudged until we reached the Iron Gate where there once stood two famous bazaars. Daulat Khana Chowk and Singhar Chowk bustled with merchants and luxury goods from all over Asia. More than once these merchants must have seen the arrival of a new princess hidden away in her gold and jewel-studded howdah. More than once they must have shouted, "Welcome. Welcome." Princesses were always welcome. Their coming was good for trade.

How frightened those princesses must have been. Forced to cross a wasteland to greet a husband they'd been promised to at birth with only a miniature painting, done with a paintbrush made from one squirrel hair, to show them what he looked like. How slowly the days must have dragged as their royal elephants plodded west, ever west, taking them away from the forests and lakes of their homeland to a desert kingdom that they would never return from.

The custom of selling off princesses to produce royal offspring who would not attack their mother's homeland was what royal alliances were all about. But what sort of lives did these princesses have? Cosseted and confined in their father's zenana until puberty; sent halfway across the country to become the first, second or third wife of a stranger; then, after being loved or abandoned for years, when their husbands died being expected to commit suttee, or suicide off a wall if their palaces were being attacked. How sad.

"What is she like?" whispered the court women pressing their kohl-painted eyes to the Pleasure Palace's marble latticework as the royal elephant swayed by.

"What is he like?" murmured the child princess, already dressed in her red wedding sari, her heavy dowry jewelry cutting into her eleven-year-old neck.

"Will she produce an heir?" whispered the first and second wives who had produced worthless girls.

"What is his palace like?" whispered the princess, while lifting the curtain to see where she would spend the rest of her life, partaking in intricate toilet rituals to render her body sufficiently devastating to charm her over-indulged husband. With a sigh, she let the curtain fall. She could see nothing but men and walls. One palace was pretty much the same as another to a princess, once she was locked inside.

At last we reached the Surajpol Gate, the official entry into the palace of angels, fairies and giants. Inside we saw halls full of golden howdahs with Belgian glass windows, kilometers of miniature paintings, dozens of silver-framed photographs showing the princes' twenty gold-and-silver trimmed Rolls Royces, and a cradle room with six royal cradles hanging by golden chains.

As we walked around the cradles, I had the mental picture of twelve turbaned princes lying head to toe in each one, all being rocked by hairy-chinned British nannies in stiffly starched pinafores, each one holding a bottle of castor oil or a bowl of porridge in a free hand.

In the costume hall, an old man in a yellow turban, sitting cross-legged holding a red silk-sheathed sword and highly decorated shield, told us that the custom of *mujira*, which is the respectful touching of the royal feet of a maharajah, maharani or rajmata, was still performed along with a small present. Then he waited and we waited. I wondered how many people kissed his feet. Not us. Giving up on us, the old rogue then showed us how to wind a turban of twenty-five meters and told us what the different colors of the turbans meant.

"A wearer of a saffron turban is a high-caste Brahman. The wearers of red and green check or yellow and mustard are large landowners of the middle castes. The wearer of a white turban is a small landholder of the middle caste. Dark colors are worn by low castes or Untouchables."

"What would happen if an Untouchable wore a saffron turban?" I asked.

A look of incomprehension crossed his face. Either no one had asked him this before or an Untouchable had never tried it.

"The way the moustache is brushed upwards or downwards," he continued, feeling his own upwards moustache, "signifies a man's caste, while his dhoti knot signifies his sub-caste. Among women it is jewelry and dress color. Midnight blue is always worn by female royalty."

My Taj Mahal ghost had worn midnight blue.

We exited through Fatehpol Gate (the gate erected by Maharajah Ajit Singh when he defeated the Moguls), and plunged into the old city. Painted blue to ward off evil spirits and mosquitoes, it consists of a jumble of overladen electric light poles that would defy any electrician, washing lines full of saris capable of strangling an unwary walker, and steep laneways winding between houses that centuries ago were owned by Brahmans but are now owned by those who can afford them. That's progress.

Continuing downwards, we arrived at a dusky pale blue clock tower square and a deep-blue cafe which produced the best saffron-flavored lassis in the world. So far we had only seen men drinking in cafes but this cafe was full of happy families on a day out. The Jodhpur women are smaller and darker than those in northern Jaisalmer or Bikaner and the Western-dressed men with their short black hair are finer-boned. None wore turbans.

Two saffron lassis later, we headed for the spice market. I cook with spices and wanted to take home some pink-colored "black" salt and some Bikaner pepper. Sally, who never cooks, wanted to take photographs of the brilliant colored spices piled up, pyramid style, in their bright plastic bowls. I was savoring the pungent smells of green ginger, cardamom, turmeric, saffron, cloves, chili, nutmeg and garlic, when who should rush up to me and throw her arms around my neck as if I was a long-lost amigo? English Evelyn, that's who. As the last time I had seen her was when she was disappearing, sobbing copiously, into the night of the Thar Desert in a jeep driven by our singing trio, I was somewhat surprised.

She then announced that she'd run away. When I didn't react sufficiently to this dramatic declaration (running away at twenty-seven isn't the same as running away at fourteen), she declared it again at the top of her voice, causing passers-by to stop and stare.

"I'm catching the Delhi train then flying to London. I've emailed my boyfriend and he's waiting for me," she shouted.

As I had not managed to email anyone, this was a feat worthy of admiration far more than her running away, and I said so.

While taking sniffs of cinnamon and cardamom, I heard Sally suggest that Evelyn tell her parents her plan. But avenging Evelyn was adamant that as they had kidnapped her, they deserved to suffer. We left her hurrying off to the railway station. Had we known where her parents were, we would have told them that she was safe, but there were too many hotels in Jodhpur.

Next day we bought our first saris. We did this in Nai Sarak, the city's main street where the stallholders sell tins of Norwegian sardines, mirror-worked cushions and Himalayan bedspreads, jumbled up together under black umbrellas. Our reluctance until now had been because we thought that Europeans looked silly in saris, but we succumbed when we saw two stalls piled high with the same brilliant colors as the spice market. Two small children, collecting cardboard in onion bags, helped us. The little girl's hair was tied in rigid dust-dry bunches and the boy's stuck up in dirt-stiff spikes. They were filthy, but they had definite opinions on saris. They grimaced, smiled and pointed; all without coming too close, as it was evident by the stall-holder's glares that should their fingers or shadows touch the saris, they would be unsalable. How difficult it must be to always have to be conscious of where one's shadow is falling.

Taking our ragamuffins' advice, I bought an orange cotton sari that I intended wearing as a scarf in "Daniel of Jaisalmer" fashion. Sally chose a red one to match her hair. To thank the children, we gave them mandarins and, when we reached Sojati Gate, an ice cream each. That was the end of our peace. A silent telegraph went out and children appeared out of cracks in the walls, out of drains in the street, out of the dust-mote-filled air. There were so many clamoring for an ice cream that we beat a fast retreat into the sweets shop. After the shopkeeper chased away the multitude with a harmless rolled-up newspaper, we felt obliged to buy a *mawa kachori* honey and nut cake from him.

On leaving this wonderful-smelling shop, Sally fell in love with a white Brahman bull and it fell in love with her. Her feeding it her honey and nut cake helped the romance along enormously. With adoration in its limpid eyes, it followed her along the road, melting her heart with each wet-nosed nudge. Even I, who have no fondness for bulls, had to admit that this one was a handsome fellow, with a small, firm hump, delicate-hoofed feet, black tail and creamy curtain of skin hanging from its neck.

"It could be a prince under a spell," Sally whispered, in a lovesick voice. "What if he is bewitched and can only become a prince one night a year?"

"Nice idea. Write it down. Get it published. You might make him famous and save his life before he dies of plastic-bag poisoning or ends up in a Pakistani's beef curry."

"You don't have a romantic bone in your body," she said, while climbing into a rickshaw with the amorous bull breathing down her neck.

"I do. Just not for bulls."

She ignored this. "I wonder how he stays so healthy?" she asked while tickling his inquisitive nose.

"Would waiting outside a sweet shop do it?" I asked.

That evening, dressed in our best, we set off for the Umaid Bhawan Palace Hotel. Smiling at the hotel guards, which was meant to imply that we ate there all the time, we strolled through the elegant garden to the palace's steps on which, our guidebook said, the residing rajmata paints little red feet, hands and swastikas to honor Diwali the Festival of Light. This yearly festival celebrates the return of Prince Ram to the Kingdom of Ayodhya after his fourteen years of exile. The festival entails the placing of thousands of flickering candles on all the roofs of Jodhpur followed by thousands of exploding fireworks to attract the Lady Lakshmi, the goddess of wealth and prosperity. I would like to see that.

On entering the Umaid Bhawan Palace one is instantly assailed with wealth and prosperity, but not an abundance of good taste. This massive unimaginative effort took fifteen years to complete and was designed by the president of the British Royal Institute of Architects, who was clearly in love with Saint Paul's Cathedral and art deco furniture. Never a good combination!

With a nod to the reception committee, we sauntered through the foyer, which has all the charm of a gun bunker and boasts of a pair of stuffed bears standing on their hind legs holding trays containing sherry bottles, and out onto the terrace.

The palace gardens have a 1930s look with square pots of bougainvillea placed around a square lawn surrounded by a square-cut hedge decorated at intervals with Grecian columns and temples. The Greek bits made me wonder if the architect had mistaken Jodhpur for Athens.

We sipped our glasses of *nimbu pani* (a cooling lemon drink), ate our club sandwiches, and watched the sun set over Grecian urns with blue Jodhpur in the distance, and then we decided to try and find a way of sneaking into the hotel's "residents only" cinema. We were wandering, although creeping could describe it better, down an ill-lit corridor, peeking into various deserted lounge rooms discussing how much we hated leopard skin wall hangings, elephant foot stools and elephant foot fire tool holders, when out of the gloom strolled a tall, slim gentleman wearing cream flannel trousers and a cream buttoned-up cardigan. So out of context was he, and so in the wrong place were we, that all three of us froze. When I say out of context I mean wrong time frame. He looked as if he belonged to a 1940s cricket team. We, on the other hand, resembled hippy burglars.

He recovered first. Nodding briefly, he took his pipe from his mouth and said with a perfect Oxford accent, "Good evening. Are you having a pleasant holiday?"

"Yes, thank you," answered Sally. "Are you?"

"Oh quite," he chuckled. Then with a wave of his pipe and a "Cheerio," he spun round and entered a side room.

"Do you think he was the maharajah?" I whispered as we hurried back to the terrace.

"Which one?"

As there were too many maharajahs of Jodhpur to remember, I suggested a second gin and tonic while I looked them up.

"There was one who, when Britain was pulling out, conspired with Muslim Pakistan and Hindu India to get the best deal for Jodhpur. He was so unhappy about signing away his power that he threatened to shoot Lord Mountbatten's constitutional adviser with a gun disguised as a fountain pen (which is in the museum). There was another who married a nineteen-year-old English nurse and brought her home as his second wife. Oh, here's something. The rajmata, although not insisting that her daughters be educated, insisted that her son go to England. The prince hated boarding school, but during school holidays he enjoyed swanking it up at the Savoy Hotel where he insisted that his thirty-five suites be filled with 3000 fresh roses every day. He also enjoyed visiting Bond Street in his pink turban, pearl earrings and opera cloak to pick up a little 'trinket' for the girl he was taking out that evening."

Sally stared out over the dark garden and the blinking lights of Jodhpur. "He didn't look like the pink turban type."

"No, he didn't, so I think I know who he is."

"Who?"

"He's your white bull and tonight is the one night in the year that he turns into a prince."

Sally crossed her long legs, flicked back her red hair then, looking at me coolly, said, "You've had too many gins."

That from someone who, only three hours earlier, had been enamored with a bull.

The following day was spent leisurely strolling through Madho Bagh Park with its thousands of rainbow-colored parakeets; visiting the beautifully sculptured Jain temples of Osiyan which are supposed to rival the erotic temples of Khajuraho and which so shocked the Victorian British but did not shock us; after all, we are readers of the *Kama Sutra*.

These temples were full of a Japanese tour group with all the men photographing the statues with lenses that would have made the naked statues the size of the Statue of Liberty, yet I doubted if they knew anything about Jainism. Did they know that Jainist followers picture the universe as a giant human figure? Did they know that a Jain ascetic carries a broom to sweep the path ahead of him lest his feet crush minute creatures? Did they know that the act of fasting until death is favored by advanced Jain ascetics? Probably not!

We ended the day by sitting beside Balsamand Lake, watching the bats that were so affected by the sunset reflected in the lake's surface that they swooped en masse into the water to drink up the flame-like liquid. "Black shadows drinking from a Lake of Fire," I wrote in my diary. Which sounded as if the lake was enchanted, so perhaps Sally's white bull being a bewitched prince wasn't so fanciful after all. It isn't hard to imagine such things in India.

# Chapter 15

## MOUNT ABU, AXES AND BOMBS

Three days later, we headed for Mount Abu. Mount Abu is where the god Krishna created the proud Hara Chauhan clan, one of the four warrior clans to rule Rajasthan. It was also the mountain retreat of the maharajahs of Jodhpur, Jaipur, Bikaner and the British Raj.

This time our bus did not travel on a state highway, which is what the previous single-lane roads were called; instead our adventurous mail-delivering driver cut across country, passing fields being plowed by elephants, camels, or both harnessed together. We stopped frequently, usually to pick up farmers, or to collect broken pieces of machinery, or to deliver mended pieces of machinery, and once in a while he dropped off the mail.

At a petrol stop, a proud tractor owner paraded back and forth showing off his shiny red machine on which sat his dogs, his wives and his four children all dressed up for the visit to the petrol pumps. He preened when he saw me photographing him. He stroked his moustache and patted his yellow turban, as if to say, "See what a success I am." I gave him the thumbs up sign to show him that I saw and was impressed. Which I was, a brand new red tractor must have cost him a fortune.

Full of petrol, the bus set off again. Only this time the driver took a wrong turn and ended up on the thrashing floor of a surprised farmer. Back we edged between two hedges with all the male passengers giving directions. It was this turn-off. No, it was that one. No, definitely this one. We were lost for an hour. It was a perfect way to see rural India, and Sally and I didn't mind a bit, neither did any of the other passengers. None of us had such pressing appointments that an hour lost here or there could cause any stress. What a wonderful life.

It must have been a propitious day for weddings because while meandering hither and yon we saw three splendidly dressed grooms wearing fanned turbans, brocade jackets and white britches, all riding white wedding stallions with red-fringed reins and gold-and-red saddle clothes.

"How do you know they're stallions?" demanded Sally.

This surprised me because being an animal lover I thought she would have noticed. "Bridegrooms cannot ride a mare or gelding to their wedding as it might make them impotent," I told her (I had read this earlier). "Grooms and brides are supposed to be virgins. Although many of the grooms have been married before, or in the case of a young prince, have already been taught the art of lovemaking by a carefully selected dancing girl, ta dum!"

Sally's eyebrows shot up. "Go on about the dancing girls."

"The British disliked this teaching system. They tried to replace it with sport. It didn't work. I can't think why."

"Oh I don't know," said Sally, putting on her posh British voice. "There is a lot to be said for sport and a cold shower."

"Not if you read the *Kama Sutra*."

We reached the base of Mount Abu in the late afternoon where we changed drivers and paid a toll. With a half-full bus we set off. Did the locals know something we didn't? Apparently so. At the sight of the first bend, our new driver turned into the gear-changing maniac from hell. Down went his foot on the accelerator, causing the bus to leap forward; around the curve we sped, causing the bus's rear wheels to swing out over nothing and its backside to dip until the rear wheels touched ground again.

With faces whiter than snow beneath our tans, we roared on upwards through the driest forest I have ever seen. Hundred-year-old trees dead from their twigs downwards surrounded by tinder-dry bamboo. There were no fire hazard warnings, only notices in English, warning walkers to beware of man-eating leopards, panthers, foxes, wild boar and bears. As the hills were so barren I was interested to know what these fierce animals lived on when there were no English-speaking walkers to devour.

"It hasn't rained for three years," explained the friendly old gentleman sitting beside me, as we swerved out over an abyss, forcing him to squash me up against a window that looked down onto a terrifying drop. "The trees die. The honeyeaters go thirsty. But still we come to Mount Abu to pray," he added, as he slid in the other direction.

"To whom?" I asked, clasping tight to the seat in front.

"Vishnu, Creator of all. Shakti, goddess mother and creator. Saraswati, goddess of learning. Shiva the Destroyer. Parvati, Shiva's beautiful consort. And of course Durga so that she will continue to ride her lion and rescue the universe from the tyranny of Mahisa the buffalo demon."

"What about the Lady Lakshmi, goddess of fortune and opportunity?" I had to ask.

"Oh most certainly. The Lady Lakshmi, consort of Vishnu, is most important. One can never have enough good fortune and opportunity."

"So say all of us," chorused Sally, sliding off her seat and being saved from landing in the aisle by the strap of one of her string bags catching on something.

"So who is your favorite?" I asked.

The sweet old man looked puzzled. "I have no favorite, dear lady. I pray to them all equally."

After driving past a tribe of monkeys throwing nuts at the bus, and barely missing three men on a motorbike who had appeared unexpectedly, we turned a bend and our rear wheel left the dirt for the last time. In front of us, lying within a circle of hills, was the town of Mount Abu built beside Nakki Lake. Legend has it that a god using his fingernails, or *nakk*, scooped out Nakki Lake. After our hair-raising ride, neither Sally nor I had any nakk left worth scooping with.

The Water Vista Hotel was advertised as a medium-priced hotel with wonderful views of the Maharajah of Jaipur's summer palace and Nakki Lake. But as there were no Indian guests it couldn't have been that medium priced. As for the view? The lake was empty except for some enterprising farmers, their families, and anyone else willing to squelch around in black mud, digging up its silty bottom, to carry it away on trailers pulled by tractors.

Our ground-floor room overlooked the garden where the women of the hotel squatted to shell peas and gossip loudly. As this was not conducive to the nap we both needed after a seven-hour bumpy bus journey, we walked down the hundred steps and back into town to explore.

Never before had we seen so many Indian women roaming around arm in arm, chatting and laughing. Never before had we seen so many tourist shops full of plastic souvenirs or jewelry shops full of glittering glass, imitation pearls and false gold, each one overflowing with women buzzing around in a buying frenzy. In the "Junk Jewelry Corporation" we watched a couple deciding between three beautiful creations of flummery laid out on black velvet. He was proudly paying and she was proudly choosing. First she asked him which of the necklace and earring sets he liked, then she asked us, then she tried each set on, then she tried them on us. All the time the salesman smiled patiently. He knew that God was in the clouds and that he had a sale. In the end she chose the most garish set that the salesman, the husband, and Sally and I, tactfully agreed suited her best.

Next we wandered up the main street to the polo oval where a row of half-starved steeds with split hoofs, plumed heads and drooping necks waited for parents to hire them for their children. It was too hot and the streets were empty so we went to eat.

On the dot at 6 p.m. just as we were leaving our cafe, an amazing thing happened. People began pouring out of doorways, out of hidden hotels, out of borrowed friends' houses and cheap holiday rentals. Holding hands, they rushed laughingly down to the lake's edge. Caught up in the gleeful crowd, we followed them out onto a dilapidated concrete jetty. Within minutes of everyone's arrival, the sun dipped into the mud and all sound ceased. There followed a communal silence similar to that of the camel safari sunset. I marvelled at how something that happens every twenty-four hours and which has happened ever since forever can still give such a wonderful feeling of communal bliss.

That night the water tank above our room sprung a leak. Although sprung a waterfall describes it better.

It started with a trickle, then began gushing down our windowpanes. I switched on the bedside lamp and saw it pouring down our walls while the ceiling above my bed bulged. Then the electricity went off and down came a ton of water. It must have been a very large tank because the deluge went on long after we'd raced outside to the safety of the garden where we stood dripping, without a soul coming to see what the noise was about.

"Where the hell is everyone?" yelled Sally.

"Hello, hello," I shouted, through the hotel's front door.

"Hello be damned," shrieked Sally, who doesn't like being immersed in water at the best of times (she's one of those people who only own a shower). "Wake up and get out here quick before we drop a bomb on the place."

As illogical as this threat was, considering how few tourists wander around India with a bomb in their bags, it did the trick. Suddenly the hotel's passageway filled with bare-chested men in dhotis, all shouting and waving their arms.

Sally shouted and waved her arms back. The sight of a drenched red-haired woman wearing a brief pair of bikini pants and bra made transparent by water, plus her long legs to die for, stopped them in their tracks. Then as it was clear she had no bomb hidden upon her person (they being able to see most of her person), their gaze switched to my baggy T-shirt which was quite capable of hiding a scud missile if I wanted to share it with my boobs.

"Our room is flooded," I said, enunciating clearly. "We need another."

"There are no other rooms, Madam," answered the closest man, while watching my hands for any movement that might resemble bomb throwing.

"Why not? The hotel isn't full," demanded Sally.

"The other rooms are not made up, Madam," he answered, averting his eyes. "There are no sheets on the beds. There are no electric lightbulbs."

"Then get some."

"That is not possible, Madam. The linen cupboard is locked and the owner has the key. Please go back to your room and we will mend everything in the morning."

"Don't be bloody stupid! The room is two feet under water," I yelled. "Unlock the linen cupboard now before I attack it with my axe."

"And I will attack it with my axe," yelled Sally.

Where we kept our axes and why we should be traveling with them in the first place didn't seem foolish at the time. Or perhaps some tourists do carry axes because our threat worked. The man took off to the office at top speed and we heard him speaking excitedly into the telephone.

Fifteen minutes later, during which time we'd heaved our dripping backpacks out into the garden without the help of the watching men, the hotel owner arrived.

Tearing up the driveway in his brand new four-wheel drive, he leaped out shouting, "Who is attacking my hotel with a bomb and axe?"

"We are," we shouted back.

"Did you bring the linen cupboard keys?" added Sally.

Now one would have thought that as it was this fellow's water tank that had collapsed on us, that he would have been apologetic, forthcoming with assistance, even helpful. Not so. This Head of God had been woken up in the middle of the night, or perhaps this Head of God had been interrupted while performing one of the sixty-four Kama Sutra positions. Whichever. He was not happy. By the way he carried on, one would have thought that we had climbed up into the ceiling and attacked his water tank with our legendary axes. All he could talk about was how expensive it was to truck in water, how much a new tank and new ceiling would cost, and how it would be days before his hotel had hot water.

"Listen here," announced Sally, thoroughly fed up with his upper-class whining. "If I don't get a room soon I am going to scream rape at the top of my voice."

"But you were not raped," he gasped, finally noticing she was only wearing wet underwear.

"You don't know that," she retorted.

"She's right," I interjected, for once perfectly attuned with Sally arguing the rights of the global traveler. "You don't know because you weren't here. So if we do not get a room with linen and hot water immediately, we will go to the police and complain of rape. Not to mention writing to the *Lonely Planet* and every other guidebook to tell them about your hotel so that you will be black-listed in their next Indian editions."

I think it was the latter threat that convinced him, because suddenly the linen cupboard key appeared, and within seconds we were installed on the first floor with fresh sheets and hot water. Apparently the tank above our room was only for the cheaper ground floor rooms. The first floor had plenty of water. Later we realized his complaining act had been for the benefit of his staff to cover the fact that two lowly women had managed to drag him out of bed.

As there were no bed-making caste servants to make our beds, we made them ourselves and fell into them.

The next morning over breakfast we were informed by a waiter, with a twinkle in his eye, that he was sorry about Madam's rape, but because of it, our breakfast was gratis and the hotel owner had arranged for a taxi to take us to the Dilwara Jain temples free of charge. But before we went, would we like to put our axes and bomb in the hotel safe? With serious faces we said we would, then we all laughed. This brought the rest of the staff, minus the owner, to our table to laugh with us while two of them mimed Sally dancing around the grass waving an axe and another mimed me throwing a bomb.

Our free taxi took us halfway down the mountain to two rows of religious stalls and a temple complex. Inside were two temples and some lean-to sheds where four stone carvers worked at restoring carvings. It was seeing these semi-naked men chipping away in the half dark that reminded me of the eight illegal Indians discovered in Sydney living in the most putrid conditions in a portable shed on a construction site. These non-English-speaking stonecutters had worked seven days a week for three-and-a-half years for the sum of $45 a month paid to their families in India. The Indian-owned company employing them was not providing workplace insurance or superannuation nor paying tax. Their excuse being that the men were donating their time. The Indian company was taken to court, the workmen were paid all their back wages at Australian rates, and they returned to India rich men. But it made me wonder how much these Jain craftsmen earned or if they were donating their time?

We paid our entry fee and left our shoes and my leather backpack with the shoe-minder as no leather articles are allowed in Jain temples. There was also a notice forbidding entrance to menstruating women. We wondered how the ticket seller would know. Through a small temple, called the House of Elephants, we entered the famous Vimal Vasahi temple built in 1031 by Vimal, a government minister of the fabulously rich city of Gujarat. Here in a sunken courtyard stood a forest of forty-five magnificently carved pillars. Among them sat a flower-decked statue with shoulder-length ears, short curly hair and heavy-lidded Nepalese eyes. This was Mahavira the first tirthankar, or great Jain teacher.

Around the courtyard were fifty-two candle-lit rooms, each with a cross-legged tirthankar inside. But it was the passageway connecting the rooms that intrigued us. The walls, ceilings and archways were covered in carvings of bosomy, ample-hipped *gopi* milk maids with come-hither eyes, hooped earrings, swaying girdles and nothing else. All were in voluptuous poses, similar to those in Angkor Wat, Cambodia, and all were guaranteed to give any Jain worshipper ideas that he should not have. I looked in my guidebook to find out more about them and discovered an eighteenth-century poem written by an Indian poet describing his perfect woman.

"Her throat should be thick and round, her shoulders soft and wide, her breasts full and the shape of young coconuts. Her waist slender enough to be clasped within ten fingers, her hips rounded, her limbs willowy, the soles of her feet without arch, and the surface of her skin delicate and smooth and seemingly without bones, sinews or angles."

"Definitely not me, but what a pity you weren't around in the eighteenth century," said Sally.

It was in the second temple, the Temple Tejpal, dedicated to the twenty-second tirthankar, and while we were comparing the more modern gopis to the more sensual older Vimal Vasahi ones, that we met our own gopi, a handsome French male called Paul, who asked us to join him for saffron lassis later on.

That evening as the three of us sat overlooking Nakki Lake, the same lemming-like rush to watch the sun set took place. Paul said it happened every day of the year. He was charming. We were charmed. He was funny. We were amused. He was interesting. We were interested. He was "fatigue" from walking around temples so he went back to his hotel. Sally was annoyed.

Back at our hotel, I searched the *Kama Sutra* for something to do with gopis or fatigue from walking around temples but found the chapter entitled "displays of passion" instead.

"What does it say?" demanded Sally, grabbing her pillow as if it were Paul and if she was about to strangle him.

"It's quite explicit," I warned her, not liking the pillow's chances of survival.

"We're adults," she snarled.

So I read. "Making love can be compared to a quarrel. The places of striking with passion are the shoulders, head, between the breasts and back. As this causes pain (I should imagine so!), striking gives rise to the eight kinds of crying, and eight kinds of kissing of forgiveness."

"Oh heaven spare me!" The pillow went flying across the room. Poor Paul.

"When a woman sees that her lover is fatigued (from too much temple walking, for instance), she should, with his permission, suggest more adventurous positions. She may also do this to satisfy her own curiosity. There are three pictures if you are curious."

"Show me."

I handed her the book.

"I don't believe it!" she exclaimed. "It's impossible!" She closed the book with a snap. "Where is the romance in that?"

"The *Kama Sutra* is full of romance," I argued.

"No it isn't. It's full of positions," she yelled. "And I don't believe he was tired from walking around temples either. I think he had someone else."

The next day we caught the bus to Udaipur.

The ride down Mount Abu was as scary as the ride up, only this time our driver became a speed freak with ambitions of entering the French Grand Prix. Down we hurtled, past devotees with worn faces and cracked hands, down past colonies of grey monkeys with fists full of nuts. But we were going too fast. Pitter-patter went the nuts on the road behind us. Sucker monkeys! You'll have to throw faster!

Halfway down, our driver skidded to a stop to pick up four men who, after climbing aboard, discovered that they had left their bus tickets behind. They begged the driver to wait while they ran back. The driver agreed. I'm sure he felt that he could make up the lost time by not using his brakes until we reached the bottom.

A Brahman family got on the bus. This family consisted of two elderly grandparents, two fat aunts, two very fat little boys in English sailor suits, a wife with a distant expression wearing a beautiful blue sari, and a handsome husband in a tight cream Nehru suit. The first thing the husband did was demand that the lower-caste passengers vacate the eight front seats so his family could sit there. Fortunately we were sitting up the back, as we would not have moved. Next he complained that the bus's tires didn't have enough air in them; that the jarring would upset his aunts; then he informed the driver that the men we were waiting for were liars, thieves and swindlers, and he insisted that their luggage be left on the road and for the bus to depart immediately.

Nobody else said a thing and before Sally and I could interject that the family would not have been able to catch the bus if it hadn't been waiting for the men, and before we could argue on the unfairness of leaving the men behind, the driver removed the men's bags and we were off, skidding around every curve on our half-flat tires at a pace guaranteed to make everyone bus sick. The four men caught up with us at the bottom of the mountain. When they got on the bus, waving their tickets, everyone, except the Brahman family, cheered. The men told the driver how they'd found the tickets in their wastepaper basket and had caught a taxi back to the bus only to find it gone and their luggage abandoned. Someone whispered that the Brahman was to blame. This infuriated the leader of the four, who said loudly in English that some people were too full of themselves and that they needed to be brought down a peg or two. The rest of the bus nodded. This mini-revolution had our full support.

From then on, at each chai stop, the alighting passengers divided into the Brahmans and the rest of us. I was also interested to see that it was the Brahman grandfather who took the two fat boys to the side of the road, unzipped them, held them, aimed them, shook them, and then zipped them up again. At what age would they be allowed to unzip and hold themselves? Twenty-one seemed a reasonable guess.

Our next drama was a punctured tire. The bus lurched to a lopsided stop and everyone but the fat aunties got out while the driver changed the tire on their side with a shaky jack.

Our third drama, and by this time we were expecting them, took place in the middle of a market in the center of a village. A puffball-truck coming around an elbow bend had met a local bus going in the other direction. The bus driver would not back up as he was of a higher caste than the truck driver, and the truck driver couldn't move unless the bus moved because his truck was jammed. Our driver, who was of a lower caste than either bus or truck driver, turned off his engine and fell asleep. Everyone waited. The truck driver read the newspaper. The men on top of his enormous load dozed off. The bus driver drank chai while his passengers, including us, got off the bus to buy soft drinks. We all waited. No one became angry. No one was stressed. No one did anything while a hot sticky hour ticked by. I believe we would be there yet if the Brahman husband hadn't taken charge. Over to the low-caste puffball-truck driver and the medium low-caste bus driver he marched in his buttoned-to-the-neck suit and his white joolis, and with a few sharp words, he had the bus edging backwards and the truck edging forwards.

"So why didn't they do that before?" I asked our driver.

"They couldn't," he explained. "It is only because he is of a higher caste that they both save face from moving first."

"So why didn't he tell them to do it earlier?"

"He had to let them have their moment of power before he exerted his, otherwise they would have been resentful."

And this is a country that has entered the computer world with such an enormous bang that European countries are begging to set up call centers all over the place. This is the country that has invented an English dictionary that covers all slang and verbal idiosyncrasies of at least ten English-speaking countries. Amazing!

Our bus started up and the hero of the hour swung on board to the compliments and gratitude of his family and everyone else.

Five hours later, we drove through Hathipol Gate and into the walled city of Udaipur.

# Chapter 16

## UDAİPUR, CRYSTAL CİTY OF MORNİNG

Beautiful, golden Udaipur where the Maharana of Udaipur, who is a direct descendent of the Sun God, resides in his white marble palace in the center of Lake Pichola. A maharana is more distinguished than a maharajah, and this maharana is the last reigning monarch in India so that makes him extra special.

The state of Udaipur covers 33,450 square kilometers. Maharana Udai Singh II founded it in the sixteenth century after Ali Akbar rode his elephant all the way from Fatehpur Sikri to burn down the then-existing Hindu capital. This elephant ride was no mean feat considering the distance we had traveled by bus. I wonder what the elephants ate?

Udaipur is built on a range of hills skirting the edge of a lake. Every street, lane or alley running across the hills is so narrow that only a rickshaw can squash through, while those running from top to bottom are as steep as ski slopes and equally slippery. Along the top of the ridge balances Lake Palace Road, Udaipur's main street, so narrow that it was built for elephant-traffic only, which is why the bus station is nowhere near it.

Our guesthouse was up over the ridge and down a lane so narrow our rickshaw pedaller dumped us off at the nearest corner. The guesthouse was also narrow. Four stories of two rooms per floor, with views over a lake that contained the Maharana of Udaipur's two island palaces, hundreds of guesthouses, hotels and roof-top cafes. All constructed cheek by jowl, with windows facing windows, balconies bumping balconies, walls against walls, all sharing the same spaghetti lines of electricity. Blind Freddy could see that there were no building permits or zoning rules applied in Udaipur. Only the intense desire to build more accommodation for a growing tourist trade.

Our hotel receptionist informed us that every night one of the guesthouses below showed the James Bond 007 film *Octopussy*, which was filmed in Udaipur when Sean Connery still had hair. He could book us a table to see the film if we liked. We said we liked.

Dumping our bags, we took off to explore this enchanting fairy-tale city before it got too dark. Along the narrow lane we walked, past a row of whitewashed houses decorated with paintings of horsemen being charged by men on war-elephants, and men on camels charging the men on horses, past a silk shop full of rainbow colors and an owner who beckoned us in with a look that said he knew he would snare us in the end. Why? Because God was in his heaven, that's why.

Hindu temples are best visited in the evening when the worshippers bring their leis of tangy marigolds and their handfuls of spicy jasmine and place these offerings around the necks of their gods to thank them for a good day. As we'd had a good day we bought marigolds from a preschool boy and climbed the steep steps. Up we went between columns painted with portraits of well-dressed Rajasthani men, around four beggars curled up under sun-faded umbrellas, between life-sized marble elephants with trunks curled up for luck, and through a yellow-framed gateway covered in red and blue writing. Inside, all was silent.

Jagdish Temple was built a hundred years after Udaipur was founded and a hundred years before Captain Cook discovered Australia, or Napoleon was born, or America's Boston Tea Party took place. Inside its main doorway stands a brass *garuda*, the half-bird half-beast that Vishnu flies around on. We tiptoed past its cruel curved beak to where three women were laying flowers in front of Jagannath, Lord of the Universe, and one of Vishnu's twenty-two incarnations. Placing flowers before one's god must be one of the most relaxing and joyful things to do.

After we'd placed our marigolds in front of Jagannath, we returned to Lake Palace Road to find it blocked by an elephant with hips only its mother could love, jammed between two stone-latticed balconies. Urged on by its owner, it was pushing with all its might. The balconies shuddered and the latticework shook, then, as if either the balconies or the elephant had magically shrunk, the elephant popped through, brushing white plaster from the balconies and taking most of the washing from one.

"Poor elephant," sympathized Sally. "Its pads must be wrecked from the cobblestones and all the garbage it has to step on. I hope there aren't any broken bottles in Udaipur."

I hoped so too. Bandaging an elephant's foot would be difficult. Not to mention finding an elephant vet. But then I expect all elephant mahouts are vets in India. We followed the elephant as it swayed down a street so steep that the animal had to bend its back legs to stop from sliding while its mahout had to dodge electric light wires, television aerials and washing lines to stop from being strangled or decapitated. Behind us came a string of salivating camels bouncing along on splayed pads, carrying sheaves of fresh coriander down to the lake to be washed.

At the bottom of the road, through a huge gateway, we saw the city's elephant stables. Inside were bales of straw, great globs of manure, and big, middle-sized and small elephants being tended to by women stable-hands with diamonds in their noses and hessian bags tied over their saris. The women were feeding green branches to the elephants. How far did those branches travel? We had seen no trees on our way to Udaipur.

Beside the elephant stables was the local *dhobi* or laundry ghat where the town's women bathed. Washing oneself and one's clothes at the same time certainly alleviates the drudgery of trying to get clothes white in a lake the color of mint tea.

We left the stables and followed the signs to a German bakery. There were quite a few of these in Udaipur, mostly owned by Indians who had gone to Germany to work and had returned with a new trade. On the way I saw a poster for Shri Mataji.

"Look at that," I called to Sally. "I've missed Shri Mataji yet again."

In an instant a curtain across a doorway was pulled aside and a slim brown-skinned woman asked, "Are you a Sahaj yogi?"

I shook my head. "But I've heard Shri Mataji speak and I would love to hear her speak again."

The curtain was pulled wider. "Then we would have performed *puja* [our prayers] together. Please come inside and have tea."

So we took off our sandals and stepped inside her neat, sparsely furnished home. Proudly she showed us the room for cooking, eating and resting in, and the room for sleeping in. This second room contained mattresses laid out on a spotlessly swept floor and all the family's clothes hung neatly from nails in the walls. There was no toilet. That was done while washing in the lake. No water taps. Drinking water was fetched from a well every day. Which made the gift of tea special.

Ouna, our hostess, fetched two chairs from her neighbor, then sent her daughter to find her husband while we played with her one-year-old son. Above the doorway hung a photograph of a fierce-looking Shri Mataji. Ouna's husband arrived almost immediately. Slight as a feather with the same innocent black currant eyes as his baby son, he shook our hands and wished us good fortune. Then picking up his son, he nuzzled the baby's neck, before adding, "How wonderful that you have seen and heard Shri Mataji speak. She is our mother, you know."

"She doesn't come to Australia very often," I said.

"She is advanced in age," said Ouna as she blew on the coal fire to heat the water for our tea.

Within minutes, sweet, milky chai appeared. We drank it from cups with broken handles while admiring the daughter's drawings that were labelled in English. Ouna's husband, whose name we never got and were too embarrassed to ask again, explain that he only worked when the rickshaw owner wasn't working; that he must earn the rickshaw's rent before he could earn money to live; and that as it was the end of the tourist season they would live on his wife's money (she painted hands with henna), while they waited for the cool weather and the return of the tourists.

"How much does a new auto-rickshaw cost?" I asked.

He told me a sum of around $1000. Then he went on to explain that to save this amount was impossible with two children.

"Will you have any more?" asked Sally, whose answer to India's poverty was for the women to have no children. (So who looks after the old when they get old?)

"Shri Mataji says it is better to educate two than to enslave six in a lifetime of poverty. So I am having a vasectomy."

"He is a very modern-thinking husband," concluded Ouna, proudly. I should say so.

Over our second cup of tea, they questioned us about our homes.

Refraining from mentioning the size of my modest house which would have sounded like a palace to Ouna, I spoke about my inner-city garden. Ouna sighed and said she would love a garden, but only the wealthy had gardens in Udaipur, as it was the City of Light, which meant that all the land belonged to the Maharana of Udaipur, otherwise known as the Light of the Hindus. Before we left, we booked Ouna to henna my hands and her husband to take us to the Monsoon Palace the following day.

By the time we were ready for our big night out at the Octopussy restaurant it was pitch black outside. Udaipur's alleyways were unlit so we felt our way to the restaurant with the help of lighted windows. *Octopussy* was being shown on the restaurant's back balcony, but the video was in such bad condition we decided to forgo Sean Connery with hair, and eat where we could see the lake. The restaurant was packed with Indian tourists which should have meant good food. It didn't. So far no food could compete with that of Mr. Laxshmi's second Jhunjhunu hotel.

On returning to our guesthouse, we discovered that the hotel staff slept, head to toe like sardines, on mattresses beneath our window. Apparently it doesn't rain during tourist season so sleeping outside was fine. But as they understood English we refrained from reading the *Kama Sutra* out loud and instead we looked at the pictures.

Next morning we breakfasted overlooking an island palace that glittered and sparkled due to one of the maharanas having had each cupola tipped with a diamond-cut globe of Baccarat crystal. In fact this particular maharana was so enchanted with crystal (being tired of gold and rubies) that he'd had entire rooms furnished with crystal furniture.

To reach the island palaces we had to catch a boat from a jetty off the Bansi Ghat. To reach the Bansi Ghat we had to pass through a military checkpoint into the Shiv Niwas Palace Hotel gardens. This necessitated a certain amount of flirting, because just as western builders are obliged to whistle at a girl walking down the street, so Indian military are obliged to flirt with all females, bless their little khaki cotton socks. There isn't enough flirting in the world, especially in Australia, although India and Jamaica probably make up for all the non-flirting countries.

Flirting over, we walked through a garden of shaved lawns and orange hibiscus, down a staircase with a marble balustrade already too hot to touch, to a canopied flat-bottomed boat with a captain who resembled Sinbad the Sailor. We stared across a four-kilometer long lake searching for telltale crocodile snouts although Sinbad assured us that the crocodiles were asleep under the water hyacinth. I asked him, how had the crocodiles reached Udaipur? Were they descendants from a prehistoric time when the hills were covered in steamy tropical marshland? Were they brought here as a deterrent to enemies wishing to attack these "flights of fancy" palaces? Or did the film crew of *Octopussy* leave them behind when the film was finished? What happened to them when the lake dried up, which it has done a few times in living memory? Did hungry crocs wander the streets of Udaipur looking for unsuspecting tourists? He stared at me fascinated. Obviously I had offered him too many explanations.

As his boat sailed over Udaipur's opal-white reflection, he pointed to the fishing boats ahead of us and told us that as the fish were sacred, only those working for the royal family were allowed to fish in Lake Pichola.

"Sacred to whom?" I asked.

"The maharana's French chefs?" answered Sally.

Our Captain Sinbad giggled.

Behind Shiv Niwas Palace, the city walls climbed over beige-colored hills that disappeared into a distant purple haze. In these hills, announced Sinbad, were Jain temples, hill stations, isolated forests, wolves, blackbuck deer, monkeys and lions. But he assured us, there hadn't been a lion sighted for years.

"All shot up," he said, showing not a tiny bit of remorse for these extinct Asian cats. "They used to keep them as pets in Jagmandir Palace. Each little prince had his own lion cub, his own peacock and his own elephant. But now, all shot up."

"Puts owning a dog into perspective," said Sally, as we putted around a small headland, and there it was, the Palace of Jagmandir. *Jag-man-dir*, the word rolled off my tongue. There it was rising out of the water with its eight life-sized marble elephants balanced on columns guarding its waterlogged entrance.

"Maybe lions and tigers still there," whispered Sinbad in his "scare the tourist" voice. Then as we bumped against a submerged flight of marble steps, four kingfishers flashed past us, like black-and-white darts. A second of hovering with blurred wings, then they dived with dive-bomber precision to capture the long-legged insects skating across the waterweeds. Snap went the kingfisher's beaks. Buzz went the captured insects. Gulp went the kingfishers. Then up they flew to hover and swoop again in a frenzy of gourmet dining.

Sally photographed the kingfishers. I photographed the stone elephants, and then we climbed out of the boat and entered the empty, forgotten Palace of Jagmandir. Begun in 1628 by Maharana Karan Singh and finished by Jagat Singh I, it is written that while hiding here from his vengeful father (the one who'd blinded his eldest son), Shah Jahan was so inspired by the palace's fragile beauty that when he built the Taj Mahal he copied it, but I could see no resemblance between Mumtaz Mahal's austere tomb and this pretty folly.

Our visit was too brief as we were only allowed to stroll a short way into the overgrown gardens, which meant we didn't see the famous frescoes now damp and peeling. Back on board Sinbad turned his prow towards the second island and the more favored Jagniwas Palace. This beautiful scalloped-walled palace (built 127 years after Jagmandir Palace) became the Lake Palace Hotel in 1974 in an attempt to support the then maharana in the manner to which he wished to remain accustomed.

The House of Udaipur's lack of fortune is attributed to the Udaipur Mewar dynasty (the longest on earth due to its uninterrupted line of seventy-five monarchs), refusing to taint their bloodline by breeding with the marauding Moguls. In other words, they could boast of being pure Hindu but they had no ready Mogul cash to splash around. So what did they do? They turned a palace into a hotel.

Lying across the water like an indolent white cat, Jagniwas is the ultimate experience with its hundreds of frescoed walls, three-sided bay windows, famous Light of the Moon ballroom, lotus ponds for the trailing of one's De Beers diamond-ringed fingers in, and crystal-clear swimming pools surrounded by mango orchards crowded with green parrots dining on plump, erotic fruit. Non-guests can visit for lunch if the hotel is not full. But only if they are wearing Gucci or Armani, *and* only if they are prepared to spend squillions of U.S. dollars.

Still entranced by the two palaces, we spent the rest of the day wandering around the city's narrow streets having an impromptu back and head massage in someone's front room (fully dressed this time), by a tall woman that Sally swore was a man in a sari, while three Indian women had their hair washed in enamel basins by three even taller women wearing saris who did look like men. Then off I went to have my hands hennaed while Sally went shopping.

I once had my feet and ankles hennaed in Zanzibar. It was a laborious business with the painter squeezing orange mud out of a goat teat sack. Her design of swirls, twirls and fishing spears took three hours to do and three hours to dry. The Indian way is faster. Ouna painted the henna on with a brush and it dried instantly. The pattern was mango-shaped which she said indicated sensuality. While she painted, we talked about children, health, education, women's stuff and husbands. It was very relaxing.

Sally arrived at five, Ouna's husband soon after, and off we went to see the sun setting behind the Monsoon Palace. Or as it was called in its heyday, the luscious Shivniwas Palace. Which makes four palaces within an hour of each other. Built as a monsoon retreat, the nineteenth-century Shivniwas Palace was once considered modern. Occupied only once a year, it took the court of Maharana Sajjan Singh a week to transfer by elephant all his wives and children and those necessities important to his exalted lifestyle.

As we approached the austere fortress it was hard to believe that this neglected vultures' nest had once hosted the Queen of England, Jacqueline Kennedy, Henry Kissinger and the Shah of Iran. Most likely all at once, as the mighty do like to mingle with the mighty. Now it is a forgotten ruin with a bolted gate the height and width of an elephant carrying a load of furniture. Prompted by Ouna's husband, we offered the gatekeepers a tip and the gates were opened for us to slip through.

There were other tourists inside (those gatekeepers make a packet), but we walked the parapets alone, admiring the view of chiffon-grey hills against an oyster-pink sky, while brown and cream kites wheeled in slow motion around a Rapunzel-style tower.

"Rapunzel, Rapunzel, let down your hair," I shouted.

Two Japanese on the second floor of the crumbling tower waved at us. They were posing for a "pretty" photograph against the background of a sunset, swallows and swifts. We waved back, then leaned over the wall and spied two young Europeans camping on a rock with their sleeping bags laid out towards the sunset. The girl looked up to us, and then magically, she called up, "Rapunzel, Rapunzel, let down your hair."

Great minds think alike.

The sun on its way to Persia slid behind the black tulle-covered hills and a velvet night engulfed the couple below. Feeling completely alone, which of course we weren't (no one is in India), we sat on the wall with the fairy lights of Udaipur reflecting in Lake Pichola and imagined a chain of heavily laden elephants plodding towards us. Behind them, revving impatiently came the maharani's Chevrolet; its purdah curtains closed against the prying eyes of lower-caste lantern carriers. Or decades later, after the unpacking has been done by one thousand servants, the speedier arrival of the widowed maharani's Cadillac with its deerskin upholstery and lace-curtained windows hiding her and her guest, the American president's wife.

On the way back to our hotel, we saw a white-haired, white-bearded holy man sitting beneath a boab tree surrounded by five circles of flickering candles.

"How does he live?" I asked Ouna's husband.

"Some of them live on air."

Which I know is not possible but the holy man was not skinny. Not as skinny as Ouna's husband.

Outside our hotel, we said good-bye and tipped him generously. He had no sooner disappeared than we were lassoed by an enchanter of color, a purveyor of dreams—the silk scarf salesman who knew he would catch us in the end. Winding a gorgeous emerald-green scarf around Sally's neck, he led her into his shop. Leaving our shoes outside, we sat on a white sheet while he unfolded scarf after scarf, each one more brilliant than the last. Yes, we would buy one, our admiring eyes told him as he calculated what to charge us, or maybe two if he kept unfolding. Soon the floor and our knees were covered in rivers of color. To prove that it was pure silk, he offered to burn a little of it. "Silk burns, synthetic silk melts," he told us. With visions of his shop going up in rainbow flames, we assured him that we believed him.

I couldn't decide between a deep blue with flecks of gold or a malachite green.

Sally, covered in scarves, and trying on more, wanted them all because, "They're so cheap."

Oh Krishna, Lord of the Universe, oh Lady Lakshmi, goddess of good fortune and opportunity, prayed the salesman silently. Send me one like this every day.

Then, as if we needed any more persuading, he danced for us. Whirling the scarves in the air around his head, he twisted and turned in slow motion as his feet stamped out a rhythm and his body swayed to the silent music of the seven veils. We were entranced. I bought two and Sally bought four. Exhausted, we collapsed onto our beds still wearing them around our necks.

"Want to read the *Kama Sutra* before the waiters settle down to sleep?" I asked Sally. "There might be something in it about scarves being seductive."

Sally nodded as best she could without strangling herself.

So I flicked through the book and found something about shampooers and masseurs instead.

"Eunuchs normally lead the life of shampooers. Under the pretense of shampooing, a eunuch may draw towards himself the thighs of the customer whom he is shampooing. If he finds that the customer is interested the eunuch scolds the customer for being forward. Then, if after knowing the eunuch's intention, the customer does not tell the eunuch to stop, the eunuch proceeds."

"To do what? And what has this got to do with scarves?"

"Let me finish! If the eunuch is ordered to proceed, the eunuch must dispute coyly, scold gently and only do so after pretending that he is most reluctant. I guess this lets him off the hook if, halfway through, the client decides he isn't interested or he's being interfered with."

"What if the customer is offended?" demanded Sally. "What if the customer punches the eunuch on the nose?"

"Then the customer shouldn't go to a eunuch shampooer in the first place. Or, as it says here, if the eunuch is enamored by his customer he can tie his customer's hands with a scarf to stop the customer from beating him."

"You made that up!"

"Only because Vatsyayana forgot to put it in."

The next morning we went to see the la crème de la crème of Udaipur. The Palace museum, Shiv Niwas Palace Hotel and Udaipur Palace. Three amazing buildings joined together are equal in size to Saint Petersburg's Hermitage Museum. We entered through the Baripol Gate, which overlooks the elephant fighting pits, deep grey-stoned pits without doors. So how do they get the elephants into them? Then we walked through Tripolia Gate, where once the maharana was weighed in gold or silver and whatever he weighed was distributed among his subjects. As the maharanas of Udaipur were a notably slender bunch I bet his subjects wished that tubby Madho Singh II had ruled them.

We spent hours climbing up towers and turrets, gazing into lacy-walled kiosks, gasping at the Sun God dynasty court with its lapis lazuli mosaic peacocks, photographing the Moti Mahal with wall-to-wall mirror-work, and exclaiming over the Ruby Mahal with its inlaid red-and-white chevrons of glass. Hot and tired and completely befuddled with so many works of art, we arrived at a terrace garden planted six floors above the ground.

It was here beneath the cool trees and beside the burbling fountain that the maharana had come to relax and chuckle over the disapproval his refusal to walk backwards away from the King of England's throne had produced at court. Or to remember the gasps of shock when he'd placed the highest honor the King of England could give, the Grand Commander of the Star of India, around the neck of his favorite Arab steed. He might have sat on the same marble bench we were sitting on rehearsing his refusal to sign away his monarchy while Lord Mountbatten the British Viceroy waited downstairs. How he must have prayed for a mouthful of honeyed lies to use against these persistent, mosquito-like British; these tea and cotton farming conquerors; these greedy, pink-skinned unbelievers who refused to budge, leaving him at a loss as how to rid his kingdom of them.

Quitting the terrace, we stepped into the Zenana Mahal with its walls full of paintings done by bored and lonely princesses and concubines, although they did move palaces three times a year, and the favorites could go out on the lake in purdah-curtained boats rowed by women guards. They could also watch romantic plays and listened to romantic love poems through fretted purdah walls, and they could play games together or with their children (one concubine was married at nine, had a child at eleven, and gave birth to sixteen more, so she had plenty to play with). So if one remembers that the culture of India is one of seductive titillating anticipation (and what woman would say no to that?), rather than one of ultimate pleasure, the Zenana Mahal wasn't such a bad place to live. They were well fed, beautifully clothed, and expensively cosseted. Millions of today's women would give anything to be so well treated.

Next we saw the Krishna Vilas rooms with their hundreds of miniatures inspired by the frivolous love affairs of the god Krishna. Here we approached an amazingly handsome Krishna look-alike wearing the traditionally low-slung cummerbund over his white uniform, and asked him why Krishna was always painted blue and why was he always painted chasing milkmaids (gopis), or stealing their clothes while they were swimming.

"Lord Krishna's skin is blue, Madams," answered our Indian Adonis. "And he chases milkmaids because his one true love is Radha, who, alas, is a virtuous married woman. As their love cannot be consummated, and as the milkmaids were well rounded from drinking so much milk, Lord Krishna could not help himself. He was forced to play the flirting game."

"I can understand that," I said.

"I too, Madam," said the guard.

We left the palace with hearts a-flutter and decided that

to recover we absolutely had to have afternoon tea at the Shiv Niwas Palace Hotel.

On our arrival, we were told that the entrance to the smaller Fateh Prakash Palace with its rare collection of table crystal, crystal chairs, crystal tables and crystal beds was through the Durbar Hall. That we could use the blue marble swimming pool for the small price of $12 per person, and that a bagpipe band would be playing in a few minutes if we wished to swim to music. Durbar Hall, with its imposing Belgian chandeliers and its portraits of former Mewar rulers, was set for 300 dinner guests. Further on, afternoon tea was laid out on a billowing curtained verandah overlooking the lake.

What a motley crew we afternoon-tea people were. Sally and I wearing trousers and shirts that could only be described as *Vogue* travel-weary beige. To our right, sat six English teenagers in crumpled school uniforms with a teacher who looked even more crumpled. To our left, sat a tizzy sixty-year-old blonde wearing a tight white punjabi outfit undone in the front far lower than any modest Indian woman would deem proper. Opposite her sat a woman with a face so deeply lined that it resembled a clown's mask. She wore a black punjabi outfit, a very unfashionable color in India, although immensely popular in the eastern suburbs of Sydney.

As we sat there spying on our fellow afternoon-tea takers, we overheard the woman in black, who sounded American, tell the waiter that she had seen a leopard in the hotel garden that very morning.

The waiter nodded, as if leopards in the palace garden were a common occurrence, "Madam need not fear, that leopard is a known dog eater and not a man eater."

"Did you hear that?" hissed Sally. "They feed dogs to their leopard."

"That wasn't what he said," I argued.

"Will Madams be having afternoon tea?" asked a second waiter who'd crept up on us.

Afternoon tea, which cost a mere 300 rupees, was wonderful, especially after a diet of curry. Cucumber sandwiches, scones with jam and cream, a platter of cakes each and a pot of the most wonderful Indian tea (freshly made not stewed, or should that be shaken not stirred as we were in 007 country?). Sitting at a petal-shaped window with the curtains swelling softly and the sound of bagpipes serenading us from below, I could have stayed there forever (I'm very fond of bagpipes). I could have been the English-born Maharani of Udaipur. Although after the maharana's death she returned to Gloucestershire so maybe I should be the Indian Maharani of Udaipur instead. But then hers was such a lonely life after her husband married his English love.

It was odd to think of these two maharanis residing in the same palace, sitting on identical rose-satin chaise longues, drinking from identical Belgian crystal, yet (through choice) never meeting. Although, perhaps not so odd. All they had in common was the maharana. I wonder if their children had met? Although I'm not sure the English wife had any children.

All the Udaipur royal children were brought up by English nannies who fed them rice pudding and custard and refused to allow them to eat Indian food until they reached puberty. But surely the childrens' indulgent Indian servants must have slipped them tidbits of spiced mutton and tangy Indian sweets. No one can live on rice pudding and custard for eleven years. Not unless they want their ears to stick out. For it is well known that rice pudding and custard has that effect on royalty.

The guidebook also said that when Maharana Baghwat Singh died, there raged a bitter legal dispute. In a fit of anger, Baghwat Singh had disinherited both his sons and the courts couldn't decide if Mohendra the elder, a devout religious scholar, or Arvid the younger, a successful businessman, should rule Udaipur. Maybe this is when the English maharani returned to England. Being a traditionalist, the Indian maharani wanted her older son to rule. Being a realist, her daughter preferred her younger brother to rule, as it was he who kept the family in spending money. Finally, the courts allotted Mohendra the title of Light of the Hindus but left the running of the Mewar inheritance to Arvid. A wise choice, I thought. Mohendra, a bad loser, never spoke to his brother again.

# Chapter 17

## VARANASI, LIFE AND DEATH

We left Udaipur for Delhi in the overnight train. When we arrived at our sleeping compartment, we found four Indians rolled up on their bunks with their dhotis or saris over their heads. We did the same and were soon asleep with our heads on our bags. But not for long. Every hour, almost on the hour, the train braked at a station. Jaundiced-yellow lights went on; raucous fruit sellers knocked on the train's outer walls; water carriers, pushing carts with large earthenware jars, stuck their brass ladles through our unshutable windows; sweet-meats sellers, with trolleys piled high with toffee twists, sugar-coated pastries, syrup-covered dough balls and insect-infested coconut icing, set up business outside our compartment. The Indians slept through it all. We gave up.

We arrived in Delhi at 5 a.m. and went straight to the Hotel White Empire, which is a block from the station, to shower and sleep. We slept all day.

Next morning we arrived at Delhi station at the crack of dawn in time to watch the cows wandering along the platform; to stare at the waiting families sitting on the dirt-encrusted platform eating from their tiffin tins (lunch boxes); and to join the groups of men clustering around the chai seller. Nothing prepares me better for a long train journey than a cup of chai. Indian women do not go to the chai seller, so from whom do they get their tea?

Once again no one understood our tickets and the seats we thought were ours were taken by soldiers who sent us back-wards and forwards, until a toilet cleaner in a fancy, faded red felt jacket resembling a brass band uniform, led us to our seats miraculously upwind from the toilets, which although clean were highly urine smelling.

Opposite us sat two adult uncles (the size of thirteen-year-olds) who were taking their two seven-year-old nephews (the size of three-year-olds) to their grandparents in Lucknow because their mother had died. The anxious father was outside the window saying good-bye to the tearful boys. He pressed a ten-rupee note into each of their hands before hurrying away. During the trip the uncles bought food for the boys but not for themselves, so we shared our sandwiches with them.

Next to the uncles sat a jolly telephone engineer who informed everyone in English that he was going home to visit his wife and that life without a wife was no life at all. The uncles agreed but said that they hadn't been fortunate enough to acquire wives yet.

Beside Sally sat a fat businessman with a briefcase and a suitcase chained to each wrist. He complained that there was no place to put his luggage but when we offered him the space under our seats, he declined. Then a poorly dressed Indian sitting beside me offered to remove his bags and put them under our seats so that Fatty could put his suitcase under his own seat. But we declined. If Fatty didn't trust us to sit above his suitcase then he could sit with it on his head for all we cared.

Time disappeared with me reading, Sally dozing, and a constant procession of hawkers hawking. First came the chai man with his bucket of sweet-smelling chai, then the French toast man with toast made at least a week ago, then the chewing tobacco man with his packets of betel nut, lime and leaf, followed by the salty-smelling potato-patty man, the candy man with little bags of crumbling musk, the salad man with a bucket of the most unappetizing salad I'd ever seen, the soft drink man with his bottles of highly colored fizz in a bucket of dirt-speckled ice, and finally a woman with brightly painted toys and drum. Then it started again with the chai man.

More people squashed into our compartment. Benches meant to hold five held eight and nine with children on their knees. The four bunks above were stacked with luggage and men who'd climbed up from the corridor to sleep on top of the bags. A trip to the toilet took half an hour and meant clambering over people, dodging airborne legs and outspread tiffin tins.

One of the funniest moments of the journey was when two transvestite beggars, whose ploy was to find a middle-class passenger and embarrass him until he paid up, came into our car. Our entire compartment burst into laughter when the older transvestite, with smudged make-up, five o'clock shadow and work-stained hands, threatened to sit on Fatty's knee. It was only when he began stroking Fatty's face and tickling his double chin that Fatty handed over some coins. A minute later the ticket inspector hurled himself into view and the transvestites disappeared out of the open train door with the train going at full speed.

"Want to know about real women in India?" I asked Sally, aware that Fatty and the entire compartment were listening.

"May as well."

"There are over 4000 million women in India. Three-quarters are illiterate and don't know the map of India due to never having traveled farther than twenty-five miles from their place of birth. Legally they cannot own or inherit property. They receive half the wage a man does for the same work. And should they give birth to a girl, and should this girl be allowed to live, she will get less food and schooling than her brothers, plus she must be married off by age twelve."

Sally glanced accusingly at Fatty.

"One of the reasons for female baby infanticide is that there are not enough boys of the right caste born to marry them. Also if they are of high caste a large marriage dowry must be produced, so it is better to put them to sleep permanently with an opium pill or opium rubbed on the mother's nipples, than lumber the family with an unmarried daughter in twelve years' time."

Sally glared at Fatty again.

"When a woman becomes a widow, her black-beaded marriage necklace is cut and her head is shaved by her female in-laws as punishment for not protecting her husband from death. Then if her family won't take her back, which normally they won't, she goes to Varanasi, navel of the world, mother of all cities, city of light, where she dies or begs until she dies."

We arrived at Varanasi at peak hour. Being midway between the eastern coast and the western border, the Varanasi station is a changing point for all trains and buses going to and coming from all over India. We had been warned by the uncles that Varanasi rickshaw drivers were famous for saying the hotel you asked for was burned down, then they take you to a hotel that paid them to, so we were surprised when an ancient sage pedalled up and said he knew our hotel. Perhaps ours was the hotel he always took tourists to.

Our ancient pedaller turned out to love Varanasi with a passion. "It is the most holiest city in the world, Madams. This is because it lies between the Varuna and the Assi rivers, both originating in the beginning of time from the body of the primordial person."

"Which primordial person?" asked Sally.

But our sage was on a roll. "Varanasi has been a place of learning for over 2000 years, Madams. There were Buddhist temples and *stupas* [funerary monuments] here four centuries before Christ."

"Yes, but who is ..." asked Sally.

"Varanasi is one of the oldest living cities on the earth."

"Who ..."

"It is the only place on earth for a Hindu to die because it is so holy that dying here ends the circle of rebirth."

Sally gave up on the primordial person. As for me, it was all too deep after a thirteen-hour train journey. But we soon found out that deep is very Varanasi.

The Temple of the Ganges Hotel is situated in the south of the city inside a walled kampong built on the riverbank. The owner greeted us with bowed head and hands pressed together. He was dressed in yellow with one red vertical stripe and two yellow horizontal stripes painted on his forehead. These are the signs of a holy man, which does not stop the wearer from making a profit from his six-room hotel, his silk shop or his travel agency.

Over chai he told us that he'd once been a schoolteacher earning fifty-five rupees a month. In desperation he'd begged Shiva to help him earn more and Shiva had answered him by giving him a business opportunity. He became a salesman of tourist items. This allowed him to become rich enough to send two of his sons to a holy ashram in Rishikesh, thanks be to

Shiva, and for him to become a guru. Would we like to be his disciples?

Just then, the electricity went off and all the fans ground to a clunking halt which sent our holy man into a flurry of annoyance. It was everyone's fault. The government's, his servants', ours, our arrival must be inauspicious, even the poor were to blame; they took too much electricity for themselves and didn't leave enough for his hotel.

"The poor are the lucky ones. They don't have to worry about all this." He waved his arms around, indicating his hotel. "All they have to do is eat and sleep all day. Shiva has blessed them," he ranted.

"So why don't you give everything to the poor?" I asked.

He looked shocked. "And offend Shiva?"

We found our room by touch while he rushed off to start his private electricity-making machine that the poor didn't have to worry about.

Next morning we awoke to the tinkling chimes of many bells, the sweet smell of incense, and the soft hypnotic sound of mantras being chanted above our room. I got up and looked out of our window. It was about seven o'clock and already the heat of the day was almost touchable.

Our hotel overlooked mud flats, flood-flattened grass, distant sandbanks and the Ganges, which was no more than a slick of pale ginger water. Beside it ran a dirt track leading to a distant curve of ghats and temples.

"Benares," I whispered, liking the ancient town's old British name more than Varanasi. "Famous for brass, brocades and burials."

"Let's go in to town and get breakfast," said Sally.

The first of the fortress-like ghats started a block from our hotel. Its crumbling steps tapered into thin wedges then disappeared under the river with its flotilla of plastic bottles. The next ghat had steps half-a-meter high. Up and down we went, stepping over suspicious-looking rubbish and acres of dust, sniffing in the scent of dung and decaying marigolds, just two more figures that no one noticed among the determined cows climbing the steps and disappearing into dark-mouthed alleyways; the starving dogs lying in the knife-sharp shadows; the orange-clad pilgrims asleep on the cement; and the occasional, obviously insane, swimmer striking out for the eastern bank.

The western cliff bank, once home to a jungle forest and now home to over eighty ghats, is nothing like the eastern bank which is flat and empty, but around the bend, so our guide book said, was the seventeenth-century Ram Nagar Palace belonging to the former Maharajah of Benares, famous for its elephant traps, vintage cars, antique clocks, silver palanquins and gold-plated howdahs.

"Oh no! Not another howdah!" cried Sally, while wiping cow poo off her sandals.

We reached the Assi Ghat, one of the five special ghats that pilgrims must bathe off if they are partaking in the Panchatirthi Yatra route ritual, and sat down to rest. We stared at the paint-peeling temple expecting something special to happen, nothing did. It wasn't this ghat's special day.

Farther on, a sign attached to a ghat wall advertised the Benares Aquatic Association. This was when I formed my theory of how, if or when aliens visit our planet, the first people to greet them should be Indians. As they are the most germ-tolerant race on earth, I am sure they would survive any galactic bugs the aliens brought with them.

We stopped at a coffee shop tucked into the foundations of a temple. Here, we were approached by an old man who did massage on a mattress jammed into a space neither he nor his client could stand up in but at a squeeze could have room for four chickens. He had an album of photographs and comments that he insisted we look at. Some of the comments written by women mentioned that he'd become a wee bit familiar while massaging their inner upper thighs. So we declined and had coffee instead.

The cafe was full of male American backpackers, all sporting long hair, bushy beards, "holy man" gear and dirty feet. Two went bathing in the river, which although we agreed was a very holy act, we also agreed we wouldn't do for a million dollars, but might consider for eternal youth and perpetual beauty. Our coffee was delicious, but afterwards we saw the cafe staff washing the coffee glasses in the river, and as we'd read that the Ganges is rumored to have a fecal coliform count of 250,000 times the World Health Organization's permitted maximum, we decided that the partaking of river-side coffees was not for us.

We left the Americans aglow with their conversion to Hinduism and crossed more ghat steps, many covered with marigold leis that had probably floated there from Rishikesh. We stopped to watch a white goat dancing most prettily on top of a woman's changing shed and a cluster of orange-clad sadhus and nude manure-ash-covered gurus sitting in meditation on octagonal platforms. We passed stacks of wood ready for the burning of bodies and a huge scale on which the wood was weighed according to how much the family could pay, and I wondered if the faster you burned had anything to do with the faster you reached the Western Paradise.

Finally we reached the second ghat on the Panchatirthi Yatra route. This is the famous Dasaswamedh Ghat where the god Brahma is supposed to have sacrificed ten horses. Thronging around this ghat was a huge number of people, all preparing for the festival of Kali which would begin the following day. It was so colorful and exciting Sally didn't have time to go on about the slaughter of the ten horses.

After milling, staring and milling about some more with what felt like half the population of the world, we decided to walk back to our hotel through the tiny, twisted back streets. Unfortunately the laneways and alleyways of old Benares, like the city's open sewers, loop round and return to the river and we were soon lost. So after eating our breakfast at a curd stall, and after being almost knocked down by a group of dhoti-wearing men banging cymbals while running through the narrow streets behind a litter carrying a body, we came out at an unknown crossroads ruled over by a brave white-helmeted policeman busy directing a permanent traffic jam.

The space above the policeman's head was so infested with knotted cables and low slung wires fanning out from a heavily laden central post that we no longer wondered why the electricity went off in Varanasi. One misjudged turn of a bus, one too high puffball-truck, and the electric maypole would be dragged down on top of the policeman, not to mention the hundreds of shoppers, tourists, commuters, rickshaw pedallers, motor-rickshaw drivers, cars and buses, all resembling a huge nebula that spewed out into side streets when it became too dense or when someone actually took notice of where the policeman was pointing.

The traffic jam was impossible to walk through so we hailed a rickshaw and for a minimal price this amazing man pushed through the oncoming tide like a butter knife through butter.

Back at our hotel we decided to ring the airline to confirm our departure tickets. The hotel owner's son, who ran his father's travel agency, which was through his father's silk shop, allowed us to use his phone. We gave up after an hour; phones, like the Internet, don't always work. Instead we booked a dawn boat-ride for the following morning.

On the way out of the silk shop, we saw a North American girl and her mother dithering over the choice of silk for the daughter's wedding gown. "Which silk was it you said Princess Diana had?" asked the mother.

"Kali preserve us," muttered Sally.

Next morning we were woken at five by a houseboy who led us along a dirt track to the hotel's jetty. Here, in a rowboat, waited an old man with a shaved head wearing white pajamas and a black bead necklace. Beside him sat his cloned grandson with the same shaved head, wearing a striped T-shirt and jeans. Without a word of greeting, which was unusual as Indians are the most sweetly mannered of people, the man and boy rowed us unevenly out onto a river awash with a glowing scarlet light that made the water look blood red. Downstream we drifted, leaving behind a blazing golden trail. Past Tulsi Ghat which had subsided into the river; past three Jain temples and countless seven-storied red brick fort-palaces turning cerise; past the Maharajah of Amber's ghat, which he visits all the way from Jaipur and where he means to die; until we reached Shivala Ghat which belongs to the Maharajah of Varanasi who boasts of being a direct descendant of the god Shiva, Lord of the Universe, also known by 1008 names. And wouldn't that be a memory test.

As we floated downstream, the mist lifted from the façades of the 2000 temples, revealing blank limestone walls rising up like Crusader castles, palaces of four and five levels with their plethora of fairytale windows, cupolas, towers and spires. Above this lacy roofline shimmered the Alamgir Mosque, constructed upon the foundations of an ancient Vishnu temple expressly to show Aurangzeb's lowly Hindu subjects who was boss. It hadn't worked. One mortal emperor does not amount for much in rose-colored Varanasi where the lords Krishna and Shiva, and the goddesses Durga and Kali reign supreme, and if our ancient rickshaw pedaller was to be believed, had done so since before the dawn of time.

Although it was early, the ghats were already busy with pilgrims having their first wash, swim or prayer for the day. Each glowing face showed its owner's joy at communing with a god they believed would cure their ills, cleanse their sins, keep them alive, and when their time came, would carry them straight to heaven where they would sit on a lotus throne and cease to exist.

There were businessmen, white sari-wearing widows gracefully holding their brass begging bowls aloft (not all old either, a widow can be a ten-year-old married off at the age of four), brightly sari-dressed women whose movements reminded me of beautifully executed dance steps, and gurus whose swimwear consisted of a strip of material put on by holding one end in their teeth while swinging the other end through their legs and up over their buttocks, then tying the ends around their waists. There were no flower offerings. Flowers are for evening prayers. Morning prayers have to do with light. Brilliant, luminescent light. God's gift of the day.

Everything was fascinating: the spicy smells, the soft dipping of the oars, the swimmers who swam out to grin up at us with teeth as white as Himalayan snow. Then we saw where the spicy smell was coming from. We were passing the Harishchandra Ghat. On a platform built in the center of this ghat's steps was a burning pyre. We could see the female body wrapped in orange material, its head and feet protruding from each end.

There was no family attending this cremation so even though the ghats on either side were crowded with bathers and worshippers, it was a lonely ceremony. So different from the funeral of a Tongan friend I'd attended two months ago, where, in a cemetery full of multi-colored plastic windmills circling in the wind, 200 mourners sang good-bye to their friend Shawny. Where was this woman's family? Where were her sons, daughters, husband and friends? Who would throw her ashes into the Ganges to send her on her way to oblivion?

"There is fire in every Hindu ceremony," read Sally softly from behind me. "Wood is expensive, so if the family can't afford enough to burn the entire body what is left of the corpse is thrown into the river."

We gazed down at the water searching for body parts, then over to the ghats where pilgrims were cleaning their teeth, cleaning the teeth of their babies, gargling, spitting, hawking, peeing and praying.

We drifted past a third burning ghat where only the privileged are cremated. This is because on this ghat's steps there is the footprint of Vishnu. We couldn't see the footprint but we were so close to the male body wrapped in white that we could hear the crackling of the sandalwood and the spitting of body fat. Beside the fire stood a naked man smeared in red-and-black paint holding a three-pronged fork.

"That fork is called a *thrishool* with which he picks out bits of burned flesh," read Sally. "The eating of the cremated flesh is a highly mystical and magical tantric practice."

"And stops one from dying of starvation," I added.

Well, what other comment can one make about ritual cannibalism?

"The burners of these fires and bodies are Outcasts called Doms," read Sally. "They collect the body at dawn and run with it through the city. If the corpse is a rich Brahman it will be covered in orange and white flowers and there will be a band of cymbals players and pipe players running after the litter."

"Like the lot who almost ran us down yesterday."

Sally nodded. "Once at a burning ghat, the litter is placed with the corpse's feet in the river where the cows will bring it good luck by eating the marigolds from around its neck. The body is completely submerged then placed on the pyre where, depending on how rich the dead person was, their first son or a Dom will crack open the skull because skulls burst when heated. Incense is then thrown over the lot and the fire lit."

We gazed over at the ghat and agreed once again that there were benefits in not being the first-born son in India.

"For the next four hours, the burners will turn the body to make it burn faster. A man's chest and a woman's thighs take the longest. When the burning is over, the Doms rake the ashes for valuables, and the family offers rice ball pindas to symbolize the soul's journey, and to celebrate the end of the person's many reincarnations and their entry into oblivion.

"Mothers and wives are not allowed near the pyre. During the thirteen days after a death they are forbidden to cook or enter the kitchen. On the thirteenth day, the deceased's ashes are scattered over the Ganges and the wife and daughters are pronounced ritually pure. Holy men, children, lepers and small-pox victims are not burned. They are lowered into the water with a weight. Which means they are reincarnated so they can return to suffer more."

I stared down into the river, imagining weighted bodies swaying in the current beneath us.

"Oh," gasped Sally, "listen to this. People who are dying have Ganges mud stuffed into their mouths, noses and ears. Once this is done, if the patient recovers they are considered Outcasts. In other words, when you're supposed to die, you die or else."

Slowly we drifted by the two-towered, pink-painted Lord of the Moon Ghat, the pretty Munshi Ghat and Ahalya Bai's Ghat, the only one of the eighty named after a woman. When we reached halfway, the old man indicated with his chin that we should turn back, and although we would have loved to see all the ghats, he looked tired, so we nodded back. We could walk the other half later on.

"Want to hear about the famous Benares enameled jewelry?" asked Sally, as we turned round. "The enamel of this antique jewelry was produced from a paste of crushed emeralds, sapphires and rubies. This type of jewelry is no longer made because the craftsmen died refusing to share their knowledge. I guess they thought they might need it when they were reincarnated."

Just before we reached the jetty of the Temple of the Ganges Hotel, a rowboat scraped against ours and a shaved-head man offered us carved statues of elephants with howdahs and maharajahs. He looked exactly like our grandfather and grandson rowers. This is not surprising as the boatmen of Varanasi are a sub-caste of Dalits and can only marry within their caste.

Leaving grandfather with a tip and grandson with Sally's sunglasses, we hurried back to our hotel where we slept until midday, and then we set off by rickshaw along the main road to see the Dasaswamedh Ghat celebrations.

"Varanasi has 140 cinemas," I read, as we were pedalled

along. "It also has a Vishwanath Temple dedicated to Shiva with 800 kilograms of gold on its towers, and a well which is rumored to contain Shiva's lingam hidden there to protect it from Muslim Emperor Aurangzeb."

"What did Aurangzeb want with Shiva's lingam?" demanded Sally.

"It doesn't say. But non-Hindus aren't allowed in the temple. There are stalls around the well where we can buy copies of Krishna's flute, colored lithographs of the god Vishnu, and glass, marble, sandstone and slate eggs which are the symbols of Shiva's lingam held within a glass, marble, sandstone or slate bowl which is the symbol of Parvati's *yoni*—her female fertility."

"What a fabulous word," cried Sally. "I want a marble yoni."

Our rickshaw pedaller took us deep into the crowd. When he could go no farther, we got out and pushed along with everyone else. Since the day before, stalls and sideshows had sprung up along the streets leading to the ghat. There were jugglers, souvenir sellers, food sellers, plastic toy sellers, and women in yellow with painted yellow faces and three-pronged forks stuck through their tongues. Music blared from loudspeakers hung hastily, and swinging dangerously, from temporarily erected poles. But there were no yogis sleeping on beds of thorns, holy fakirs swinging suspended by hooks piercing their chests or backs, or fakirs climbing up ropes coming out of wicker baskets and disappearing into the air. *Fakir* is where the English word "fake" comes from. Which is not to say these yogis and fakirs don't sleep on nails or hang themselves up with hooks, only to say that the English, unable to comprehend anyone wanting to do such things, thought them tricks.

There was so much to see, hear, touch and smell that in the end we sat under a tree and stared and listened. Here we met young Krishna selling bars of highly perfumed hotel soap, and although we had plenty, we bought more because he told us that he was the sole supporter of his mother and sister as his father had drowned while fishing.

"Fishing in the Ganges?" I questioned. "Aren't the fish holy?"

He nodded while thinking of the right answer to give us. Then he added that his family always thanked Shiva before eating them.

An hour or so later, time being elastic in India, we decided to find the Vishwanath Temple and buy our lingams and yonis, so once again we dived into the crowd. Two blocks on, we arrived as close as we were ever going to get. The Vishwanath Temple is built on top of, or close to, the place where a temple has existed for the last 1500 years so it is a very, very holy spot. Beside it stands Aurangzeb's Great Mosque, guarded by Hindu soldiers for fear of it being bombed by religious fanatics. On a day like this it would be a brave Muslim who pushed through to worship here.

The entire area was packed solid so after finding no pleasure in swaying backwards and forwards in a crowd that evidently found great pleasure in doing so, we burrowed our way back to the Dasaswamedh Ghat steps where a huge platform had been erected for that evening's performance. All the steps, from the water's edge to the temple entrance, were occupied.

Waiting for the performance wasn't difficult, there were so many people to watch, and night fell amazingly fast. One minute it was daylight, next minute it was dark with strings of candles floating on the river, fairy lights blinking all over a VIP barge and spotlights lighting up politicians in homespun caps to prove they are one of the people as they arrived by exclusive motorboat or chauffeured cars to take up their front row seats. The crowd's excitement was electric. Drama was everywhere.

Suddenly, striding out onto the stage came the star singing at the top of his voice. He commanded immediate attention. He looked exactly like an Indian Pavarotti, pale skin, trimmed beard, yellow ziggurat hat with peacock feather, raw silk woven scarf thrown over left shoulder, cream pajamas, hands held wide, eyes shut and mouth open. A nearby Indian explained that he was singing about a saint and that he would act out the story of this saint's life. Which he did, with much changing of voices, singing and storytelling. It wasn't hard to guess the stories. They were about wives and husbands, fathers and sons, and women arguing. Everyone arguing. Each came to the saint for advice. I got the idea that the saint's life was a succession of weary "I told you so" or "You should have" lectures, but the audience loved it and laughed when they recognized themselves.

After intermission the actor returned in a different pair of pajamas, scarf and hat. This time he performs a story from the Ramayana in which Surpanakha the beautiful sister of the evil King Ravana of Sri Lanka attempts to entice King Rama and King Rama's brother Lakshmana. They are enticed, much to the glee of the audience, but in retaliation for his weakness, Lakshmana cuts off Surpanakha's nose. She goes crying to her brother, the evil King Ravana who, in turn, spirits away King Rama's wife, the virtuous Queen Sita. King Rama, his brother Lakshmana, and his friend, Hanuman the monkey god, rushes off to Sri Lanka to kill the evil King Ravana and to rescue Queen Sita, who eventually burns herself when her husband refuses to believe she was untouched. This story is so well known that the audience sang along with the performer. It was wonderful entertainment and we were sad when it was over.

"He is on again tomorrow night," a police officer informed us. But sadly, our time in Varanasi was over.

Next day we packed our bags and took a rickshaw to the station via the famous Durga Temple which is mostly occupied by monkeys. On the way our rickshaw driver told us about Varanasi's October festival. This is the Devi Deepavali festival famous for its boat races, martial arts competitions, more than a million earthen lamps lit on the ghats, and an equal amount placed upon the Ganges in small leaf boats. We agreed it sounded beautiful and that we would love to see it.

"So you'll come back in October. Everyone comes back to Varanasi, it is the best place to die," he said confidently.

# Chapter 18

## Reluctant Daughter-in-Law's Lament

On boarding the Delhi train, we discovered our bunks were occupied. Mine by a pile of luggage, a father, a mother and three daughters. Sally's by two old, sari-wrapped women, one resembling the Witch of the North, the other a tiny crumpled-up ancient resembling Agnes, my Rajasthani camel. Nothing we said would move them. The showing of our tickets, the miming that the seats were ours, the losing of Sally's temper as the Witch of the North spat at her. Finally, I told the father that if he did not move I would sit on his knee. At this unimaginable threat, he leaped for the doorway where a crowd of men with jet-black moustaches were watching the "War of the Seats."

I sat down next to the man's wife, causing the child she was holding to set up a piercing howl as if I were Durga come to earth. Sally's threat to sit on the Witch of the North's knee did not have the same effect as mine had.

"Do it, I dare you," the witch's fearless black eyes challenged.

So Sally took hold of the witch's bag that was on the seat beside her. At this the witch let out such a howl of protest that the first and third child of the family began to wail like a fire engine. Sally, who is not great with shrieking children, lost it. She hung over the witch menacingly while yelling that she'd paid the European tourist price for her seat, which was a hundred times more than the witch had paid for hers, and that she had no intention of sitting on the floor for the next thirteen hours. So the witch had better move before she was severely woman-handled. And would someone shut those children up!

The witch yelled back in Hindi, "Bugger off, you white-faced she-devil. I'm not moving." Or something like that.

Suddenly among all this crying and yelling there appeared a student who spoke English. Thank Krishna! Or in this case it was probably Durga. He explained to the father of the upset children and to the scowling witch that as we had paid for sleepers we should have them. A fact they knew perfectly well. But he was of a higher caste than they so they had to comply. Maybe there is something to this caste system after all.

The witch moved up a hand's width and Sally snuggled in. There they sat, hip to hip, elbow to elbow, with faces like twin Durgas, each gaining or losing a tiny bit of space as the train rocked. Beside the witch lay shrivelled-up granny. I later decided she was senile as she never spoke no matter how the witch pinched her, or shoved her towards the toilet, or berated her loudly, while pushing her to the floor.

Half-an-hour later, after we had forgotten granny and the scowling witch, the ticket inspector arrived. Out came everyone's tickets, but there was no ticket for granny. The student translated what the witch said to the inspector. Granny was the witch's mother-in-law, whom the witch, at great cost, had taken to Varanasi to die. Only worthless, ungrateful granny hadn't died. After two weeks, the witch's rupees had run out and they were returning home penniless. But as granny was meant to die, her daughter-in-law had not bought her a return ticket.

Now there is positivity for you.

Everyone inside our compartment and all those sitting on bunks to the ceiling or squatting on the floor the length of the train's corridor discussed the "Lament of the Penniless Daughter-in-Law and the Reluctant Granny." Some stared accusingly at the offending granny who in turn crunched herself up into an even smaller bundle of misery. Some told her how fortunate she was to have been taken to Varanasi. Others demanded to know why she hadn't died when she should have. The ungrateful granny didn't answer.

"Poor old thing," commiserated Sally. "It's a wonder she didn't get the 'mud stuffed into her mouth' treatment."

The student said that this granny had most likely had the mud stuffed into her mouth treatment, as her daughter-in-law was a very determined daughter-in-law.

"This is a dilemma," announced the ticket inspector in English. In other words, granny was taking up space that someone who did have a ticket could use.

Then the ticket inspector had a brilliant idea. Nay, an inspiring idea! "The two foreigners (us) had paid European prices for their tickets and so the space between their feet was well and truly paid for," he informed the entire car.

"I'd say handsomely paid for up to the ceiling and ten feet in every direction," added Sally.

"And so," continued the ticket inspector, "if granny can

squash into the space between the foreigners' feet, the problem is solved."

Too bad if we didn't want a senile granny jammed between our knees, because with a multitude of Indians beaming at us with the pleasure of having the problem settled, we were in no position to decline. So I let granny rest her head on my haversack, and Sally gave her a towel to cover her legs, and she concertinaed herself up even more until she would have fitted into a soap box and here she stayed, not moving a muscle. Three skinny students instantly filled the seat she vacated.

By ten o'clock, there were twenty people squashed into our compartment that made pulling down the middle bunks awkward. The two top bunks were already down and full of luggage and a couple of sleeping men who had taken their lives in their hands by crawling up and under the decapitating ceiling fans.

Finally the witch wanted to sleep and as her bunk was above mine everyone had to move for her. It seemed a good time to stake my claim, which I did, allowing four students to perch on the end of my bunk, while I snuggled down in my sleeping bag. Opposite me the family I had deposed claimed Sally's bottom bunk while Sally happily climbed onto the middle bunk where no one could sit on her. She shared this bunk with a large tin trunk. While she was asleep, a man sneaked in between the wall and trunk and slept in a space big enough for a full-grown frog.

Granny slept on the floor a hand's width from my nose. She could have been dead, no one would have known. Above me the witch wriggled and sighed, twisted and turned, each time hitting the wall with her elbow, her knee, her heel, until in the end I lost my temper and told her that she was a selfish, nasty piece of goods, and that I couldn't see why she couldn't share her bunk with the older woman. But, as she wouldn't, could she please keep still for five minutes at a time.

Up until then everyone in the car had presumed that the witch couldn't speak English. Suddenly she could.

"I went to my mother-in-law's house at the age of ten where she, the beauty of the village, beat me and forced me to work twelve hours a day. For years I slaved for my husband and his parents then he, the ungrateful wretch, went to Delhi and remarried. I never saw him again. Meanwhile I wasted my life looking after his parents. Now I am sixty and I have spent five years of my savings taking her to Varanasi so she can die and I can be free. So although I am forced to feed her, bathe her and clothe her, I will not..." here her voice rose a vibrating octave ... "sleep with her. And if she dies on the floor beside you, I will be eternally grateful to Shiva."

This outpouring of rage, pain, frustration and hatred in precise, near-perfect English was so shocking that not one of the twenty or so people squashed into our compartment uttered a word for at least five minutes. Then Sally spoke up.

"I'd say that answered your question."

Throughout the night, granny went three times to the toilet which was in the next car past an open exit door. Each time the witch followed her. The fourth time the witch returned alone, and I had the feeling that as the train had rocked back and forth, she had shoved the old woman through the open doorway into the fast-moving night. When I awoke in the morning, they were gone.

"They got off in the night," one passenger said.

"Both of them?" I queried.

He shrugged as if he didn't care. What was one more parcel of bones, one more bundle of unloved, unwanted unhappiness lying by a train track?

We arrived at Delhi in the morning and went straight to the Hotel White Empire to shower and then to enjoy our last day in India. We purposefully left the picking up of the monster case until we were on our way to the airport although this decision caused Sally stress as she was dying to see it.

After a day of last-minute shopping at the bazaars, more clothes for Sally, more books and jewelry for me, we arrived at the Armpit Hotel with the trunk of the taxi already full, and were astonished to find the hotel's restaurant finished.

"Please come and see," begged an army of receptionists. So we did.

The restaurant had a blue ceiling painted with clouds, walls covered in mirrors and paintings of pretty eighteenth-century women in crinolines sitting in quaint English gardens, and a garish modern stainless steel bar with purple plastic leather-topped bar stools.

"It will be used for society weddings," boasted the manager. "It will be the best restaurant Delhi has ever seen."

Back in the foyer, we watched two waiters struggling to drag the case out of the tiny elevator. But the case was stubborn, it wasn't going anywhere with these strangers, then it saw Sally. It immediately released its grip on the elevator floor and bounced free. Sally rushed to it, stroked it, cooed to it, and brushed off the dust while the case panted with joy. I suppose it had thought itself forsaken and abandoned. I know if I had owned it, it would have been.

A large tip changed hands and the waiters (both with the beginnings of back problems they would have for the rest of their lives) carried the contented case to the back seat of the taxi. With many good-byes and come-back-soons, we set off for the airport leaving behind all eight Delhis with their 2000 metric tonnes of air pollutants, their countless tons of plastic bags and bottles, and the best wedding restaurant Delhi has ever seen.

We arrived hours before we were due to leave, because Sally wanted to squash her five cloth bags and their contents into her case. So who was I to point out that it was bursting at the seams, groaning at the handle, extraordinarily bottom heavy, and over-weight by any airport standards. It was hers. She could do what she liked with it. We found a corner where she up-ended the case, her backpack and five cloth bags. Sitting in the middle of an incredible mess, she began the effort of deciding what would go into the case first. I sat on my bag and watched.

A man in black, followed by his dough-faced wife and daughter both wearing Bo-peep hats and ankle-length, ferret-grey dresses, stopped to ask what she was doing.

"She's setting up house in the airport," I told him.

"Everyone needs a home," he answered, in a deep solemn voice, confirming my suspicions that he was a man of the cloth.

"So where have you been?" I asked. If I am going to sit at an airport for two hours I will talk to anyone.

"We have been instructing the tribal people about God."

"Didn't they know already?" said Sally. Missionaries rate on a par with Indian films with her.

"They knew naught of Christ. But now they know he died for them," he answered, in the righteous tone of one who has the email address of God.

What can one say to that? Not a lot. So I turned to his two females. "Did you like tribal life?"

They didn't answer. Speaking was a male prerogative.

After they'd left, he striding forth to conquer the heathen world, his two sour-faced women trotting behind him, I wondered how the tribal people had taken to his self-sacrificing god. How willingly had they given up their handsome blue-skinned Krishna with his gopi milkmaid love affairs? How reluctantly had they forsaken their warrior god Shiva, or their beloved Lady Lakshmi, giver of wealth and prosperity? Had they truly abandoned the fearful, bloody-mouthed Kali or the terrifying Durga? Had they really renounced their lovable elephant-headed Ganesh? Or had they simply absorbed Christ and added him to their list of 1001 gods? I bet they had.

"I suppose being a Christian is better than being an Outcast or an Untouchable," said Sally, squashing down her case with the determination of a sumo wrestler.

Sometimes Sally hits the nail on the head. Not only that, she'd fitted the five bags and their contents into the monster case so I was impressed.

"So what will we do now?" she asked, sitting on it to make sure it didn't vomit forth its overload.

But there was no now. It was time for me to leave. With hasty hugs and kisses, my boarding card was issued, my little red bag whisked off to the cargo hold, and I waved good-bye from behind the barrier before hurrying towards customs.

Sally waved back. She looked so lonely roosting there on her case that I felt guilty leaving her with something she couldn't possibly move without the help of a removalist elephant or a crane. Then, as an official walked by, I dug into my backpack and handed him the *Kama Sutra*, pointing at Sally, and asked him to give it to her.

Glancing down at the title, he smiled broadly. "Certainly, Madam. Did you enjoy it?"

"Yes," I said, smiling back at him. "Although I do prefer practice to theory."

My plane took off the minute it was full. No hanging around for timetables. As it circled above Delhi, the Indian stewardess asked me, "Did you like India, Madam?"

"Most definitely. India is like a beautiful woman," I answered.

She smiled at the compliment, then turned away to ask the same question of the next passenger, while my thoughts continued. India was like a beautiful woman. A beautiful woman in a yellow sari with bare feet, bone bracelets, and three water pots balanced on her head.

# GLOSSARY

**ashram**   a community of people living together to study and develop their spirituality and beliefs

**begum**   a female Muslim ruler/ high-class court female

**betel nut**   seed of betel palms, which is flavored and chewed as a stimulant

*bhoot*   ghost

**Brahman**   a member of one of the highest castes within Hindu society

**chapattis**   a flat unleavened bread

*chinkara/ chikara*   also called an Indian gazelle (small antelope)

**dacoit**   bandit/robber

**dhal**   an Indian recipe made of lentils

**dhobi**   usually a male Indian who hand-washes clothes for a living

**dhoti**   loin cloth worn by Hindu men

*gahgra*   a full skirt worn by women in western India

**garuda**   a mythical eagle, half- beast half-bird

*ghat*   series of steps to body of water

*gopi*   milkmaid

*gula*   powdered colors (yellow, green, orange, blue, red) used during the Holi festival (festival of colors)

*havelis*   luxurious residence often built by aristocrats or merchantmen

*joolis* (or *jutis*)   traditional pointed Indian footwear

**kampong**   Malaysian or Indonesian enclosed settlement or village

*kumkum*   or vermilion, placed by Indian women on their foreheads or hair parting as a marriage sign

*kurta*   traditional clothing, loose shirt worn either above or below the knees

*lassi*   traditional Indian beverage made from yogurt, water, spices and fruit

*lei*   flower necklace

# GLOSSARY

**lingam** symbol of Shiva, phallus

**machaan** platform or foundation erected or built in a tree

**maharajah** ruling prince or king

**maharana** wife of a ruling prince and/or can rule in her own right

**mahout** elephant keeper, trainer and rider

**muezzin** Muslim cryer summoning the people to prayer

**orni** veil

**paise** coin equivalent to 100th of a rupee

**pakoras** deep-fried fritter

**puja** prayers

**roti** unleavened bread

**sadhu** Indian holy man

**salwar kameez** traditional dress consisting of a *kameez* (shirt) and *salwar* (trousers)

**sidi** title of respect

**sikhs** member of religious sect who do not believe in the caste system

**stupas** funeral ornaments

**suttee** Hindu ritual where wife throws herself on husband's funeral pyre to die with him as sign of respect and love

**thali** gold necklace used most often at weddings containing emblems. One emblem is the thali – phallic symbol placed at the center of the necklace

**tirthankar** teacher who demonstrates the path to enlightenment

**yoni** symbol representing the female reproductive organ

**vermilion powder/mark** bright red pigment made from cinnabar and mercuric sulfide used in decoration and as a sign of marriage

**zenana** designated area of a house/palace reserved only for women

# ABOUT THE AUTHOR

**Trisha Bernard** was born in Melbourne and began traveling at sixteen. She hasn't stopped since and has visited more than 100 countries, even staying to earn a bit of money in twenty of them. She has worked as an au pair in Paris and Morocco, taught English in Greece and Jamaica, worked on boats in Canada and Mallorca, and tutored in Sweden and London, just to name a few.

Trisha has written 26 young-adult books. *With the* Kama Sutra *Under My Arm* is her first adult travel title and the realization of a lifelong dream to share her stories with grown-ups!